To Joette,

Thanks for the ride!

Best Wishes!

[illegible]

The Grandfather of Black Basketball

The Grandfather of Black Basketball

The Life and Times of Dr. E. B. Henderson

Edwin Bancroft Henderson II

ROWMAN & LITTLEFIELD
Lanham • Boulder • New York • London

Published by Rowman & Littlefield
An imprint of The Rowman & Littlefield Publishing Group, Inc.
4501 Forbes Boulevard, Suite 200, Lanham, Maryland 20706
www.rowman.com

86-90 Paul Street, London EC2A 4NE, United Kingdom

British Library Cataloguing in Publication Information Available

Library of Congress Cataloging-in-Publication Data
Names: Henderson, Edwin Bancroft, II, 1955– author.
Title: The grandfather of Black basketball: the life and times of Dr. E. B. Henderson / Edwin Bancroft Henderson II.
Description: Lanham: Rowman & Littlefield Publishers, [2024] | Includes bibliographical references and index. | Summary: "The first contemporary biography of Dr. Edwin Bancroft Henderson, a civil rights activist who, as a coach, athlete, administrator, and author, is credited with introducing the game of basketball to Black players, coaches, and the media"—Provided by publisher.
Identifiers: LCCN 2023030248 (print) | LCCN 2023030249 (ebook) | ISBN 9781538163610 (cloth) | ISBN 9781538163627 (epub)
Subjects: LCSH: Henderson, Edwin Bancroft, 1883–1977. | Basketball—United States—History. | Physical education teachers—United States—Biography. | African American civil rights workers—United States—Biography.
Classification: LCC GV333.H38 H44 2024 (print) | LCC GV333.H38 (ebook) | DDC 613.7092 [B]—dc23/eng/20230725
LC record available at https://lccn.loc.gov/2023030248
LC ebook record available at https://lccn.loc.gov/2023030249

∞™ The paper used in this publication meets the minimum requirements of American National Standard for Information Sciences—Permanence of Paper for Printed Library Materials, ANSI/NISO Z39.48-1992.

Contents

Illustrations

Acknowledgments

Writing this book has been a journey for me, my greatest pleasure. First and foremost, I have to thank God Almighty, the Creator of the Universe, and the Ancestors, for inspiration showing me the way forward. I'd like to thank the folks at Rowman & Littlefield, who took a chance on me, particularly Christen Karniski for believing in this project. To my late mother and father, Betty Alice Francis Henderson and James H. M. Henderson, for their love and devotion to me and to this story through their short book *Molder of Men: Portrait of a Grand Old Man*. To my wife, Nikki Graves Henderson, for her love, patience, and devotion to this project and so many others too numerous to count. To my children and grandchildren, who have taught me patience and tried my patience. To my siblings, Ellen, Dena, and Jay, who have shared the experience of knowing our grandparents, whom this book is about. I counted on you for your perspective on this story and a second set of eyes. I want to especially thank my sister Dena Sewell and cousin Suzette Francis for taking the time in your busy days to help edit. I'd like to thank Elizabeth Dowling Taylor, author and friend, who gave me early feedback and encouragement. Thanks to Keith Irby, an actor who played E. B. in *Tinner Hill: Portraits in Black and White*, who has been helpful as the archivist for the Eastern Board of Officials. I'd also like to thank Debbie Massey, who took a look in the latter days of the manuscript but gave me some valuable lessons on writing in the final days of writing. I'd also like to thank Al Tony Gilmore, professor and sports historian, for his feedback and for reviewing my manuscript. Also, thank you to the late Dr. Leon Coursey, whom I counted on for his interviews and professional perspectives from his 1971 dissertation on E. B.'s professional career and much more. Also, a big thank-you to David Aldridge, Claude Johnson, Susan Rayls, David Wiggins, and so many others who caused me to see the wisdom in writing my own damn book. I'd like to also thank Al Bertrand at Georgetown University Press and particularly the second peer reviewer who said I was not the one to write this book. You lit a fire under me to boldly go forward and be the one to write this book. Special thanks to trustee Barrington "Bo" Scott at the University of the District of Columbia and Brian Hanlon, official sculptor for the Basketball Hall of Fame and sculptor for the Dr. E. B. Henderson statue on the University of the District of Columbia campus. Let me not forget and thank all the people at the Naismith Memorial Basketball Hall of Fame for not making it easy and pushing the envelope in an eight-year-long journey to acknowledge the root of Black basketball in your museum. And most of all, to my grandparents E. B. and Nell, who were there for me from the beginning, thank you for the road map to tell your story.

Foreword

David Aldridge

There is no motivation for me to lie to you, so let's be honest: the packet that introduced me to E. B. Henderson, and why he should be in the Naismith Memorial Basketball Hall of Fame, sat in the back seat of my car for weeks. Months, maybe.

In my line of work, you get a lot of unprompted solicitations from people you don't know—specifically, story ideas. Everyone seems to have a son or daughter who is spectacular at . . . whatever. Basketball. Coaching. Someone has a "revolutionary" idea about shooting or stats that you must drop whatever you're doing to write about. It's part of the job when you cover sports.

So it was not unusual for me to receive a packet in the mail in 2006. It came in a translucent envelope. On its cover was a picture of a young man, sitting, in uniform with a basketball in his hand. Clearly, the young man had played many, many years ago. The cover page had on it the headline: "Seven Reasons Why E. B. Henderson Should Be in the Hall of Fame." The man's name was Edwin B. Henderson, known as "E. B." by one and all.

It quickly became clear that Mr. Henderson was not being pushed for the Hall for his on-court exploits, though he was a fine player in his day, one of the better centers in the game. The packet detailed how Henderson was the first person to teach the game of basketball to Black people in the United States—and in my hometown of Washington, D.C. *That* certainly got my attention. So, too, did the rest of Henderson's story: he had learned the game, which literally had been invented only a little more than a decade prior, from a man named Dudley Allen Sargent at Harvard University.

Sargent had spent much of his life in pursuit of athletic rigor and innovation. As a teenager, he'd built his own set of Indian Clubs—weighted maces that were swung in exercises designed to increase strength and muscle mass—after seeing a picture of a man with a toned physique using them.[1] This began a lifetime of training and developing physical fitness routines, equipment and classes, which included, beginning in 1887, teaching a summer physical fitness class at Harvard for physical education teachers who would take Sargent's teachings back to their schools. In 1904, one of the budding phys ed teachers who made the pilgrimage to Cambridge was Henderson, who'd decided to become a gym teacher after completing a two-year program at a teacher training school in D.C.

Sargent had learned the game from one of his former students, Luther Gulick Jr. Gulick Jr. had become superintendent of the physical education department of the International Young Men's Christian Association (YMCA) Training School in Springfield, Mass., in 1887, at age 22, shortly after leaving Sargent's Normal School. Four years later, Gulick Jr. was in need. The Springfield Y had a football program for its male students in the fall, but after the football season ended, the players grew bored by the less-than-rigorous games and activities that were offered in the winter, and their appearances at workouts dropped significantly. Gulick Jr. sought to create a game that his athletes could play indoors during the cold winter months.

Gulick turned to one of his recently hired phys ed teachers at the Springfield YMCA whom he'd just brought down from the Montreal Y the previous summer. The teacher's name was James Naismith. Gulick laid it out to Naismith: come up with something. In two weeks, Naismith had taken a little from several of the more popular team sports of the time to create a game he called "basket-ball," named for the peach baskets he'd attached to the railings at either end of the gymnasium at the school.

Naismith taught the game to Gulick. Gulick taught the game to Sargent. Sargent taught the game to Henderson. Talk about being present at the creation.

Henderson came back to the District, and in the fall of 1904, he began teaching basketball to his students in the segregated schools of Washington. But his contributions didn't end there. Two years later, he helped form the first officially sanctioned league for African American students to participate and compete in individual and team competitions, the Interscholastic Athletic Association of Middle Atlantic States. He began coordinating play between basketball teams in cities up and down the East Coast, particularly in New York, the first city in the country where the game had taken a hold on the public, and D.C.

In 1909, Henderson organized and played on a D.C. team sponsored by the Twelfth Street Colored YMCA, which played its games in the ballroom of the True Reformers Hall on 12th and U Streets, NW. (The hall was the first building of its kind in the country—designed, developed, financed, and built entirely by African Americans.) The team thus became known as the "Washington 12th Streeters," won the third annual Colored Basketball World Championship, a consensus among sportswriters at Black newspapers nationwide as to which team was the best in the country.

It was not coincidence that the Y was central to basketball's development.

Almost all of the involved players—Gulick, Naismith, Sargent, Henderson—were adherents of what became known as "Muscular Christianity," the notion that regular, taxing activity, particularly among men, was central to their development, both physically and spiritually. The idea was that regular exercise—and, in some circles, the more dangerous the better—was a balm against the supposed "softening" of America as it entered the Industrial Age. No less than Theodore Roosevelt, the nation's twenty-sixth president, was a fierce advocate of the philosophy; Roosevelt had been an early champion and defender of college football, despite the game leading to numerous catastrophic injuries as it grew in popularity nationwide.

"As a nation we have many tremendous problems to work out," Roosevelt wrote in *The North American Review* in 1890, "and we need to bring every ounce of vital power possible to their solution. No people has ever done great and lasting work if its physical type was infirm and weak. Goodness and strength must go hand in hand if the Republic is to be preserved. The good man who is able and ready to strike a blow for the right, and to put down evil with the strong arm, is the citizen who deserves our most hearty respect."[2] Massachusetts Senator Henry Cabot Lodge, in a speech to fellow Harvard alumni in 1896, said, "I happen to be one of those, Mr. President, who believe profoundly in athletic contests. The time given to athletic contests and the injuries incurred on the playing-field are part of the price which the English-speaking race has paid for being world-conquerors."[3]

Yet the turn of the 20th century was no different for most Black people than that which had occurred at the turn of the 19th. Slavery had been ended, through the Emancipation Proclamation. The Thirteenth, Fourteenth, and Fifteenth Amendments to the Constitution, along with the Civil Rights Acts of 1866 and 1875, had guaranteed, at least on paper, equal rights and protections for the former slaves still living in the United States, as Reconstruction began in earnest after the end of the Civil War. But these freedoms were short-lived. Virulent, state-sponsored racism, starting in the South and spreading to all corners of the country, had taken a blowtorch to those protections in practice. The Compromise of 1877, the Mississippi Plan, the 1883 Supreme Court ruling declaring the Civil Rights Act of 1875 unconstitutional, *Plessy v. Ferguson*—they all fell, in order, dominos of discrimination and division that would clear the runway for Jim Crow, and three-quarters of a century of institutionalized, government-sanctioned racism nationwide.

In this era, African Americans were, of course, not only subjugated to second-class status as human beings in America, but blamed for that second-class citizenry. Pseudo-science "proving" the intellectual inferiority of Black people was propped up and promoted, often by newspapers and other media that were financially and otherwise motivated to keep White America the de facto America. Among the canards, whose tendrils exist to this day, was ignoring the impact of institutional racism on generations of Black people. White communities in the early 1900s enjoyed a boon in recreational spaces. But while White neighborhoods and communities were able to enjoy the benefits of playgrounds and other open areas, most Black neighborhoods were excluded. And when that lack of activity relative to White people contributed to poorer health outcomes, such as larger incidences of tuberculosis in Black communities, many posited that the overarching reason was the poor "habits" of Black people.

Washington, D.C., thankfully, was the exception. The capital city's large Black population lived in a city where funds for school activities were allocated not only to the segregated White public schools in the District, but to Black schools and students as well. Thus, Henderson could not only teach the game to his increasingly interested students, they had many more spaces, such as True Reformers, in which to play after they learned the rules.

But Henderson—and this was all in the pamphlet—had a lot more to contribute to the game's development.

He took the 12th Streeters team and moved it, essentially, to Howard University, creating that school's first basketball team, in 1910. That year, they won the Colored Basketball World Championship. Henderson was an editor of the ISAA's *Spaulding Official Handbook*, the first publication in the country that chronicled participation by Black athletes in all major sports. He founded the Eastern Board of Officials, the first entity that trained Black referees to work basketball games. He fought to integrate local swimming pools and other athletic facilities in the D.C. region. And, in 1939, he wrote *The Negro in Sports*, the first book to ever provide a comprehensive history of Black American participation in sports. And in the last three-plus decades of his life, E. B. was a stalwart member of his local NAACP, fighting vigorously for change at the local and national levels.

Nearly five decades later, the legendary tennis star and historian Arthur Ashe penned his own three-volume academic summary of the history of Black athletes in America, *A Hard Road to Glory: A History of the African-American Athlete,* an offshoot of the course "The Black Athlete in Contemporary Society" that Ashe taught at Florida Memorial College (now Florida Memorial University), an HBCU in Miami Gardens, Florida.

"In preparing my course syllabus," Ashe wrote in his book, *Days of Grace*, published just after his death in 1993, "I quickly discovered, to my surprise and chagrin, that virtually nothing had been written by scholars, black or white, on the history of black involvement in sports in America. Hunting in the New York Public Library on Forty-Second Street, I found only two books: Edwin B. Henderson's *The Negro in Sports*, published in 1938, with a revised edition in 1948; and A. S. "Doc" Young's *Negro Firsts in Sport*. I was baffled by this poverty of information." [4]

Ashe told *Sports Illustrated* in 1991 that he paid $40 to secure a copy of the original Henderson book, and $35 for the updated version. "I wouldn't mind having 20 copies," he said then. [5]

And all of this information—all of this glorious and noteworthy history, this compelling and detailed argument correctly making the case for a true pioneer's case to be enshrined in what is officially known as the Naismith Memorial Basketball Hall of Fame, named after James Naismith, in that very same Springfield, Mass., where he invented the game—sat in a once-read packet in a translucent envelope, in the back seat of my car, for weeks. Months, maybe.

I wish I could tell you why I didn't take the packet and immediately demand airtime on TNT, where I worked at the time, or space to write a couple thousand words on the subject on NBA.com. But there's no dramatic narrative, no Act II that put me in peril. I just didn't jump on it. I had a job. I had a family and kids. I had a mortgage. Life got in the way. Your excuse here.

Fortunately for all of us, Edwin B. Henderson II and his wife Nikki aren't the type of people who took the world's initial shrug, of which I was a part, as their final answer.

Edwin II was, and is, E. B. Henderson's grandson. Armed with the truth, in the papers and correspondence that E. B. kept in his Falls Church, Virginia, home, Edwin II and Nikki began a polite, firm, and consistent campaign to get him into the Hall. A note, a call, a reminder: *Why E. B. Henderson Should Be in the Hall of Fame*. They kept at it, for eight years, slowly pushing the rock up the hill. The Hall doesn't inform people that they're making progress—or, not making any. It just lets you know when you get in. So, year after year, there was nothing from the Hall for Edwin II and Nikki. But they kept striving. Slowly, the idea took root in my muddled, mortgage-paying head. I didn't have a gargantuan platform as a reporter for TNT and writer for NBA.com, but it was a decent-sized one.

Fortunately, someone more qualified than me was already on the case—Claude Johnson, the founder of Black Fives Foundation, an organization and companion website dedicated to telling the stories of the forgotten men (and, women) who paved the way as basketball's first pioneers, at the turn of the century and soon after. I'd met Claude just after he'd left the NBA, in order to fulfill a calling. In doing so, Claude was picking up the baton for the great Howie Evans, who worked at the *Amsterdam News*, and whose columns over several decades arguing on behalf of the great Rens teams, players and coaches led to many of them receiving induction into the Hall in the '80s and '90s.

Claude, too, knew the history of the Black teams and leagues, whose contributions had been forgotten by time, like John "Wonder Boy" Isaacs, Dolly King, Ora Washington, George Crowe, and others. Claude quickly began advocating for E. B. on his site as one of the top contributors who deserved HOF consideration and election. Edwin II and Nikki kept pushing. Claude kept writing. And, finally, they gained traction. Who knows which drop of water is the one that finally dislodges the rock?

In 2011, the Hall announced it would establish an Early African-American Pioneers of the Game committee that would specifically address the candidacies of Black players and contributors to the game who'd played or worked before the establishment of the NBA, in 1947. Equally importantly: this committee would be empowered to vote to enshrine candidates directly to the Hall, rather than them having to receive the votes of three-fourths of committee members, the practice for other Hall selection committees. Finally, in September 2013, the Early African-American Committee announced that E. B. had been directly elected into the Hall of Fame. I "broke" the news on Twitter. But that was an accident. I assumed that everyone who needed to know had been informed. The news should have been given, first, to Edwin II and Nikki. It was their work that made it possible.

"How hard is it to bring a man to life who has been dead for 36 years?" I asked in writing about Edwin and Nikki's journey. As it turned out, it was very hard. And very much worth it.

David Aldridge is a sports journalist, writer for The Athletic, *and winner of Naismith Memorial Basketball Hall of Fame's Curt Gowdy Media Award.*

Introduction

Who Was E. B. Henderson?

On September 8, 2013, Dr. Edwin Bancroft (E. B.) Henderson was inducted into the Naismith Basketball Hall of Fame. At the induction ceremony, Ahmad Rashad, emcee for the affair, said, "When you consider the true pioneers of the sport, that discussion should begin with Dr. Naismith and then quickly shifts to Dr. Edwin Bancroft (E. B.) Henderson."[1]

When E. B. Henderson went to Harvard University in 1904 to attend the summer institute of the Dudley Sargent College of Physical Training, he was exposed to the fundamentals of basketball. Basketball had been officially presented to the public at the 1904 St. Louis World Fair by the Fort Shaw Indian School girls team. At the time, basketball was not popularly played by boys, but E. B. had a different idea. At the end of the summer, upon his return to his native Washington, DC, he began to introduce the game to young African American boys in the Washington, DC, Colored School System, where he became the first African American male certified to teach physical education in the United States.

Within the next six years, E. B. formed the Inter-Scholastic Athletic Association (ISAA), the first African American athletic league; the Eastern Board of Officials (EBO), the first organization to train and organize officials; and the Public School Athletic League (PSAL) for the Washington, DC, Colored schools, the first school league in a segregated division. At that time, even the White schools in Washington,

DC, didn't have an athletic league of their own. In 1907–1908, Henderson helped to form a championship series against the newly formed Olympian Athletic League of New York City's Black athletic clubs. After the Crescent Athletic Club of Washington lost the first two years to the Smart Set of Brooklyn, Henderson organized his own team at the Twelfth Street YMCA to challenge for the championship. The Washington Twelfth-Streeters went undefeated against all comers, including all the New York club teams, and captured the Colored Basketball World Championship for the 1909–1910 season.

> In 1908, EB wrote letters to the American Sports Publishing Company, the publishers of all the Spalding Equipment Company handbooks and manuals, inquiring about publishing a handbook that for the first time would highlight the athletic activity taking place among African American leagues and teams in New York; Washington, DC; the Black colleges; and high schools around the country. EB coedited the *Official Handbook for the Inter-Scholastic Athletic Association of Middle Atlantic States* from 1910 to 1913. This publication was the first handbook Spalding produced that included pictures of Black athletes and Black teams, thus becoming the first chronicle of African Americans participating in sports. In 1911, EB published "The Colored College Athlete" in *Crisis Magazine*, the official magazine of the National Association for the Advancement of Colored People (NAACP), which was edited by the renowned African American scholar Dr. W. E. B. Du Bois. In the article, he boldly predicted, "When competent physical directors and equal training facilities are afforded the Colored youth, the White athlete will find an *equal, or superior*, in nearly every line of athletic endeavor."[2]

E. B. was the first African American male to be certified to teach physical education in the schools of the United States. He devoted fifty years to teaching, coaching, and advocating for athletic facilities, physical training, and education in the Washington, DC, Colored School System and nationally. For much of that time, he was the director of physical education, health, and safety in DC public schools. Additionally, E. B. became a reknowned author, writing the Spalding publications, three books, chapters in several books, and had more than three thousand letters to the editor during his life.

E. B. was also a fearless advocate for the civil rights of African Americans through his activism in the NAACP. He was active in the Washington, DC, branch of the NAACP and was instrumental in establishing the first branch of the NAACP in his rural hometown of Falls Church, Virginia. As chairman of the Committee against Segregation in the Nation's Capital and the Committee against Segregation in Recreation in the Nation's Capital, he pushed to open doors for Black people. After the landmark Supreme Court decision in *Brown v. Board of Education*, E. B. was elected and served as president of the Virginia Conference of NAACPs to lead the fight against "massive resistance" to desegregation of the schools in Virginia.

I coined the title "grandfather of Black basketball" for my grandfather because Bob Douglas is considered the father of Black professional basketball for his role as the founder and manager of the New York Renaissance basketball team and John McLendon is considered the father of Black college basketball for his coaching at North Carolina College of Negroes (now North Carolina Central University) and Tennessee A&I (now Tennessee State University), winning national titles, and then successfully coaching in the American Basketball Association (ABA). Both are well deserving of fatherhood status, but introducing basketball to Blacks on a wide-scale organized basis predates both these fine gentlemen's worthy accomplishments. So if Bob Douglas and John McLendon are the "fathers of Black basketball," then E. B. Henderson is the "grandfather of Black basketball."

E. B.'s scope of work, not only in basketball, but also in physical education, sports history, civil rights, and public school athletics, gives credence to what Arthur Ashe said in his book *Hard Road to Glory: Basketball*:

> Black players have weathered many difficulties since 1908, when Edwin B. Henderson began the first serious inner-city competitions between New York City and Washington, DC. . . . Henderson himself *cannot be thanked enough* for his contributions. In addition, coaches and officials

> like Cumberland Posey, Robert Douglas, Abe Saperstein, Holcombe Rucker, Clarence "Big House" Gaines, Johnny B. McLendon, Vivian Stringer, Dave Whitney, and K. C. Jones have been outstanding.[3]

Through this book chronicling the life and times of Edwin Bancroft Henderson, it is my hope that those who make their livings playing, coaching, managing, and owning basketball teams will begin to thank Henderson for introducing basketball to African Americans by putting in place the infrastructure and then nurturing the game while it was in its infancy, which has now evolved into the phenomenal enterprise it is today.

On February 3, 1977, I was with friends at the WBIL radio station in Tuskegee, Alabama, recording a commercial, when something nudged me, and I heard a voice in my head saying, "Go check on Grandpa." So I left my friends in the middle of the recording session and went to John A. Andrew Hospital on the campus of Tuskegee Institute, where he had been for the past three weeks. When I got there, I saw several people struggling over his body and then a still calmness. As I experienced his last breath releasing from his lifeless body, I wondered, "Why was I the one who heard his voice beckoning me to come to him?"

After shedding some tears, I called my parents and then reached out to my siblings to let them know that E. B., the man we affectionately knew as Grandpa, had passed away. He was ninety-three years old. After everyone arrived at the hospital, we said a prayer and then began contacting our pastor and making the arrangements for funeral services. At the funeral, I cried inconsolably. The man for whom I had been named was gone. Although I had learned so much from him, there were still so many unanswered questions. Nell and E. B.'s desire was to be cremated and placed in a common crypt at their summer cottage, Loafing Holt, overlooking Black Walnut Lake at Highland Beach.

When E. B. died in 1977, there weren't any monuments, buildings, statues, or other manifestations of his contributions to athletics, physical education, sports history, or civil rights anywhere. His books were no longer in print, although they existed in libraries. The Spalding booklets that showed the first pictures of Black teams participating in athletics were rare items only found in the hidden stacks of libraries and archives. The Washington, DC, Public School's athletic conference was no longer named the PSAL but rather the DC-ISAA (ISAA—like the first league for Blacks initiated by E. B.), but no one made any connection to where that name came from. It was as if he had been erased from the annals of history.

In 1988, after finally settling my grandparents' will, my father and uncle were liquidating their assets. The house that E. B. and Nell built at 307 South Maple Avenue in Falls Church was on the list of things to sell. Upon learning this, I told my father that I wanted the house because I was his namesake. I was shocked when they agreed to not sell the house and put me on the deed. In the fall of 1993, I moved into that home. I started a nonprofit organization to preserve the history of the early civil rights movement, which my grandparents were instrumental in establishing. To a large degree, I was preserving the legacy started by E. B. and others in Falls Church, when they formed the first rural branch of the NAACP after the segregation ordinance in 1915 that would have made my grandparents move out of their new home.

In 1997, twenty years after E. B.'s passing, my sister Dena and I were looking at things that had been stored away in the attic and came across a box. Upon closer inspection, we observed faded papers that mice had gnawed around the edges. In the box, between the lettered dividers that one usually finds in someone's file cabinets, there were documents, letters, saved programs, photographs, and copies of Spalding handbooks, among other things. In little time, we knew we had run across a treasure trove of E. B.'s very valuable items that had been saved for some unsuspecting person to find. Someone had emptied his file cabinet into this box, and I asked my sister if I could have it.

These items were meant for me to find. This was the road map my grandfather left for me to tell his story. Even though I grew up around him, I have spent the better part of the past thirty years on a journey of finding E. B. Henderson. It was as if a light had come shining through the attic window, like in *The Blues Brothers*, when John Belushi and Dan Aykroyd said, "We're on a mission from God."

With this book and all the honors posthumously bestowed upon my grandfather, it is my hope that people will come to know the man who flung open the doors for African American youth to participate in organized sports, particularly basketball, and he will get the recognition he deserves.

I

Sunrise

Where We Begin

On one frosty November morning in Southwest Washington, DC, near the waterfront, a newborn baby cried out and took its first breaths into a new world full of challenges. The year was 1883, and the child, Edwin Bancroft "E. B." Henderson. Young Edwin was the son of Louisa and William Henderson. Being the firstborn, a lot would be expected of young Edwin as the family grew and moved from place to place. But for now, Edwin's parents adored their son with wonder and amazement. As the midwife gathered her things to leave after another successful birth, mother and father marveled at their newborn baby. He was a handsome and healthy child. Even with all the challenges attributed to being born an African American boy in a southern city nestled between the former slave states of Maryland and Virginia, hope for the future was enough to be joyous for now.

Edwin's birthplace was the home of his paternal grandmother, Eliza Hicks. She was born enslaved on the Fitzhugh Plantation with her family mostly intact, including her mother, Elizabeth Mimetou Foote, and her grandmother Rachel, until their separation after Mordecai Fitzhugh passed. After the execution of Mordecai's 1858 will, three generations of Edwin's ancestors were split up and sent to different plantations.[1]

In 1670, William ("the immigrant") Fitzhugh, Mordecai's grandfather, immigrated to Stafford, Virginia, where he established the family's principal residence. William was a successful lawyer, an officer in the

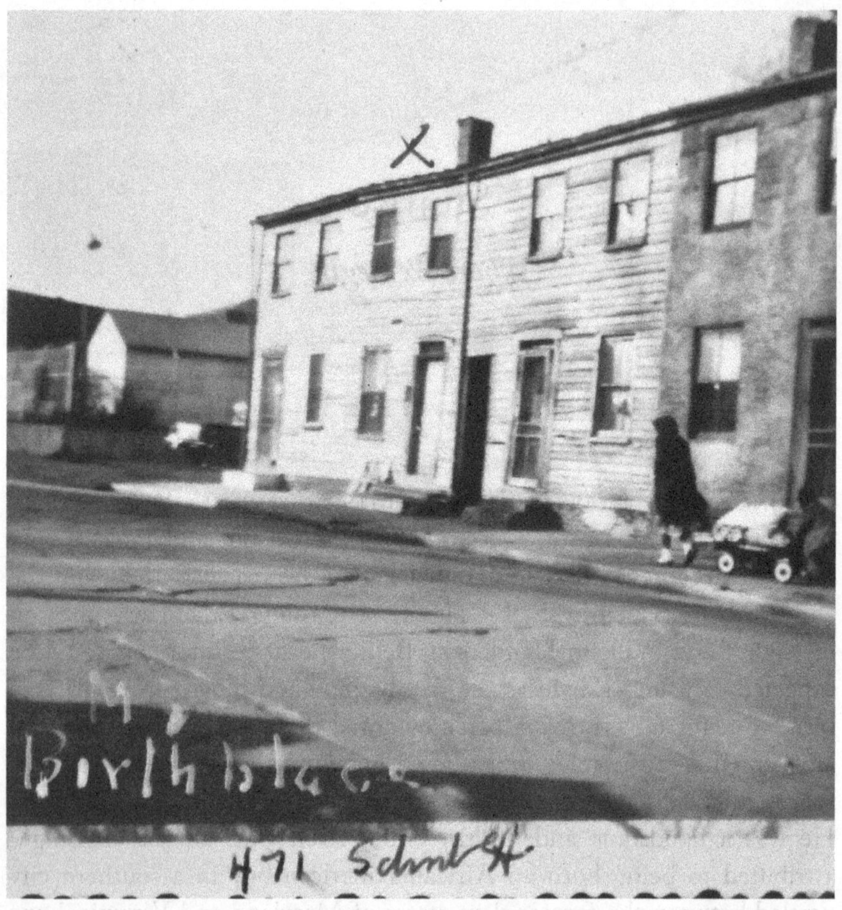

Edwin Henderson's birthplace in Southwest Washington, DC. *Courtesy of Henderson Family Collection*

local militia, and representative to the colonial legislature. He was a very successful land investor who served as an agent for the proprietor of the Northern Neck (of Virginia) Grant, which provided him knowledge about prime parcels of land—and of which he took full advantage. William Fitzhugh's total land holdings consisted of 54,000 acres, including his estate in both Stafford and Fairfax Counties. The Ravensworth Plantation (consisting of 21,996 acres) was the largest plantation in Fairfax County, Virginia. Upon William Sr.'s death in 1701, William Jr. and his brother, Captain Henry Fitzhugh, divided Ravensworth Estate in Fairfax County equally. Two generations later, Henry's grandson Mordecai Fitzhugh's portion of the original estate was 2,300 acres, on which E. B.'s ancestors were enslaved.[2]

According to *The Story of Ravensworth* by John Browne, "The 1810 federal census recorded two free adults, four children under 10 years old and 34 slaves in the household. . . . His house in the northeast part of his 2300 acres was located near the planned road (Leesburg Pike), where it passes through today's Seven Corners intersection with Arlington Boulevard."[3] Edwin's grandmother Eliza was born on Mordecai's plantation to Elizabeth Mimetou Foote and Charles Andrew Hicks. Eliza's ancestry can be traced back to Chief Mimetou, the eldest uncle of Chief Powhatan, the father of Pocahontas. Chief Mimetou was born in the mid-1500s and was an archenemy of the English settlers, leading his tribe in the 1622 assault on the English tobacco plantations along the James River, when he was killed in the effort to stem the advances of the English.[4]

Mimetou's great-grandson Chief John Logan, apparently the offspring of his Native mother and a Scotch Irish father, was the victim of Indian removal. In 1753, Colonel Charles Broadwater was ordered to the property of William Fitzhugh III to remove the Indian presence on the Fitzhugh Plantation. Chief John was old and refused to move, so he and his Native wife were killed, but their young papoose was thrown to the side during the skirmish. One of Broadwater's soldiers, Andrew Hicks, saved the boy, gave him his name, and placed him on the Fitzhugh Plantation among the enslaved, there to be raised. The pistol powder horn belonging to Colonel Broadwater was given to the child to pacify him and remained in the family as a memento for more than two hundred years.[5]

The rescued boy grew strong and sired a son named Charles Andrew Hicks. In 1846, on the Mordecai Fitzhugh Plantation, Charles Hicks and his wife, Elizabeth Mimetou Foote, gave birth to Eliza, Edwin's grandmother. In 1858, Eliza was willed to Mordecai Fitzhugh's daughter Lucinda Henry as an inheritance.[6] At the age of twelve, Eliza was expected to become a breeder (Virginia was known as a "slave-breeding state," as were many of the more northern border states once tobacco was no longer the major cash crop). Eliza, rather than remaining the property of Lucinda Henry and being forced to give birth to children who would be sold into slavery, decided to run away to find her mother, who had been dealt to Mordecai Fitzhugh's other daughter, Julianna Slade, on an adjoining plantation.

After running away, Eliza was "sold down South" into Mississippi, into what was known as the "Cotton Kingdom," by one of the several slave auction brokers in Alexandria, Virginia. Arriving in New Orleans, she was pregnant with William, Edwin's father. Eliza was transported to the New Orleans slave market, the largest in the South. Both Eliza and her son ended up on a plantation in Vicksburg, Mississippi.

During the months-long assault in 1863 by General Ulysses S. Grant's troops at Milliken's Bend around Vicksburg, US Colored troops under the command of Colonel Hermann Lieb repelled the Confederates under the command of Major General John G. Walker, who were trying to disrupt the Union supply lines on the Mississippi River. Grant's victory was a turning point in the Civil War, as it would split the Confederacy in half, separating the states to the west of the Mississippi River from the states to the east. It was during this battle that Grant recognized how hard US Colored troops would fight for their freedom.[7]

During the Battle of Vicksburg, Eliza hid young William in a trunk and, along with others on the surrounding plantations, fled to the Union lines, where they sought asylum from their Southern enslavers. She did not leave Mississippi directly afterward and was married by a chaplain of a Massachusetts regiment to a young soldier by the name of Henderson, whose real name was Shadrach Rodogruis, the son of a Portuguese sailor.[8] Feeling the need to be among family, Eliza and William followed the trail of contraband back to her home near Washington, DC, where she might receive protection and opportunities in the contraband camps. She never saw or heard from Shadrach again.[9]

Eliza settled in Southwest Washington, DC, near the waterfront, where work was plentiful. Southwest Washington, DC, was a mixed-race, working-class community; one could find work from the ships that were coming in, loading, and unloading cargo at the wharf. Many workers lived in the alleyways, where they would remain out of sight of the White residents, like the soldiers at the Washington Arsenal (today's Fort McNair). But for the most part, Southwest Washington was a mix of newly freed Blacks, Irish, German, Jewish, and other European immigrants.

In 1870, Eliza obtained a loan from the Freedmen's Bureau and bought a new two-story building on School Street SW, Washington, DC, where she opened a grocery store on the first floor. Her cousin Frederick Foote Jr. in Falls Church owned the largest grocery store in the Greater Falls Church area. Almost 40 percent of Falls Church was populated by Blacks. When it became a town in 1875, Fred Jr. was elected town constable, or sheriff, and in 1880, he was elected the first African American town councilman in Falls Church, becoming one of the first elected African American officials in Virginia. Because everyone knew Fred Jr., the people in Falls Church, both Black and White, bought their groceries and provisions at his store.

In 1874, when William was fifteen years old, Eliza tried to enroll him into Howard University, but he rebelled and joined the US Navy.[10] He served six tours of duty on four different steamships before being honorably discharged in 1880. As a coal heaver aboard his second steamship, the USS *Tallapoosa*, he was injured with a hernia and was continually sick with intermittent fevers, bronchitis, and adenitis. These ailments would follow him for many years even after he was discharged and may have been the reason he was denied a pension from the navy when he applied in 1898. After he was discharged, he moved back to Southwest Washington, where he met and fell in love with his wife, Louisa.

Louisa Mars was born in Williamsburg, Virginia, the daughter of an enslaved woman, Annie Thomas, and her White master. Louisa was fair enough to pass for White. As a young teenager, she moved to Washington, DC, to live with her sister and her sister's husband. Louisa, or Lulu, as she was often called, worked as a domestic in several Washington, DC, households. Louisa and William were married in February 1883, and Edwin "E. B." Henderson was born nine months later, in November 1883.[11]

As William and Louisa embarked on starting a family, they may have wondered where life would lead them. Washington was a very progressive city for African Americans after the Civil War, and many African Americans were doing quite well there. Although inequality and discrimination still existed, access to good schools, medical care, and jobs made Washington a better place to live and raise a family than almost anywhere else, including just across the border in Maryland or Virginia.

2

The "Black Mecca"

Washington, DC, 1861–1904 and Beyond

African Americans in Washington DC

Washington, DC, was known as a welcoming place and the "Black Mecca" for African Americans almost from its inception. In 1791, the District of Columbia was established as a brokered deal between Alexander Hamilton and Thomas Jefferson, two of America's Founding Fathers.[1] Major Pierre Charles L'Enfant, who fought in the American Revolution under the command of Marquis de Lafayette, was hired by President George Washington to design the plan for the capital of the new country. L'Enfant's idea was to create a city to mirror Paris, the capital of his native France.

L'Enfant was assigned a brilliant gentleman of African descent, Benjamin Banneker, to assist in drawing the plans for the new city. Banneker was a renowned mathematician, astronomer, inventor, and publisher of an early almanac. His enslaved maternal grandfather was from the Dogon Tribe of Mali in Western Africa, known for their advanced knowledge of astronomy, which was passed down to Banneker.[2] Banneker's neighbor Andrew Ellicott was hired to conduct the survey for the new capital, and Ellicott commissioned Banneker to set the astronomical azimuth for laying out the plan for a one-hundred-square-mile plot of land that would become the District of Columbia. Banneker laid on his back for three consecutive nights at the southernmost point of the proposed city, Jones Point, in what is now Alexandria.[3]

George Washington became increasingly irritated with L'Enfant's delays due to his desire for perfection, as well as his drunkenness, and fired him. L'Enfant gathered his belongings and hastily left for his native France, taking his plans for the city with him. Fortunately, Banneker, who had a photographic memory, redrew L'Enfant's plans and assisted Ellicott in surveying and laying the boundary stones for the city.[4]

Land was ceded by two slaveholding states to create the District of Columbia, so it was natural that Washington, DC, had several slave markets and auction houses within its borders. Once tobacco was no longer the colonies' major cash crop, the upper Southern states supplied the cotton-producing states with labor through what was called the domestic slave trade. Virginia, on Washington's southern border, was known as a "slave-breeding state":

> Virginia's domestic slave trade grew substantially in the early nineteenth century. It became the state's most lucrative industry, with more money being made by the exporting of enslaved people than was made from tobacco. . . . Two million enslaved people are believed to have been transported or marched on foot from Richmond to the Deep South, where they were needed to labor in the cotton fields.[5]

In 1849, Abraham Lincoln introduced a bill in Congress to compensate slave owners in exchange for abolishing the practice of buying and selling slaves in the District of Columbia. Fearing the sentiment in Washington to outlaw slavery, many Virginians in 1846 urged the slave-trading and -brokering companies in Alexandria and Richmond to demand the retrocession of the lands in the District of Columbia back to Virginia.[6]

Many Whites, especially those visiting from European countries, were appalled by the slave coffles marching through the city on their way to the "Cotton Kingdom" in the Southern states. Visitors and foreign diplomats from other countries around the world were shocked at the hypocrisy of American freedom. Charles Dickens, on a visit to Washington, noted, "The sensation of exacting any service from human creatures who are bought and sold and being for the time a party as it were to their condition, is not an enviable one." Many view the bondage in a nation that prided itself on the concepts of liberty and freedom as an embarrassment, thus giving the city a bad reputation.[7]

Abolitionist sentiment was commonplace in Washington. Slave revolts and uprisings increased as the nineteenth century progressed and caused more to consider emancipation of all enslaved persons in the nation. The 1848 *Pearl* incident, where seventy-seven enslaved African Americans attempted to make their strike for freedom on the schooner the *Pearl* at the Seventh Street wharf in Washington, DC, caused both pro- and antislavery groups to demand more attention to the institution of slavery in the nation, especially in the nation's capital. Several of my own ancestors were among those on the *Pearl*.[8]

As the city grew and the population of the enslaved in Washington increased, free people of African descent also increased. By the 1830s, there were more free Blacks in Washington than there were enslaved, and by 1850, there were 8,461 free Blacks, compared to 4,694 enslaved. Still, because of the infamous Black codes, Blacks could not vote, testify against White people, or hold political office. By 1860, the census records show that, of the 89,080 people living in Washington, DC, 14,000 were Black, 11,131 of whom were free, almost 80 percent. In Washington, there were a good number of "free people of color" who owned businesses and provided services to the White citizenry of the city. Another name for these people was "free dealers." However, there existed the prevailing attitude of White supremacy and the realization of inequality during these times. Washington, DC, was sandwiched between two slaveholding states, where African Americans could enjoy some semblance of freedom during a time of legal bondage, even though the prevailing reality was that people of African descent were a commodity to be bought, sold, leased out, and used as collateral.[9]

Before the Emancipation Proclamation, all enslaved people in the District of Columbia and several from the areas around Washington were freed by the Act for the Release of Certain Persons Held to Service or Labor in the District of Columbia by Reason of African Descent, signed by Abraham Lincoln on April 16, 1862. Those in Washington,

DC, who freed their enslaved would be compensated. With the government having jurisdiction over Washington, DC, Lincoln, as president, was able to accomplish what he had attempted thirteen years previously, in 1849.[10] Today, in Washington, DC, April 16 is celebrated as Liberation Day.

In the 1860s, Washington was about to swell in population. With the Civil War in progress and the country in disarray, enslaved people were encouraged to tempt fate and try to find their way to Washington and to freedom. After the news of Southern aggression, attacking Fort Sumter in Charleston, the race was on to escape from slavery.

Another impetus to strike for freedom took place in May 1861, when three enslaved men in the Hampton Roads area of Virginia rowed their boat out to Fortress Monroe. These three men asked for asylum from their slave masters, and the soldiers under General Benjamin Butler took them in. The next day, the owners went to the fort demanding that their property be returned to them under the Fugitive Slave Act of 1850. To this, General Butler told the three men, "Since Virginia is no longer a state under the laws of the United States, I do not have to return your property, but rather, these are 'Contrabands of War,' and as such, the law does not apply." The next day, a stream of enslaved people found their way to Fortress Monroe. The stream became a river of enslaved people finding their way to Union lines and Washington, DC, where contraband camps were set up to accommodate the people who sought freedom.[11]

Most have been taught erroneously through simplistic terms that "Abraham Lincoln freed the slaves" by issuing the Emancipation Proclamation. However, upon further analysis, it was a rather clever executive order and wartime act that freed the slaves in jurisdictions over which Lincoln had no legal authority. It states further, "[S]uch persons of suitable condition, will be received into the armed service of the United States," so with this edict, Lincoln freed no slaves but rather prompted disruption, inviting slave insurrection and escapes. It also invited African Americans to join the fight against the Confederacy to attain the emancipation they sought.

After the Emancipation Proclamation went into effect on January 1, 1863, the mission of the United States shifted from the preservation of the Union to ending the institution of slavery in the United States. More than 200,000 African Americans enlisted and fought in the Civil War. Many were former slaves who made their way to the Union lines during battles. Many were recruited at contraband camps set up to care for those who had escaped slavery. But also many free African Americans believed in the fight and volunteered now that the purpose had shifted to freeing their enslaved brothers.[12]

This would not happen without resistance from the Confederacy, who promised that Black soldiers captured during the war would be reenslaved, and the White officers commanding the Negro soldiers would be killed or kept alive and treated more severely than officers of White troops. The most heinous act of the war against Black troops came at Fort Pillow, Tennessee. Black troops were outnumbered and attempted to surrender, but the Confederate troops would not give them quarter, as they would have done for White Union soldiers. The Confederate troops, under the command of Nathan Bedford Forrest of Ku Klux Klan fame, slaughtered them all. This proved to US Colored troops that they must fight to the death in battle. They would not be allowed to surrender. From this point forward, the rallying cry for US Colored troops was "Remember Fort Pillow."[13]

The U Street area, what is now U Street and Florida Avenue, was essentially rural at that time. U Street was known as Boundary Road because Washington, DC, beyond that point was totally undeveloped. The federal government initially bought this land along Vermont Avenue NW just north of Logan Circle on Boundary Road to build a camp for Union soldiers. But shortly after the war began, camps to accommodate the contrabands became more essential. Many parcels of land in the Washington, DC, and Northern Virginia areas became contraband camps. In late spring of 1862, Camp Barker became one of the first of several hundred of these camps, near the corner of Twelfth and U Streets and what is now Howard University. At one point, Camp Barker housed as many as four thousand formerly enslaved people, but an outbreak of cholera caused the camp to be disbanded. Many inhabitants in contraband camps found work, bought property, and built homes in the areas of the camps, and that is what happened along U Street, as well.[14]

After disease ravaged Camp Barker, Freedmen's Village was established on the grounds of the Robert E. Lee Plantation, where Arlington Cemetery is located today. The Confiscation Act of 1861 and 1862 authorized the government to seize the property belonging to Confederate sympathizers. There were many other camps, as well, like Camp Wadsworth and Camp Beckwith in McLean, Virginia; Camp Rucker, near Falls Church; and Camp Todd in Alexandria, all of which were used as recruitment centers for the US Colored troops. Camps were scattered all over nearby Washington, DC, on both sides of the Potomac River to accommodate the influx of enslaved people seeking refuge. The men were encouraged to enlist in the US Colored troops. The women were enlisted to do cooking, laundry, and other activities to support the troops. And the children were placed in schools, learning to read and write.[15]

Almost simultaneously in 1862, Freedmen's Hospital was established to provide medical care for those who had made their way to the camp. Five years later, in 1867, Howard University was established to accommodate a college, and a "Colored school system" was established to provide education for the children who found their way to Washington, DC. The camp, the hospital, and the university created the synergy to bring commercial enterprise to the U Street area, which years later would be given the moniker Black Broadway by Booker T. Washington.[16]

During the Reconstruction era, African Americans were elected to Congress and sent to Washington, as well as to statehouses in the Southern states. However, toward the end of Reconstruction, violence and retribution resurfaced once the federal troops who were in the South to protect the rights of Black people under the new amendments to the Constitution were taken out. Many of those, like Blanche K. Bruce, decided to stay in Washington rather than return to Mississippi, where he was elected as a senator in 1874. Other enterprising African Americans came to pursue business ventures to provide goods and services to the new inhabitants.

Scholars and academics were teaching or being educated at Howard University. Freedmen's Hospital provided medical care for African Americans arriving in Washington. And many parents came to Washington because it meant their children would receive an education. This environment created a vibrant African American culture centered along the U Street corridor, in an area known as LeDroit Park. Although society was strictly segregated, this section along U Street provided most of, if not all, the goods and services essential for African Americans to survive and thrive between 1862 and 1900.[17]

Another area of Washington set aside for African Americans to settle after the Civil War was along the banks of the Anacostia River. In 1867, General Oliver Otis Howard, the superintendent of the Freedmen's Bureau, purchased 375 acres from the descendants of James Barry for $50,000 in what was officially named Uniontown but was more commonly known as Barry Farm. Although the land was purchased to provide opportunities to African American refugees who had recently been emancipated from slavery, purchasing land for those of means was also an attractive proposition. Frederick Douglass's three sons, Charles, Lewis, and Frederick Jr., purchased lots in Anacostia. Frederick Douglass's home in Rochester, New York, burned down in 1872, and he moved to Washington, where he was known as the "Lion of Anacostia." Douglass moved with his wife, Anna Murray Douglass, to Cedar Hill in Anacostia, overlooking the federal city he called home, in 1878.[18]

Frederick Douglass's reputation as a champion for abolition and social justice for Blacks and women made him a fixture in Washington society at this time. From 1872, when he moved to Washington, until his death, he would hold several federal appointments. He could be seen walking around Washington, emboldening other African Americans with a sense of pride and dignity. Shortly after the Civil War, his three sons played baseball with the Washington Mutuals, where he would be seen in the audience watching the games.[19]

Douglass became the US marshall for Washington, DC, in 1877; the recorder of deeds in 1881; and finally the ambassador to Haiti (1889–91), where he advocated for autonomy for the island nation that had thrown off the shackles of slavery only to be made to pay reparations to their former colonial master, France.[20]

In the 1870s and '80s, a group known as the Grand Fountain of the United Order of True Reformers was established in many progressive African American communities around the country. This organization expanded under the leadership of William Washington Browne. At first, it was associated with the all-White temperance movement but changed under Browne's leadership to become a mutual benefit society, issuing a death benefit to its members, much like an insurance company. In 1881, it expanded its services to include a Black-owned and -operated bank, hotel, printing office, grocery store, concert hall, and real estate office. It had more than seven hundred chapters with more than 40,000 members.[21]

In 1902, the True Reformers Hall was built in Washington, DC, at Twelfth and U Streets. The first floor was commercial and retail space. The second floor was a ballroom. Physicians and lawyers rented the upper floors, and the basement was an armory and drill room for Washington's Black National Guard unit. Amazingly, the building was built without incurring any debt. This was a testament to the progress of African Americans, when most of them had been enslaved less than forty years previously. This building would later become one of the hotbeds of Black basketball in 1907 because it was the only place large enough to put a close-to-regulation basketball court for Blacks in Washington at the time.[22]

Mary Ann Shadd Cary, a Howard University Law School graduate and the second African American woman to earn a law degree, referred to Washington, DC, as the "Mecca of the [C]olored pilgrim seeking civil, religious, social, and business enlightenment, and preferment of protection."[23] Is it any wonder that the synergy of African Americans seeking freedom and coming to a place where there was an opportunity for land ownership, a hospital for medical care, a university, and a "Colored" school system to educate their children made Washington, DC, in the late 1800s home to the largest population of Black people in the United States?[24]

In the short time between slavery and freedom, African Americans were making great strides toward proving to Whites that Blacks were not an inferior people. I beg to differ with the common conception that the renaissance of African American culture took place in Harlem. The renaissance moved north to Harlem *after being born and cultivated in Washington, DC.* Many of the musicians, intellectual thinkers, writers, and artists spent their formative years in Washington, DC. During the first wave of migration during and after the Civil War, those individuals landed in Washington, DC. In the second wave, in what we call the Great Migration, those individuals proceeded in Harlem, Chicago, and other industrial cities in the North.

When one looks at African Americans in Washington, DC, from the Civil War to the turn of the twentieth century, one must take into account that (1) in the short span of time, Blacks had advanced further than most would have ever imagined; (2) Black exceptionalism had debunked the false narrative of White supremacy; and (3) Blacks had accomplished all this against the odds, overcome seemingly insurmountable obstacles, and were successful in building a self-sufficient community despite racial segregation.

But by far, the major reason Washington, DC, was the best place for African Americans to live after the end of slavery and during the Jim Crow era was because there was a dedicated public education division for African Americans. The Washington, DC, Colored School System was equally funded and catered to a Black constituency that believed that African Americans were not inferior. The Colored schools of Washington were better funded than any other segregated school divisions in the country. An essay from the 1935 *Journal of Negro Education* includes insight from Dr. W. E. B. Du Bois:

> "Does the Negro need separate schools?" His answer was an emphatic "God knows it does." Du Bois's attitude toward racially segregated schools was pragmatic: as long as [W]hites believed in the inferiority of [B]lack people, [B]lack children and young adults were better off in separate schools and universities.
>
> Du Bois continues: "I have long been convinced . . . that the Negroes in the public schools of Harlem are not getting an education that is in any sense comparable in efficiency, discipline, and human development with that which the Negroes are getting in the separate public schools in Washington, DC."[25]

This is the world EB was born into. Although it might not have seemed like a time of African American prosperity, it was a time of great opportunity. It was a time when a young man could make his mark and create

Edwin Henderson at two years old with mother Louisa and brother William.
COURTESY OF HENDERSON FAMILY COLLECTION

something for the greater good. EB was able to find a need and fulfill it, giving opportunities to young people and bettering his race by introducing sports, emphasizing physical training and healthy and clean living, during the Great Migration.

However, for William Henderson, now that a second child was born, he needed to make a better wage than he was afforded in Washington, DC. He found it hard to find a job that paid enough to support his growing family, but he heard about great opportunities in Pittsburgh's steel mills.

3

Pittsburgh

Learning the Value of Work

In mid-1885, Louisa gave birth to another child, a son named William, after his father. With two young children to care for, Louisa would not be able to work. And with another mouth to feed, William knew, as a day laborer, he would need more money and steady work to provide for his growing family.

Meanwhile, events across the river in Falls Church, Virginia, were causing Eliza to consider moving back to where her cousin Fred Foote Jr. was trying to run his store. Fred, as a member of the Falls Church Town Council, was dealing with a difficult racial situation. The town council was a very combative environment. Falls Church was experiencing a backlash stemming from the ending of Reconstruction, the disenfranchisement of Black communities, and the "redemption" by many Whites in Virginia wanting to take back their land and to take away the rights granted to African American citizens through the new amendments to the Constitution.

Debate and deliberations were often difficult, if not outright hostile. The politics in the town were dominated by the Democratic Party's anti-Reconstructionist and anti-Black mentality. Fred Jr.'s ideas and influence were blocked or marginalized at every turn by the Democratic majority on the town council. And although Fred, still a relatively young man, dealt with this situation as best he could, the negativity and constant bickering affected his health and longevity.

The town council did not like the idea of Black people, who always voted Republican, the party of Abraham Lincoln, having a say in town matters. The Democratic majority proposed a plan to gerrymander and retrocede one-third of the town, where 232 Black registered voters lived, back to Fairfax County and out of the jurisdiction of the town of Falls Church. This caused Fred Jr. much distress and, some would say, ultimately led to his untimely death.[1]

Eliza was phenomenal and doing well with her store in Southwest Washington. She was a smart, savvy, and very shrewd businesswoman. She would eventually buy out Fred Jr.'s store, sell the portion of the lot that faced Leesburg Pike (which was the main street in the town), and use the proceeds to pay off Fred Jr.'s loan on the property. She built a new home and a new store down the block closer to the Episcopal Falls Church, for which the town is named. Now that she was free and clear of her debts, she became a land speculator, purchasing several strategic parcels of land near the Falls Church in the center of town.[2]

A couple of years after the birth of William Jr., William Sr. had grown increasingly frustrated with his prospects of finding good-paying work along the wharf in Washington, DC. It seemed that his service in the navy meant little to those who were hiring watermen to work on the boats and the waterways, as those jobs were kept from him and saved for those of a lighter complexion. Only the more menial labor was afforded African Americans in Washington, DC.

William had heard of how Pittsburgh was a booming industrial city with good-paying jobs in the steel mills. Pittsburgh was the fastest-growing city in the country in the mid-1880s. He made up his mind and convinced Louisa that Pittsburgh would be a better place to raise the family. So in 1888, William, Louisa, and the two children said goodbye to Eliza and Washington, DC, and moved to Pittsburgh, Pennsylvania. William felt good about his prospects of better employment in Pittsburgh's steel mills. Months after their second child was born, this young family boarded a train with all their belongings and moved to Smoketown, with William's high hopes of making a better wage to support his growing family as many others would do:

> Black migrants [moved] from the farmlands of small towns of the South, where wages for African Americans averaged less than $3.50 per week. That went up to $9 a week in big Southern cities like Louisville. But in the urban North, the average weekly wage for Black employees was as much as $14 per week, and no Northern city was more financially promising than Pittsburgh.[3]

After arriving in Pittsburgh and spending most of the money they had saved for a place to accommodate their small family, they settled into the Hill District of Pittsburgh, "located on a slope overlooking Pittsburgh's downtown from the East."[4] William went job hunting, and though he had no experience as a steel worker, he found a job relatively quickly as a laborer in one of the steel mills. Still, the pay for the menial jobs were several times better than the wages one was able to make in southern states: $1 or $2 versus $0.25–0.50 a day to raise a family on.[5]

Now five years old, E. B. was enrolled in the Franklin School, a racially mixed school just a few blocks away, at the corner of Franklin and Logan Streets, near the Golden Triangle.[6] A third-grade teacher recognized how well Louisa had homeschooled young Edwin. E. B. remembered, "One White teacher of the 3rd grade had me read her pupils and gave me a quarter, one-fourth of a laborer's pay in those days."[7]

The Henderson family was growing. Everyone was expected to pitch in, even the two young boys. Louisa wasn't able to help much. She had all she could handle with the two boys and another one on the way. Charles was born in 1889, and Annie was born in 1891. On Sunday mornings, Louisa would bake hot rolls and send Edwin and William to sell them in front of their home to people walking home from church. Additionally, the boys would light fires in the furnaces of Jewish homes because people of the Jewish faith were not allowed to do such work on their Sabbath. The family also raised chickens in the backyard and sold eggs. The Henderson household was an industrious one, with everyone helping as much as they could, no matter what age they might have been.[8]

Amenities for Blacks were much better in Pittsburgh because society there was not segregated. The Hendersons lived a block away from the bustling intersection of Wylie Avenue and Fulton Street. Harlem

Renaissance poet Claude McKay nicknamed this section the "Crossroads of the World" as the epicenter of African American life at that time.[9]

But there were also certain unsavory elements lying in the shadows of this thriving community. Many a steel factory paycheck was squandered on drinking and prostitution. Gambling dens and policy games, or "numbers running," was prevalent in this area of town. Many poor factory workers would spend their hard-earned money on these leisurely activities, hoping to expand the little earnings they made in the factories.[10]

During slavery, many African Americans were skilled laborers: blacksmiths, carpenters, horse farriers, and so on, but despite this, African Americans were not allowed to join labor unions, which were the conduit to opportunities for skilled workers in the factories in the northern United States. African Americans had moved north from the plantations to the "plants" to take advantage of industrial production, but White workers in the North did not want to compete with them for the skilled positions. Labor unions were created at factories and prohibited African Americans from joining, thereby preserving skilled jobs for Whites only. Many factories openly advertised, "Whites only need apply."

So the only jobs offered to African Americans were the manual-labor jobs or the most dangerous jobs in places like the furnace area, where accidents happened regularly. African Americans were commonly used as strikebreakers, where they could get a foothold on the skilled positions. But there was always the real danger of violence against strikebreakers, commonly called scabs.[11] For William, as a laborer, working in the steel mills could be dangerous, and there were not many opportunities for advancement. He was stuck on the bottom rungs of the work scale. But an opportunity was about to present itself that would change everything for the Hendersons, as well as many African Americans working in the steel mills.

Carnegie Steel was making massive profits just before the 1892 confrontation, and the union, the Amalgamated Association, wanted a raise commensurate with the profits made by Carnegie Steel Company. The 1892 strike at the Homestead Steel Plant of the Carnegie Steel Company morphed into a bloody battle instigated by the steel plant's management and would become one of the deadliest strikes in US history.[12]

In 1891, Henry Clay Frick became chairman of the Carnegie Steel Company. Frick despised labor unions, particularly the Amalgamated Association, which represented eight thousand skilled workers. Pittsburgh labor historian Charles McCollester later wrote in the *Point of Pittsburgh*, "The skilled production workers at Homestead enjoy wages significantly higher than at any other mill in the country."[13] The three-year contract with the Amalgamated Association of Iron and Steel Workers was up for renewal, and management was not negotiating in good faith. The factory wanted the skilled workers to take a pay cut, even though they had taken a pay cut in the previous three-year contract. Instead of offering proposals, management issued ultimatums. After the negotiations broke, the company advertised widely for strikebreakers and locked out the workers. William Henderson was hired as a strikebreaker, a scab.[14]

According to McCollester, the union "established pickets on eight-hour shifts, river patrols and a signal system."[15] Frick hired the Pinkerton National Detective Agency to infiltrate and break the strike from the inside. Then, on July 6, before dawn, three hundred Pinkerton agents approached the steel mill on a river barge. Thousands of workers and their families rushed to the river to keep them out. A battle ensued, gunfire broke out, but in the end, the Pinkertons surrendered when they were beaten by the angry mob.

Four days later, the National Guard sent in 8,500 troops to quash the strike. Frick announced, "Under no circumstances will we have any further dealing with the Amalgamated Association as an organization. This is final." This effectively broke the union, causing its membership to plummet from 24,000 to just 8,000 within a matter of three years.[16]

To make matters worse, the Panic of 1893 and a depression that would last almost a decade started shortly after the strike. With the downturn in the economy, workers were being laid off. With more people looking for work than there were jobs to fill, the competition for even the menial manual-labor jobs was extremely difficult. Retaliation against those African Americans who crossed picket lines during the strike meant danger for people like William, who were hoping they could move into skilled-labor jobs and make a better wage. The economic downturn and the extreme competition for even the most menial jobs meant Pittsburgh was starting to look a lot less favorable to William and Louisa.

Meanwhile, back in Washington, Eliza left the store in Southwest Washington to take over the operations for Fred Jr.'s store in Falls Church. Before Fred passed in 1889, he sold his store to Eliza. The house and store at 477 School Street needed someone to manage things there, so it was time for the Hendersons to bid Pittsburgh goodbye.

4

Back Home to Washington

In 1893, the Pittsburgh adventure was coming to an end. The Panic of 1893 caused many banks, railroads, and steel mills to downsize or outright close. The price farmers were getting for their crops went into a precipitous decline year after year until the turn of the twentieth century. As a result, railroads began to reduce the cost of shipping crops to market. Everyone felt it; as banks began to fail, runs on the banks became more and more prevalent, and many people lost their life's savings when the banks closed. The stock market crash of 1929 is often discussed, but in many respects, the Panic of 1893 was just as bad, if not worse. Grover Cleveland's incoming administration was blamed, and the Democratic Party would not win another presidential election until 1912.[1]

As a result, the steel mills began to cut back, meaning layoffs. Whether William lost his job due to the layoffs or from retaliation for participating as a strikebreaker is unclear. Regardless, the Hendersons decided to leave the hostilities of the strikes, the Pinkertons, and the militias and return to Washington, where family and opportunity awaited them. After Fred Foote Jr. passed away in 1889 at the young age of forty-three, there was a need for them to return to Washington to manage affairs there. Although the experience in Pittsburgh ended without them achieving a financial foothold in the industrial city, the valuable lesson of being industrious in all his endeavors would benefit a growing young man in later life. E. B. took this lesson to heart, and it was a constant mantra for his own life.

As they settled into the two-story flat on School Street, the Henderson family felt some security having a grocery store because it was always going to be a needed commodity. Louisa would run the day-to-day operation of the store, while William found work as a waiter and a porter in Washington.[2] The economy of Washington, DC, was not dependent on industry or farming; rather, the business of Washington was to provide goods and services to accommodate the federal government. Therefore, food, lodging, transportation, schools for children, and other family and personal essentials sustained the Washington economy. And because of William's employment and Louisa's store management, the family was set on sound financial footing, especially because they did not have to pay rent. Eliza's home in Southwest Washington was owned free and clear.

Edwin was now ten years old, and he began the year in fifth grade at the Eliza G. Randle Intermediate School at the corner of Delaware Avenue and H and First Streets SW, about ten blocks from their home on School Street. The Randle School was beyond capacity, and starting on the first day, E. B. got into a fight with another student who teased him because of the way he talked, or his "western twang," which he may have picked up while in Pittsburgh.[3]

The following year, seeking a change for sixth grade, E. B. was enrolled in the Anthony Bowen School at Ninth and E Streets SW, only four blocks from his home. The Bowen School was named for Anthony Bowen, who was quite an iconic figure in Washington, DC, in the mid-1800s. He was an enslaved man who purchased his freedom in 1826 and became the first clerk in the US Patent Office. His home on Ninth Street in Southwest Washington, DC, was a known station for the Underground Railroad, where he built an extra attic to hide runaways.

In 1839, Bowen helped set up a Meeting House for Free Blacks. In 1841, he helped establish one of the few schools for free Blacks at the Metropolitan (Wesley) AME Zion Church, the Sunday Evening School, where students learned the Bible, reading, writing, and arithmetic. Bowen is probably best known for organizing the first Colored branch of the YMCA in 1853, but it hardly resembled the YMCAs we are accustomed to seeing today. It was little more than a club, with the only activity being Christian Bible study. Unfortunately, there was not a permanent facility from which to operate until 1908, when they broke ground to build the Twelfth Street YMCA.[4]

The Anthony Bowen School was established in 1867 as the first free school for Black children in Washington, DC, in first through sixth grades, and it was made possible by combining two side-by-side row houses together to form one school. Because the school was retrofitted by combining two existing row houses, the building soon had structural problems. It lacked proper ventilation, lighting, and heating. The school's principal, Julia C. Grant, wrote a letter to the editor of the *Washington Times*, explaining, "The rooms were heated by 10 pot belly stoves in the classrooms which emitted dangerous fumes that made pupils and teachers sick." The *Times* sent a reporter out, who confirmed her story, and labeled the school a "death trap for children."[5] It may well have been Ms. Grant's example that influenced E. B. to write letters to the editors of newspapers to affect change. If so, she made a huge impression on E. B., who would publish more than three thousand letters to the editor during his life span.[6]

After school, children would play in the streets and parks, which were designed to accommodate leisure play and relaxation. Southwest Washington was a mixed-race working-class neighborhood when E. B. grew up there. Regardless of race, children played together, not caring about their parents' mundane concerns about race. Among E. B.'s many friends and playmates were Al Jolson, who was a star in Hollywood's first talkie, *The Jazz Singer*, and Kate Smith, who as a singer is best known for her renditions of Irving Berlin's "God Bless America."[7]

After finishing the sixth grade at Bowen, the school board condemned the school. However, the school board made the case that the historical nature of the school was too important to simply tear down, so Congress appropriated funds for the reconstruction of the school with modern amenities and safety provisions to preserve the school on its original site. Edwin would move onto seventh and eighth grades at the Bell School at First Street and Southwest Drive, in the shadow of the Capitol and the Library of Congress.[8]

The Bell School had a playground, which was rare. Many of the schools in E. B.'s day were buildings without adequate recreational or leisure space. Even though the plans for Washington provided plenty of open space, much of it was segregated and off-limits to Washington's African American population.

E. B. would frequent the Library of Congress after school, sitting and reading before making his way back home on School Street. This place was not segregated, open to all, regardless of race. The assistant librarian was a Black man named Daniel Murray, who was an example of Black exceptionalism during a time of abject condemnation of Blackness in our nation. He was a member of Washington's Black elite, W. E. B. Du Bois's "Talented Tenth," and a "race man" in the capital and the nation, as well. Because of this, E. B. felt welcomed at the Library of Congress and proud of this institution for having such an upstanding person in a high position.[9]

On occasion, one could find E. B. wandering the halls of the Capitol and sitting in the galleries of Congress and the Senate, listening to debates on the social, economic, and political issues concerning African Americans in the late 1800s. Henderson later recalled, "On the floor of the Senate there were two senators of particularly ill repute to me—Tillman and Blease of South Carolina, who often referred to 'damned niggers' in speeches on the floor. Another was the Alabamian Heflin, who once shot at a colored man on a Washington, DC, streetcar because he did not move from the front of the car."[10]

From the time school was out in fifth grade until his third year in high school, E. B. would spend his summers with his grandmother Eliza in Falls Church. There, he met many of his extended family, who lived in what was a rural farming community at the time. The Footes, Hicks, Scipios, Richards, and others of his extended family had a reputation as being dependable and respected members of that community.

After saving Fred Jr.'s store when he became sick and died, Eliza sold half of his property along Leesburg Pike to satisfy and pay off the loan that she assumed upon buying it from her cousin. Now, with the residual from the sale, she had enough money to build a home and a new store, which bordered the Episcopal Falls Church. A smart businesswoman, she also purchased several parcels of land that once belonged to Falls Church along Fairfax Court House Road and were used to store tobacco, and colonial farmers would pay their taxes to the Episcopal Church. The Episcopal Church was England's representative body during the 1600s and 1700s before the American Revolution in 1776, when America broke away from England. Here is where hard work, clean living, and good food contributed to making E. B.'s strong muscular body and work ethic, which Eliza exemplified through all the obstacles she overcame during her lifetime.

On February 18, 1898, the USS *Maine* exploded in the harbor of Havana, Cuba. The United States declared war on Spain, and thus, the Spanish–American War had begun. The US military established Camp Alger in Falls Church to train troops for fighting in Cuba, Puerto Rico, and the Philippines. The Ninth Battalion Ohio Volunteer Infantry, commanded by Major Charles Young, was among those training at Camp Alger. As told by E. B., one afternoon at his grandmother's store, there was a White enlisted man sitting on the steps of the store. As Major Young approached and entered the store, the White soldier refused to salute his superior officer. The soldier insisted, "I'll never salute a damn n——." E. B. continued,

> I thought Young had not seen the soldier against the wall. In a great cloud of dust, Young whirled his horse around and yelled, "Get up! Salute!" There stood this soldier listening to as severe a tongue lashing as ever I heard one adult giving another. Young's finals words were "You're saluting the United States Army." He returned the salute, spurred his horse around, and was on his way back to Camp Alger. That evening I went across the street to home a proud youngster.[11]

Soon the summer would be over, and E. B. would embark on another horizon-expanding experience at the prestigious M Street High School. School until now had been pretty easy for E. B., and he was always at the top of his class. At M Street High School, he would be competing academically with students from wealthier, middle-class backgrounds. More would be expected of him there.

5

M Street High School

An Introduction to Washington's Black Elites

In 1898, E. B. graduated from Bell Junior High School, and as one of the highest-achieving students in the District of Columbia, he could now enroll in the prestigious M Street High School, the academic high school for African Americans in DC. M Street High School was one of the first high schools in the nation for African Americans. It provided a classical education that included Latin and advanced science and mathematics courses. Many of its students would later go on to attend Ivy League and other prestigious colleges in the northern and western states.

At M Street High School, there were two course tracks to which students could apply themselves: the academic track, where Latin was required, and the scientific track, where German or French was required.[1] E. B. enrolled in the academic track and remained on the honor roll his entire M Street career. Every male student was required to participate in military drill, which he detested as a waste of time because he would rather be at the river fishing or swimming. Probably for the first time in his academic career, he was challenged to compete against people who looked like him but were wealthier and had more privilege than he had growing up.

Shortly after the DC Emancipation Act of 1862, the Act Providing for the Education of Colored Children in the Cities of Washington and Georgetown, District of Columbia and for Other Purposes was passed:

> A separate board of trustees for Black schools worked parallel to the board of trustees for White schools. With the onset of mandatory education for all children of school age, that same year Mayor Richard Wallach moved to obtain funding for the construction of a series of new school buildings throughout the community. This was quickly followed by a restructuring of the school system that by 1864 saw the introduction of a graded system that was introduced as well as high schools and teaching schools. Legislation also provided for a more equal distribution of funding for White and Black schools.[2]

One of the foremost advocates for African American rights was Charles Sumner, senator from Massachusetts. Sumner was a leader of the Radical Republicans, who overrode several of then president Andrew Johnson's vetoes that were this Southern sympathizer's efforts to marginalize Reconstruction. Sumner advocated for and introduced a bill on the floor of the Senate in 1870 that would have guaranteed all citizens, regardless of race, access to accommodations, theaters, public schools, churches, and cemeteries as an amendment to a general amnesty bill for former Confederates. Of course, it did not pass. After his death in 1874, a compromise bill, the Civil Rights Act of 1875, passed as a symbolic gesture to honor Sumner for his long service in the US Senate. This bill stated,

> [A]ll persons within the jurisdiction of the United States shall be entitled to the full and equal enjoyment of the accommodations, advantages, facilities, and privileges of inns, public conveyances on land or water, theaters, and other places of public amusement; subject only to the conditions and limitations established by law, and applicable alike to citizens of every race and color, regardless of any previous condition of servitude.[3]

Although the bill passed, the US Supreme Court ruled the Civil Rights Act of 1875 unconstitutional in 1883, ushering in a period called the "Nadir" of African American history (1890–1920). It was characterized by lynching, Jim Crow segregation, and second-class citizenship in much of the nation, in both the North and South.[4] The Civil Rights Act of 1964 ninety years later would finally address public accommodations enumerated in the Civil Rights Act of 1875. Public schools for African Americans began with the building of the John F. Cook School (1867); the Thaddeus Stevens School (1868); and the most elaborate and equal school to White schools at the time, the Sumner School (1872).[5]

Senator Sumner had a permanent room in the Wormley House Hotel at the corner of Fifteenth and H Streets NW, where he lived when the Senate was in session. This way he could take his meals in the exclusive dining room and have his room made up every morning. James Wormley was a renowned chef and caterer who had been the chef to the Court of Saint James while serving the ambassador to Great Britain during the Civil War.[6]

Wormley was also well known for his soothing and healing remedies, which he concocted to care for his hotel guests. This is why he was called to the bedside of Abraham Lincoln after he was shot at Ford's Theater.[7] It may have been for this reason that Sumner stayed at the Mr. Wormley's hotel. In 1856, while advocating for abolition, Sumner was viciously beaten on the Senate floor by Congressman Preston Brooks of South Carolina. Sumner may have needed some of Wormley's remedies for the long-haul effects of that incident.[8] Wormley was also a strong advocate for a Colored school division in Washington, DC, and after his death in 1884, the Wormley School was built in 1885 at 3325 Prospect Street NW, a few blocks from Georgetown University.[9]

Washington, DC's first Black high school, the Preparatory High School for Colored Youth, began instruction with an enrollment of forty-five students in November 1870 in the basement of the Fifteenth Street Presbyterian Church.[10] The school moved several times, from the Fifteenth Street Presbyterian Church to the Thaddeus Stevens School (1871–1872), to the Charles Sumner School (1872–1877), and to the Myrtilda Miner School (1877–1891). Finally, in 1891, it received its first permanent home on M Street NW, between First Street and New Jersey Avenue in Northwest Washington, DC. The M Street School had no playground, a gymnasium, sports fields, or organized athletics and had no space where its students could participate in athletics and physical training.[11] Years later, in 1917, M Street High School was replaced by Paul Lawrence Dunbar High School a couple of blocks away at First

A weekly "flashback" comic strip in the *Kids Post* was done to celebrate African American History Month in the February 2010 *Washington Post*.
COURTESY OF FEBRUARY 2010 WASHINGTON POST, *RED ROSE STUDIOS, PATRICK REYNOLDS*

and N Streets in Northwest DC. Although the physical structure was a vast improvement, there was very little space where its students could participate in athletics and physical training.

The principals at M Street High School included a list of notables: Emma Hutchins was the first and the only White principal. Next, Mary Jane Patterson was the first Black woman to receive a college degree in the United States, from Oberlin College in 1862. Francis Cardoza graduated from the University of Glasgow in Scotland and the seminary in Edinburgh and served as principal from 1882 until 1896. The principals during E. B.'s attendance at M Street High School were Judge Robert H. Terrell and Anna J. Cooper.[12]

Robert H. Terrell was principal at M Street from 1899 to 1901, when he was appointed the second justice of the peace for Washington, DC. In 1911, he was the first judge to the municipal court of Washington, DC, appointed by President William Howard Taft. His wife, Mary Church Terrell, was a founder of both the National Association of Colored Women (1896) and the National Association for the Advancement of Colored People (1909).[13]

Judge Terrell was replaced by Anna J. Cooper, an author, educator, and activist sometimes referred to as the "Mother of Black Feminism" because of her book *A Voice from the South: By a Black Woman from the*

South (1892), which won her great acclaim. She received bachelor's and master's degrees from Oberlin and a PhD from the Paris Sorbonne University. She taught Latin at M Street before becoming the principal in 1901. In 1900, she attended the first Pan-African Conference. She would step down as principal after being entangled in a controversy, supposedly over those who advocated for a classical education versus the Booker T. Washington model of vocational education, but it was probably more about her stance on gender equality. She would continue at M Street as a model teacher of Latin, mathematics, and science for several decades, instilling in her students high ideals of scholarship, racial pride, and self-improvement.[14]

This was the caliber of educational leadership at M Street High School. These two principals set high standards that exemplified the excellence expected of its students (and later Dunbar High School). Most teachers at M Street had advanced degrees and high expectations for their students. Many were exceptionally trained professionals, but because of discrimination at that time, they were unable to find employment in their fields of expertise. Many were contributors to the Harlem Renaissance, including Jessie Fauset; Angeline Grimke; Mary P. Burrill; Ida A. Gibbs Hunt; and Carter G. Woodson, the "Father of Black History," who taught French, Spanish, English, and history.[15] Dr. Woodson earned his PhD from Harvard University in 1912 and would go on to found the Association for the Study of Negro Life and History (1915) and Negro History Week (1926). He wrote his seminal work, "The Mis-education of the Negro" in 1933, and later, E. B. would cultivate a relationship with him for his own seminal work.[16]

M Street High School produced a long list of students who accomplished great things. Among that list are Benjamin O. Davis Sr., Nellie Quander, Julia Evangeline Brooks, Mary Gibson Hundley, Nannie Helen Burroughs (founder of the National Trade and Professional School for Women), and Charles Hamilton Houston (who graduated from M Street as class valedictorian at the age of fifteen). Houston would later matriculate to Harvard Law School. He became the first African American elected editor of the prestigious *Harvard Law Review*; served on the faculty of Howard University's Law School; and established the

NAACP's Legal Defense Fund, where he mentored Thurgood Marshall. Another graduate from M Street as E. B. was first enrolled was Garnet C. Wilkinson, who would become the superintendent of Washington, DC, Colored schools and a friend and colleague of E. B. during his storied career.[17]

This was the new environment that E. B. was being exposed to. He would rub shoulders with, compete with, and influence people who would help to shape his aspirations for a better life. With his good looks, charm, and personality, he made friends quickly and was one of the top students at M Street. Though he came from a working-class family from the Southwest, he found he could compete intellectually with the best and brightest from more prominent sectors of Washington's population, such as U Street, LeDroit Park, and Shaw communities. Families like the Syphaxs, the Wormleys, the Francises, the Evans, the Cooks, and Murrays were among his friends, and although from the upper-middle class, they felt he was one of them when it came to school and intellectual endeavors.

E. B. walked to school and back every day, missing only two days in four years. He recalled that there was no organized recreation for students during his high school years. The students organized their own teams to play with other school teams because there were no coaches and no referees to call the games. He was a star pitcher for M Street's baseball team. E. B. was also a member of the M Street High School football team, playing guard and tackle. They had a rivalry with the Colored high school teams from Baltimore, Maryland. Because M Street had no facilities for athletics, they used the public fields located near the National Mall, where the Washington Monument lay unfinished and future monuments would later stand. This was a sandlot, when students actively participated in sports before the leagues and referee organizations provided structure for organized sports.[18]

Much of this was probably noticed by Ms. Anita Turner, who knew of young E. B.'s interest in athletics and physical fitness. Turner was the only Black certified physical education teacher in the DC Colored schools. She studied physical training and obtained her certificate by attending the summer sessions at the Harvard University Dudley Sargent School of Physical Training in 1897. She was one of the first African Americans certified to teach physical education in American schools. In those days, only girls played basketball in physical education classes under the tutelage of Turner. Because participating in basketball in those days was strictly for girls, it was perceived as a "sissy sport" among E. B.'s male colleagues.[19]

The boy's physical education teacher was a White ex-wrestler named Bill Foley. Foley spent one day a week teaching in the Colored schools while teaching physical training four days a week in the White high schools. Nothing beyond calisthenics was taught to the male students during their physical education classes in the Colored high schools and usually only for about fifteen minutes in the hallways or corridors of the school.[20] To obtain more physical activity during his time at M Street and Miner Teachers College, E. B. and a few of his friends took up long-distance walking. On weekends, he, Milton Francis, and Haley Douglass would walk to Annapolis, Maryland, where their families had a summer cottage at Highland Beach.[21] This was when E. B. was introduced to the resort community on the Chesapeake Bay that he came to love. Highland Beach was founded by Frederick Douglass's son Charles. Many of the Washington elite families, like the Francises and the Wormleys, purchased property as a retreat for their families on the Chesapeake Bay.[22]

E. B. would also go on long-distance walks with his friends Nat Guy, J. Hume, R. Bruce, Dixon, and Montgomery to the Great Falls, along the Potomac River in Virginia. There, they would swim in the river upstream, where it was probably much cleaner than it would have been closer to the city. Another option for long-distance walking was to Baltimore, an industrial city that had a prosperous Black middle class that predated the emancipation in 1865.

It was also at M Street that he noticed from afar a gorgeous, petite young lady from a prominent family of Washington, DC: Miss Mary Ellen Meriwether. In polite social society, it would have been considered forward to approach her directly, to say the least. Anyway, to the serious-minded young Henderson, girls were taboo until he would be able to support a spouse. So he concentrated on his academics and making friends among his more socially elite male colleagues at M Street.

E. B. went on to graduate from M Street with honors, distinguishing himself to Washington's "Black bourgeoisie." Being from a working-class family, his striving to excel made him acceptable to the affluent Black middle class of Washington, DC. He was intelligent, charismatic, handsome, and driven to be successful. He was self-assured and confident about his prospects for the future.

6

Miner Teacher's College, Normal School No. 2

AFTER GRADUATING FROM M STREET HIGH SCHOOL, E. B. DECIDED TO enroll in Miner Teacher's College, Normal School No. 2, where he would train to become a teacher. Miner Teacher's College was segregated into two divisions. White students attended Normal School No. 1. African Americans or any other race attended Normal School No. 2. So in the fall of 1902, Edwin Bancroft Henderson enrolled in Normal School No. 2, where he would distinguish himself further.

Although he would have loved to follow in the footsteps of many of his well-to-do friends who aspired to become doctors and lawyers, he knew he could little afford the time or expense of a four-year college degree, taking classes in the daytime, let alone attending law or medical school for another three to four years before being able to settle into a profession and earn a living.

Normal schools were two-year colleges specifically intended to train teachers. The curriculum included teaching methodologies, as well as specific subject content and discipline.[1] Miss Myrtilla Miner was a Quaker involved in abolition who started her school, the Normal School for Colored Girls, in 1851 in Washington. She was associated with many other members of the Friends societies, such as Emily Howland; Johns Hopkins; and Henry Ward Beecher, brother of Harriet Beecher Stowe. Stowe was the author of the best seller of her time, *Uncle Tom's Cabin*, and gave a generous donation of $1,000 of the proceeds from her book to Miss

Miner's efforts to start the school. One of her first students was Emily Edmonson, who would stay and become an assistant to Miss Miner.[2]

Emily and her sister Mary were part of the famous attempted Washington slave escape in 1848 onboard the schooner *Pearl*, where seventy-seven enslaved individuals made a strike for freedom but were caught and sent to a slave penitentiary in Baltimore before being transferred to New Orleans to be sold. Luckily, there was an outbreak of yellow fever, and they were sent back, eventually ending up in a slave pen in Alexandria, Virginia. Their father, a free man, traveled to New York, where he was able to obtain an audience with Henry Ward Beecher, who approached his congregation to raise the money to purchase Emily and Mary. Both girls would go on to attend Oberlin College, but Mary, suffering from her ordeal in the various slaveholding cells in Baltimore, New Orleans, and Alexandria, died a year later. There is a famous picture of both girls and Frederick Douglass at an abolition gathering in the 1850s.[3]

Ms. Miner and Emily Edmonson taught African American children and adults in the contraband camps around Washington, DC, during and after the Civil War; in 1863, when received a charter from the Senate as the "Institute for the Education of Colored Youth." At a time when African Americans were coming out of bondage in the South, where teaching them to read and write was against the law, there was a need to be filled, and Myrtilla Miner stepped up by starting a normal school. Many African Americans, especially adults, wanted to be able to read the Bible, but more practically, they wanted to be able to read and write so that they could advance in American society.[4]

> In 1851, Miner began teaching young girls in a small frame home on New York Avenue. The school offered primary schooling and classes in domestic skills. Its emphasis from the beginning was to train teachers. Miss Miner stressed hygiene and nature study in addition to rigorous academic training. The students, aged through, learned spelling, reading, geography, penmanship, composition, analysis of authors, moral philosophy, and translation. Within two months of opening, school enrollment grew from six. Despite opposition from some segments of the community, the school prospered with help of continued

contributions from Quakers and a gift from Harriet Beecher Stowe of $1,000 of the royalties she earned from *Uncle Tom's Cabin*.[5]

With the help of the Society of Friends, the first permanent location of the school was at what is now Dupont Circle:

> In 1853, a lot had been purchased in the city of Washington, comprising about three acres, with two small frame-houses upon it, situated between 19th and 20th Streets, and N Street and New Hampshire Avenue, being described on the plan of the City as Square No. 115. The cost of this property was about $4,300. It was purchased and held in trust for the purposes of the school by Thomas Williamson and Samuel Rhoads, two benevolent members of the Society of Friends residing in Philadelphia. (Johns Hopkins was another early supporter of Ms. Miner's school.)[6]

Another famous Quaker, abolitionist, and educator, Emily Howland, came to Washington to help with the teaching duties at the school. Both women lived upstairs in the teacher's quarters. The school endured violent attacks from those opposed to teaching African Americans to read and write. Emily Edmondson's family moved onto the three-acre property and were helpful in protecting Ms. Miner. Ms. Miner learned how to shoot to protect herself and the school.[7] Ms. Miner became ill in 1856, and she took a leave of absence and moved to Petaluma, California, to heal.

In 1862, an act of Congress granted a charter establishing the Institution for the Education of Colored Youth. One of the caveats of the bill was a 10 percent tax levied on property belonging to African Americans in Washington, DC, to support the school system. The bill placed the school on a solid foundation, with a board of directors: The "Institution for the Education of Colored Youth" authorized by Congress is incorporated. "Myrtilla Miner became its first president. The directors include Henry Addison, John C. Underwood, George C. Abbott, William H. Channing, Nancy M. Johnson, and Myrtilla Miner.[8] Unfortunately, Ms. Miner's health would not permit her return to the school she worked so hard for. In 1864, "she was thrown from a carriage in Petaluma,

California, and, shortly after a long journey back to Washington that year, she died of tuberculosis probably exacerbated by her injuries."[9]

In 1868, George F. T. Cook became the first superintendent of the Washington, DC, Colored Public School System. Under his leadership, it became the largest and best school district for African American students in the United States. The Miner Teacher's College was a conduit for the training of teachers in the Washington, DC, schools, as well as other schools regionally and nationally.[10]

For E. B., attending Miner was a means to a middle-class lifestyle. He excelled at M Street, but he flourished at Miner. Miner's curriculum was a two-year program dedicated to general education for someone who wanted to teach elementary school. The first year was dedicated to theory, while the second year was devoted to practice. It is unclear whether E. B. knew his path from Miner would lead him to become a physical educator. In most schools at this time, there was not much emphasis on physical education, but that would accelerate once E. B. was certified to teach.

Because of her experience at the Dudley Sargent School of Physical Training, Ms. Anita Turner taught classes for physical training at Miner, where her philosophy for teaching physical education became more practical. Ms. Turner was the first director of playgrounds, Divisions X–XIII. She also conducted classes in physical training for women at Howard:

> Under Miss Turner's leadership the emphasis in physical education was shifted from the rigidly formal to the more informal type of program. Games, stunts, and folk dances replaced formal exercises. Physical activities were correlated with classroom work in the development of units of study. Attitudes, interest, and skills were high carry-over value into outside life now and in years to come were developed.[11]

Ms. Turner's philosophy resonated with E. B., and she became his favorite instructor at Miner Normal School No. 2.

E. B. took up cycling while he was attending Miner. Cycling had become very popular in the late 1890s, and it was E. B.'s major mode of transportation rather than the local segregated trollies. An avid journal writer, E. B. often wrote about riding his "wheel" as he called it, to get around town, as well as for his journeys to Highland Beach in Annapolis.[12]

Around the turn of the twentieth century, African American interest in cycling grew, due partly to the success of cyclist Marshall Walter "Major" Taylor, the "Black Cyclone." Taylor was the king of all the sprints, from the half-mile to the two-mile. He was the world champion of bicycle racing in 1898 and 1899, and he won contest after contest in both Europe and Australia. He was only the second African American to attain a world title of any kind in cycling. Canadian boxer George Dixon was the first.[13]

Two women E. B. met at Miner would change his life forever. One of those would be his future wife, Mary Ellen Meriwether. The other was his professional mentor, Miss Anita Turner. It was because of her that E. B. was encouraged to attend Harvard University, which put him on the path to becoming the first African American male to teach physical education in American public schools.

Although it was at M Street that E. B. first met Miss Anita Turner, it was at Miner that he came under her tutelage. In 1904, after graduating number one in his class of thirty-seven at Miner, E. B. became the first and only member of his family to graduate from college.[14] He received an assignment to teach third grade in the Washington, DC, Colored schools. Miss Turner, knowing "Henderson's love for athletics, his intellectual capacity to learn, and his leadership capabilities," suggested that he enroll in the summer session of Dudley Sargent's School for Physical Training to earn his certification to teach physical education.[15]

She impressed upon him that physical education was a new discipline, and by getting in on the ground floor, he would be a pioneer on a new frontier and be able to adapt his love for physical activity into an opportunity for others to enjoy physical training and athletics. He would be providing a public health initiative to address the ailments created by the sedentary life that came with living in crowded, often unsanitary tenements and alleys in cities that were filling with African Americans leaving the South during the Great Migration. She instilled in him how much this was needed and how he could be the first male of his race to gain certification in this new discipline.[16]

Edwin Henderson in his early twenties at his graduation from Miner Teachers College, Normal School No. 2.
COURTESY OF HENDERSON FAMILY COLLECTION

Going to the Dudley Sargent School of Physical Training was an intriguing idea, one that really resonated with E. B. But how would he be able to manage it? Money was tight, and he had planned to work at a resort on the New Jersey shore to earn enough money to maintain his living situation. Miss Turner offered her assistance in any way she could to get him to Harvard. She contacted Dudley Sargent directly and obtained for E. B. a job waiting tables at Sargent's boardinghouse on campus, which made it possible for E. B. to attend the summer session. And the rest is history.[17]

7
Ned and Nell's Courtship

While it might seem in this day and age that romance is all but lost, this wasn't true in the early twentieth century. The romance between E. B. and Mary Ellen can be seen in the letters they wrote to each other. They gave themselves pet names that they used throughout their lives. For whatever reason, they both would simply add an *N* in front of their names. So, *E. B.*, or *Ed*, became *Ned*, and *Mary Ellen* became *Nell* or *Nellie*. They were affectionately known as Ned and Nell. Although E. B. was a serious-minded fellow about most things, Nell brought out a tender, gentle side that complemented his intellectual acumen. They had a long courtship that lasted six years, and their marriage lasted sixty-six years. For them, no one could argue that love wasn't real.

Coming from a working-class family and wanting to be a high achiever, E. B. always went above and beyond what was required. According to E. B.,

> As a result of my reputation for being a good lesson planner and a disciplinarian, one of my classmates, Lottie Wallace, . . . told a girl in the lower class that perhaps I could help her with a project. Until then girls were taboo. So, when at a recess period she sat in a seat in front, leaning toward my desk and ask for advice, I gave her nothing but academic attention. But I was invited to call some Friday evening.[1]

Nell's family was part of the social elite in Washington, and at this time, there was a

> certain decorum that one stayed within when courting. It was very strict and different from what we might experience today. Most often, certain families only married within certain other families that were of the same standing or class. It was understood that parents had much more control, and all interactions between the sexes were chaperoned, especially for girls, until the girl's suitor had met the approval of both parents. Parents insisted on knowing who their daughters were interested in, and their approval of a young man was generally respected.[2]

E. B. did call on Nellie on a Friday evening, soon after her invitation, and he found that there would be competition. At least a dozen young men could be found at the Meriwether home at 1822 13th Street calling on their two eligible daughters, Nell and Agnes. (The two younger Meriwether daughters, Sarah, one of the founding members of the Alpha Kappa Alpha sorority, and Edith, who would later marry Booker T. Washington's son Ernest Davidson "Dave" Washington, were not of age to receive callers yet.) But after a couple years, there were only two suitors for the two daughters left: E. B. for Nellie and Benjamin Brownley for Agnes.[3]

Nellie's father, James Henry Meriwether, was a lawyer and real estate broker who built many houses in Washington, DC. His law office was on Pennsylvania Avenue at Twelfth Street NW. His father was a White slaveholder from Kentucky, who saw his son's aptitude at a young age and sent him to Canada to be educated. He came to Washington to attend Howard University, where he graduated from Howard University's law school and later became the first Howard University alumnus to become a member of its board of trustees.[4]

Nell's mother's family (the Robinsons) were enslaved on the estate of Lord Fairfax, the Baron of Cameron, in Winchester, Virginia. The Robinson family became free when Robert Carter III's father and grandfather died, leaving him with seventeen large plantations, one of which was Lord Fairfax's estate in colonial Virginia. Carter III is known for freeing thousands of his enslaved people from these plantations in the late eighteenth and early nineteenth centuries.[5]

When Nell's great-grandfather Jonathan Robinson was killed in 1836, Nell's grandfather Robert, with his mother and four siblings, left Winchester and moved to Springfield, Illinois, where they opened a barbershop. An advertisement for their barbershop stated that Abraham Lincoln and Stephen Douglass were among their Springfield customers. Robert, or R. J., Robinson, finally settled in Wellington, Ohio, just down the road from Oberlin College, where he and his family started a church and several businesses.[6] Nell's grandfather had two daughters and four sons. All his sons fought in the Civil War, mostly with the US Colored troops. Nell's mother, Mary Louise Robinson, graduated from Oberlin College in 1870.

After graduating, Nell's mother came to Washington to teach at the first high school for African Americans, the Preparatory High School for Colored Youth, in the basement of her church, the Fifteenth Street Presbyterian Church in Northwest Washington, DC. This school evolved into M Street High School and then Paul Lawrence Dunbar High School.[7] She was also instrumental in establishing the Home for Destitute Women and Children and was largely responsible for saving the home when she testified before Congress for funding when the home moved from Eighth Street to Euclid Street NW, near Howard University. At its new location, it became known as the Meriwether Home. Elizabeth Keckley, friend and seamstress for Mary Todd Lincoln, spent her last days at the Meriwether home.[8]

Both of Nell's parents were college educated, socially and politically conscious African Americans, and solidly in the Washington Black elite. Mr. and Mrs. Meriwether believed that E. B. had great promise and therefore gave their blessing for their daughter to be courted by a fine, upstanding young gentleman. Their courtship was encapsulated by the many letters these voracious writers wrote to one another. During the time of their courtship, the US Postal Service delivered mail twice, if not three times, a day.[9] Early on, when Nell sprained her ankle, E. B. wrote,

To the Sweetest in the World,

No sun did shine for the world or me this morning and though the world may "cease to repine" for it knows that behind the clouds the sun still shines as brightly, I cannot for my sun is a little less dim, no doubt to her badly sprained ankle. I began to grow uneasy when you had not put in your appearance this morning at 9:00 and I immediately began to make inquiries which resulted in my finding out that your dear shapely, so little ankle had been slightly turned. It has not ever sprained, it has perhaps been slightly strained, that's all. I should not no doubt think so much of my curative powers, but I think if I could kiss that ankle it would come around alright but we are not M_ _ _ _ _ _ d yet. Oh, but I did miss your face this morning. My ankle which was hurt the other day and has never gotten well and is now painful with increased fury sympathy you know. I did not know whether it was the right thing to do to come around and inquire after you, but I threw all thoughts of prosperity to the wind and went to inquire. One day perhaps I may have the happiness of nursing such an ankle back to health. And I could easily lift you from place to place and rock you to a peaceful sleep if we were "M." You said the other night that I have been with you so much that I might not be able to do without you. You never spoke more true when you said you were indis [can't make it out]. I simply satisfy myself now with the thought that some day you may be my own, my verry own, every drop in sight of heaven and earth. Then if you were sick, I could be with you always. Please excuse this writing and all else not right. Every person is coming around me as I write, and I can't collect thoughts or write legibly. So, in reading forget everything but that I love you and if you let me shall love you always.

I think your ankle will be better soon and I may see you in your angelic loveliness. Until then I have your picture and my thoughts and [????] to remind me of my one dear darling sweetheart

I am your own

E Henderson[10]

Nell was also head over heels in love with E. B.:

I may meet many people, but I do not wish to love any one or have any one love me but "Ned." Often when we are both teasing I say I am going to other places and meet Drs. and Lawyers and be Mrs. Dr. so and so etc. But I will feel highly honored and only want to be Mrs. E. B. Henderson. Would you like to change my name to that? How Happy I should be if I could be in your room in your little rocking chair with you. You say just to kiss me a few times. *Never*, a few times would not do. It would have to be many times.

Here is one of my flowers. I have sent many messages to you by it. I told it to give you my love, to say oh how I miss you, how I hope the time will pass quickly when we two will live as one. And last but not least, have sent you 10 kisses by it. Now Ned don't forget to take care of yourself and write to me and to your mother. If I was there I would kiss your head ache away I am sure. I received a short note from Brownley today.

With much love I am your

Nell[11]

Many of the letters were written while he was in Cambridge, Massachusetts, attending Harvard's Dudley Sargent Physical Training summer sessions, where he paid for his room and board by serving at Professor Sargent's table. After the summer sessions were over, E. B. waited tables at the Squantum Resort in Quincy, Massachusetts, on Dorchester Bay, owned by Black restaurateur and inventor Joseph Lee.[12] In 1908, Nell came to visit and spend time with him in Quincy, Massachusetts. Another summer job for E. B. one year was at the Marina in Ocean Grove Resort in New Jersey for three or four weeks before returning to Washington for the school year.[13]

They did practically everything together in those days. Nell, being from an upper-class background, was well versed in the etiquette of polite society and was also able to share some of her social connections with E. B. to help him connect with people who might assist in his upward mobility. Nell wrote,

Dr. Atwood was here yesterday. He said he heard I was going to be married. Then he said a promotion in your salary had been talked of and

> he thought that you ought to have it and that it could be managed all right in the fall. He said although he was not on the board still his word would have some weight. He also said you got a fine mark "A" I believe the highest you could get. You were quite selfish to keep it to yourself tho. So, when you come back in the fall you had better see what can be done. If it can be done why not have it done. I am not stump speaking but just stating plain facts for your own good. I suppose Joe [Josephine] Wormley is in Boston now. All the rest of her family are away now. This is Maud Johnson's wedding morn and a beautiful one it is too; only a little hot. I truly do not wish to marry in the summer. You know I suffer from the heat, and you are very large you know and between you and the heat I believe I should die. Give my regards to Miss Davis and Keep all the love for yourself and write soon to
>
> Your Nell[14]

Probably most concerning during their courtship was finances. How would E. B. be able to provide Nell with the upper-middle-class lifestyle she was accustomed to on his teacher's salary? The Washington, DC, public schools, like many schools at that time, had the rule that, once a woman was married, she could no longer work as a teacher because she had to take care of a husband and family, so work outside the home was out of the question. Nell would have to retire once they were married. This antiquated rule was the major issue preventing them from marrying sooner.[15]

E. B. was well aware that he needed to have a profession that could provide for Nell, so he enrolled in Howard University Medical School's night classes. At the end of his first year in medical school, the American Medical Association required that the majority, if not all, classes be taught in the daytime hours, which was difficult if not impossible because he taught during the day.[16] But E. B. found a way by soliciting several doctors at the medical school to continue to teach in the early evenings, if he could prove that it was worth their while by bringing in enough students to make it viable. He succeeded in getting enough students because several male teachers were also in the night school program and wanted to continue taking classes to become doctors.

E. B. marries Mary Ellen Henderson on Christmas Eve, 1910. Picture taken in Falls Church, Virginia, where they moved into his grandmother Eliza's home to raise their family. Eliza was born a slave in Fairfax County.
COURTESY OF HENDERSON FAMILY COLLECTION

However, in E. B.'s third year, he was coaching, refereeing, and getting his team ready at the Twelfth Street YMCA, and he found it impossible to fit it all in. With great disappointment, he dropped out of medical school.[17] Years later, he earned the title of doctor in earnest by completing courses to become a doctor of chiropractic; he graduated from a course in physiotherapy and osteopathy from the Central Chiropractic College in 1922.[18] For a while, E. B. would conduct massage therapy and electrotherapy. But once again, the strain of teaching, coaching, and officiating would not allow him, in good conscience, to have a chiropractic profession on the side. For the most part, he used his knowledge of chiropractic while in physical training with the team she was coaching.

So how was E. B. going to earn enough money to support Nell after they were married? In 1904, when he first started teaching, his salary was $45 per month. By 1910, E. B. had received several promotions and was earning double that amount, $90 per month, which was what two teachers would have made.[19] They decided that they need not wait any longer.

During their courtship, they had been saving money for that eventual day when they would become man and wife. They would need money so they could move to the country, buy land, and build a house for the family they were planning. They started to plan their wedding, making 1910 an eventful year.

Aside from his upcoming marriage to Nell, going to Harvard University's Dudley Sargent College of Physical Training was the best decision E. B. would make at a young age. There he would make friends and professional colleagues who would help him to create opportunities for the youth in his community.

8

Harvard University's Dudley Sargent School of Physical Training

After waking up early on a Saturday morning in 1904 in Southwest Washington, E. B. went for a run around the wharf area. His mind was racing; he was about to graduate number one in his class from Miner Teacher's College, Normal School No. 2, and he had found the woman of his dreams, someone with whom to spend his life, move to the country, build a home, and have children. Nell was all that he had ever hoped for. Pulling himself back to the present, E. B. made it back to his grandmother's house at 477 School Street and prepared for his important day.

His parents were at his graduation ceremony. They beamed with pride as they watched their oldest child, who had worked so hard and would become the first in the Henderson family to graduate from college. As class valedictorian, he addressed the 1904 graduating class, then walked across the stage to receive his diploma. Nell was there with her mother, who was also proud and very impressed with E. B.'s speech.

Even after graduating top of his class, E. B., along with every potential teacher going into the Washington, DC, Colored schools, had to take a proficiency test to be eligible to teach. E. B. passed his test with the highest score and was assigned to teach third grade.

Miss Anita Turner, the assistant director of physical education in the Colored schools, had been aware of E. B. for some time at M Street and then at Normal School No. 2. She was impressed with E. B.'s dedication, his energy and passion for athletics, and his physical feats of endurance.

She attended Harvard University's Sargent School of Physical Training summer sessions from 1895 to 1897 and was one of the first women to be certified to teach physical education in the United States. There had been no African American male teachers who had successfully completed this course and become certified, but several notable men had previously attended the Dudley Sargent School for the practical course in physical training, such as Booker T. Washington and Theodore Roosevelt. To be fully certified to teach, one had to attend not only the practical curriculum but also the theory and demonstration curriculums, as well.[1]

In 1879, Dr. Dudley Allen Sargent became assistant professor of physical training and director at the Hemenway Gymnasium. Sargent graduated from Yale Medical School but was more interested in the development of the body and how a healthy body meant a healthy mind and helped to build character: "[T]he purpose of muscular exercise was not to attain bodily health and beauty alone, but to break up morbid mental tendencies, to dispel the gloomy shadows of despondency, and to inspire serenity of spirit. . . . [T]he grand aim of all muscular activity from an educational point of view is to improve conduct and develop character."[2]

After finishing medical school, Sargent opened a private gymnasium in New York City, the Hygienic Institute and School of Physical Culture, where he transformed the traditional gymnasium of Swedish and German calisthenics and added machines he invented for physical exercise, introducing pulleys and adjustable weights to apparatuses. Doing so allowed everyone to train, no matter what physical state or ability one might have. After becoming director of physical training at Harvard, Sargent convinced the university to develop a complete system of mechanized fitness. The Hemenway Gymnasium was renovated to include a running track, a rowing room, a fencing room, a baseball cage, and tennis courts. In total, Sargent invented fifty-six machines that lined the walls of the Hemenway Gymnasium.

Sargent was a stickler for conduct; in fact, he was blamed for the banning of football at the university in 1885 on the grounds that it triggered "rough play and fighting." It did not go over well, and it cost him the full professorship. Sargent also challenged the notion of the Victorian

The 1907 class of the Dudley Sargeant School for Physical Training.
COURTESY OF HUPSF SUMMER SCHOOL OF PHYSICAL TRAINING, HARVARD UNIVERSITY ARCHIVES

tradition, whereby women were not supposed to do anything involving physical exertion. He promoted the idea of women participating in athletics, enrolled women in his physical training school, and encouraged girls' and women's participation in athletics.[3]

Unlike most of his contemporaries, Sargent was interested in the measurements that bodies could aspire to rather than the ones they possessed. He introduced the science of anthropometrics so he could measure progress in his students and athletes. Once basketball was introduced into the curriculum, Dr. Sargent also innovated a measure that has become a valuable standard in basketball and other activities: the Sargent Test (widely known today as the vertical-jump test).[4]

Turner suggested to E. B. that, rather than simply accept a position to teach in the elementary schools of Washington, he should attend

Harvard University's Dudley Sargent School of Physical Training. This was the best place in the country for someone to attain the certification to teach physical education. She believed that he would be successful and would impress Dr. Sargent, as well.[5] E. B. could not afford attending fall and winter semesters because he had to earn a living. Instead, he would attend three summer sessions to earn the certification, like Miss Turner had done. And when he returned from his first summer session in the fall, he would be eligible to take the test to teach physical education in his first school year, receiving a provisional certification until he finished the full course.

E. B. knew that, to go to Harvard, he would need a job while he was in Cambridge, as his depleted funds could not pay the $50 for tuition for the summer session. But after taking a few days to figure things out, he borrowed the money for car fare, tuition, and lodging. Miss Turner wrote to Dr. Sargent, asking him to get E. B. a part-time job waiting on his table in his boardinghouse on campus, which would allow him to repay the money he borrowed to attend the summer courses.[6]

E. B. found Cambridge and Boston refreshing. The restrictions placed on him because of his race and segregation were absent there. He was able to go downtown to the theaters, he could eat at restaurants, and there was little or no discrimination that he observed. Then one day, needing a haircut, E. B. entered a barbershop. He told the barber that, because his hair was full and long, all he needed was a trim. E. B., not suspecting any shenanigans, sat back in the chair, closed his eyes, and felt the barber clippers, starting at the front and pressing against his scalp all the way to the back.

E. B. jumped up from his chair as the barber and others laughed at the atrocity. He felt like fighting or cursing the barber, but he did not want to make a scene and possibly be kicked out of Harvard, so he quickly left the barbershop. Embarrassed and angry, he wandered the streets until he found a Black barber to have his head shaved to match the damage. He was no longer of the impression that simply being in Boston would allow him to completely escape the stigma of race.[7]

> EB was excited to be in the intellectually rich environment of one of the most prestigious universities in the world. He found the academic environment of Harvard very stimulating. Dr. Sargent believed in the philosophy of "physical education for all." All the instructors were pioneers of physical training. All the students were brilliant, and the environment was ultracompetitive. Many of the students he was taking classes with would go on to become the foremost proponents of physical education in the country. Edwin noted, "Dr. Burnett, later director of health and physical education in Baltimore, was a student instructor. Dr. McCloy, noted western authority on test and research in physical education, and Leroy Samse, the first man to pole vault twelve feet, were in my classes."[8]

Additionally, E. B. had the opportunity to converse with some of the preeminent professors at Harvard, whom he had read and admired, such as William James, the noted psychologist, and Josiah Royce, the philosopher who would come to Hemenway Gymnasium to work out on the weights and other exercise machines Dr. Sargent had invented. After classes, E. B. played handball on several occasions with these two esteemed scholars, which was an experience he savored throughout his life.[9]

Harvard University's first director of physical training and manager of Hemenway Gymnasium and first African American professor was a broken-down boxer by the name of Abram Molineaux Hewlett. Harvard College hired Hewlett as a professor of physical training and director of the gymnasium in 1859 until his death in 1871. The *Harvard* magazine of October 1859 and the Harvard yearbook of 1887 paid high tribute to his work.[10]

E. B. noted,

> The teachers in the old Hemenway Gymnasium were some of the noted pioneers in physical training such as Eberhardt, Nissen, Schrader, McCurdy, Dr. Sargent, and others. Some of these were exponents of Swedish and German gymnastics, the Delsarte, and Danish Schools. In my classes for three summers were men [and women], who have since become the foremost exponents of physical training in our nation.[11]

E. B. attended the Dudley Sargent School of Physical Training summer sessions in 1904, 1905, and 1907. His activities in 1906 prevented him from attending that year. The course work proved far superior to what he could have gained anywhere else in the country.

The first-year courses E. B. took were anatomy, apparatus, floor work, games, physiology, and track athletics. In year 2, he received instruction on aesthetic dancing ("fancy steps"), apparatus (men), applied anatomy, clubs, dumbbells, examinations (anthropometry), first aid, floor work, gymnastics, and wand. In year 3, he received instruction in boxing, football, games, history of physical education, physiology of exercise, and wrestling.[12] In E.B.'s first summer at Harvard, he was introduced to the fundamentals of the new sport of basketball in his games course work.

Canadian Dr. James Naismith came to Springfield College in Massachusetts, where, in 1891, at the behest of Luther Gulick, he was asked to invent a game that would help football and baseball players to stay in shape during the winter months—a sport meant to be played indoors while it was cold outside.[13] Most people had never before seen the game being played. It had been taught and played mostly in the YMCAs and a small group of colleges, with most competitions being won by the YMCA teams. An early White league was established in 1898 but had little success and folded in 1904, but 1904 was eventful in basketball's evolution.[14] Basketball was officially introduced to the public at the St. Louis World's Fair by the Fort Shaw Indian School girls basketball team.[15] It was also introduced as a demonstration sport at the St. Louis Olympic Games in July 1904.[16]

The light went on in E. B.'s mind. Basketball seemed to be a delicate mix of brains, brawn, and teamwork, but notably, the main goal of the sport was a vertical one, whereas all other sports had a horizontal or linear goal. He visualized the game as a vehicle, the perfect instrument to take advantage of African Americans' innate ability of speed and vertical elevation. He would teach basketball to African American boys when he returned to the Washington, DC, Colored schools. Until that time, only girls played basketball, and some of the rules for girls were different from the boys, particularly in the half-court game. By introducing basketball to boys and creating the leagues and training referees, E. B. would be known for nurturing the sport while it was still in its infancy and helping to popularize it with a community that had never seen the sport being played.

The network of professional physical directors he encountered at Dr. Sargent's summer sessions was the most important thing to him. Another important observation for E. B. was the infinite possibilities that existed beyond the segregated borders of his world in the District of Columbia. This enabled him to know what resources were available to him to advance and promote the public health and physical well-being of African Americans. These resources would be useful in moving the needle toward equality for the next generation of African Americans and to dismantle the awful legacy of White supremacy and inequality in society.

9

Building the Infrastructure

Physical Education and Recreation

Mr. Henderson endeavored to institute the same types of physical educational programs in the Black schools that were discussed in professional circles, written in professional literature, or that were found in some White schools."[1]

Nell met E. B. at the station upon his arrival at Union Station in September 1904, and although they had written letters to each other almost every day since he left for Cambridge, the reunion was a joyous one. Returning to Washington after gaining a rich professional experience at Harvard University, E. B. was excited to apply all he had learned from Dr. Sargent and his faculty at the Dudley School of Physical Training at Harvard University.

He had already been hired and certified to teach third grade in the elementary schools of Washington before he left for Harvard, but before he would be allowed to teach physical education, he would have to take an examination to prove proficiency in his discipline. Soon after returning, he took the test, again scoring the highest on the proficiency exam. E. B. became the first African American male to be certificated to teach physical education in the nation's public schools. He replaced Bill Foley, who had been his physical education teacher at M Street High School. Mr. Foley was the last White physical education teacher for the boys in the segregated Washington, DC, Colored schools. Replacing Foley meant that E. B. would be an army of one, the only physical education teacher in the Colored schools for male students in kindergarten through twelfth grades. As such, he had to travel each week to teach at all the schools, both elementary and secondary.

E. B. recalled,

> After I left high school as a student, there was little promotion of athletics during the winter months. After football season, other than drill days, many boys would gather in the armory and dance with each other.
>
> This developed because a few older students had begun to make money by playing piano in the hot spots about the city. They used the armory piano to practice after school which led to the practice of all-male dancing.
>
> I mentioned this, because to wean the boys back to indoor practice in sports, I had to break up the dancing parties to the dislike of many of the so-called boys. In a short while I had the boys again engaging in manly sports.
>
> Basketball had not been introduced to boys in Washington until my promotion of the sport in 1904.[2]

Shortly after returning from Harvard, E. B.'s parents, William, and Louisa, moved from the two-story flat on School Street in Southwest DC to Falls Church, Virginia, where they would take care of E. B.'s aging grandmother Eliza. Meanwhile, by passing the proficiency test to teach physical training, E. B. received a 5 percent raise in pay, which allowed him to move to 760 Harvard Street NW, across from Howard University and closer to Nell.[3] Additionally, E. B. would be closer to where the action was. This area was more centrally located to the schools, Howard University, and U Street. E. B. recalled,

> I taught three days a week in the elementary schools, teaching throughout the city, mainly in outlying districts to which I traveled on my bicycle. I returned to M Street and Armstrong in the afternoons, three days a week, that were not used for military training to coach the boys in athletics. I taught the rudiments of basketball to boys for the first time in Washington, DC Negro Schools. In the next few years, I taught and developed a number of teams, trained officials, and had much

> competition. During this period, I also taught rudiments of fencing, boxing, wrestling, gymnastics, and track and field.[4]

Miss Anita Turner was assistant director of physical training in the Washington, DC, public schools, even though there was no director of physical training in the Colored schools. Being a devotee of Dr. Sargent's program at Harvard, she was the foremost leader of physical training in the Colored schools. She was impressed with E. B.'s dedication and energy in promoting the tenets of Dr. Sargent's program. In addition to teaching in the public schools, she taught physical training at Miner Normal School and Howard University. She allowed E. B. to take a leadership role in developing programs to further the teaching of physical training and promoting athletics among the boys in the Colored schools. She was confident that he was going to do a great job, much like she had done for girls' physical training in the DC Colored schools.

E. B. believed the most important reason to teach physical education and promote participation in athletics was because of the sedentary urban lifestyle, as well as the overcrowded and unsanitary conditions in which African Americans often found themselves in northern cities. He learned at Harvard University that teaching healthy living habits, the importance of good hygiene, and exercise would help to prevent the diseases prevalent in the most impoverished areas of the cities. Dudley Sargent, the director of the summer school at Harvard, was first and foremost a physician, and he taught his students, "Exercise is medicine" (a quote attributed to the Grecian philosopher of medicine Hippocrates in the fifth century BC). Henderson believed that exercise and physical activity could hold at bay such diseases as tuberculosis, dysentery, hypertension, diabetes, and several types of cancers that were killing many who moved north in the Great Migration.[5] Bob Kuska explains,

> It was no secret that Washington's Black mortality rate stood at about double that of whites, with Tuberculosis claiming nearly five hundred lives in the year 1900. The fact inspired well-meaning White public health officials to pontificate about the sickly city-dwelling Black, which rankled many Black leaders.

E. B., middle right, with the faculty of the Paul Lawrence Dunbar High School, *COURTESY OF HENDERSON FAMILY COLLECTION, ALSO DISTRICT OF COLUMBIA COLORED SCHOOLS*

> . . . Henderson knew Blacks were not the only ones dying of tuberculosis, since the "White Plague" also levied a tribute of nearly four hundred Whites in 1900. Henderson thought that Black people's aches and pains owed more to Washington's cramped urban milieu than to some inherent physical defect. . . . Henderson believed that urban life offered Blacks neither the time or space to exercise regularly, destroying their natural vitality and making them susceptible to disease.[6]

Physical education was not simply about teaching games to play at recess in school. Dudley Sargent's school taught that exercise would help to prevent sickness. E. B. found himself on the precipice of a public health epidemic. Due to transportation advances, such as the train, the trolley, and soon automobiles, not having to walk or do physical labor, like so many did living and working on farms in the South, the physical health of African Americans was deteriorating. Pollution and diseases were decreasing the life span of African Americans living in cities.

But public health was not the only concern for Henderson. E. B. hated the second-class-citizen status of African Americans, and he had a strategy to address it in his teaching of physical education:

> Henderson envisioned achievement in athletics as the best weapon for attacking and destroying Jim Crow. He believed that in sports, unlike politics, all races followed the same rules. Henderson reasoned that with formalized training, Black athletes would have a rare chance to compete on equal terms with Whites. They would have the opportunity to outperform them, capturing the nation's imagination with their poise and talent, and debunk the stereotypes that stigmatized the race.[7]

E. B. felt that teaching what he had learned at the Dudley Sargent School would help make life better for African Americans.[8]

The Washington, DC, Recreation Department

There were restrictions to African American access for many of the parks, playgrounds, and public areas in Washington, DC, during the early twentieth century. This was especially true in areas where very few Blacks lived. Many areas west and north in Rock Creek Park were off-limits for use by Blacks. The Rose Park playground in Georgetown was off-limits to African Americans until E. B. led a protest to give African Americans access.[9]

Early on in E. B.'s professional career, he was involved in advising, advocating for, and planning the activities and facilities that African Americans could access. The city had not created a playground or recreation department until around 1909, when James West, who had been the secretary of the Republican National Committee, took the job to head the Parks and Recreation Department for Washington, DC. Because he was a political appointee and knew practically nothing of the theories or the activities of recreation, he often conferred with E. B. for advice concerning appointments, facility design, and purchasing equipment. Mr. West would later become the CEO of the Boy Scouts of America and leave the city's Recreation Department.

Segregation of parks was an issue that E. B. was adamant about changing. He remarked,

> The City Park authorities continued to segregate, even going as far as to segregate areas for picnicking in Rock Creek Park. I organized a group of citizens representing nearly seventy organizations to protest the discrimination and it was some time before we had the signs taken down in the park. Eventually, the Department of Recreation liberalized many of its practices, but continued segregation until about a year before the Supreme Court Decision of 1954.[10]

In the later part of E. B.'s career, he was sought for his knowledge and opinions on physical education and recreation. Under Franklin Delano Roosevelt's New Deal, E. B. held several appointments with the Federal Security Agency (FSA). He was a member of the National Council on Physical Fitness, Schools and Colleges Subcommittee. Additionally, he

1, E. B. Henderson, Chairman; 2, M. M. Morton, M Street High School; 3, S. E. Compton, Commercial High School; 4, W. B. Hartgrove, Armstrong Manual Training High School.
HIGH SCHOOL GAMES COMMITTEE P. S. A. L., WASHINGTON, D. C.

Henderson established the first school league for African Americans in the United States for the Washington Colored schools.

COURTESY OF HENDERSON FAMILY COLLECTION, TAKEN FROM THE SPALDING OFFICIAL HANDBOOK, *1911*

served as state director to the Physical Fitness Committee for Washington, DC, and consultant to the Women's Commission, Physical Fitness Committee.

In 1935, E. B. was appointed to the Planning Committee for Coordinating Plans for Recreational Facilities in Washington, DC:

> For more than a year Mr. Edwin B. Henderson has served on the Committee for Coordination of Plans for the District Recreation System, headed by Mr. Lewis E. Barrett, Coordinator. In addition, as head of the Department of Health and Physical Education in Colored Junior and Senior High Schools and in his past relationship with playgrounds and community centers, he has probably a more complete picture of recreational facilities, their functioning, and needs than any other one colored citizen.[11]

Further,

> Never before in America has recreation been so great a need in the welfare of people as today. Although many educational, religious, and economic leaders in our group have seemingly failed to grasp the significance of this trend, yet the President of the United States in most of his major talks and special welfare planners stress the top—recreation. As an offset to delinquency of youth and crime, as a preventive of social deterioration as a means of physical rehabilitation on the one hand and of the containment of more wholesome living for all on the other. Recreation is a category of activity unexcelled.[12]

The committee consisted of three organizations and other administrative personnel. E. B. describes,

> The District of Columbia Recreation Committee was formed in 1935 consisting of Frederic A. Delano, Chairman; Commissioner George E. Allen; C. Marshall Finnan, Superintendent of National Capital Parks; and Henry I. Quinn, of the Board of Education. This committee selected for Coordinator of Recreation for Washington Lewis E. Barrett, whose qualification and experience were outstanding. The first problem considered by the committee was that of prevention

of mistakes in planning future grounds and building for recreation and improvement of existing facilities. A committee for planning comprising representatives of the National Capital Parks, the public schools, the municipal Architects Office, and the DC Playground was formed with Coordinator Barrett as chairman. The present membership consists of Lewis Barrett, Chairman, T. C. Secretary, Frank T. Gastaide, W. A. Draper, Malcolm Kirkpatrick, C. E. Cobb, E. B. Henderson, and Richard Tennyson.[13]

E. B. was the only African American on this committee. For him, the task was twofold: (1) to open up and give African Americans access to all the public spaces in the district and (2) to open the pocketbooks for the improvement of existing facilities and the building of more facilities within the schools and communities for African Americans to participate in athletics and recreation. E. B. wrote in a succession of articles in the *Washington Tribune* what was needed for the committee to make recreation more accessible to the African American community.

E. B.'s third article in the *Washington Tribune*, on April 3, 1937, noted the lack of access to public spaces:

> By far the most important facilities for recreation for Washingtonians of all ages are those under the control of the National Capital Parks. The splendid parks about our city, golf courses, many tennis courts, football and baseball fields, picnic grounds, swimming pools, large recreation centers, etc. are all planned for and administered by the Offices of the National Capital Parks.
>
> Although the general use of parks and waterways is free of restrictions, colored people have always protested the limitation placed upon the use of picnic grounds, golf courses, game fields and courts by the prevailing method of licensing and permit issuance.[14]

E. B. also addressed the lack of adequate facilities available to African Americans for participating in recreation and athletics in the District of Columbia in his second article:

Edwin B.Henderson and others of the Inter-Scholastic Athletic
Association Games Committee at the first track meet for Negro
at Howard University on May 30,1906.

The Games Committee for the Interscholastic Athletic Association (ISAA), the first African American athletic league in America, at a 1906 track meet, the first event organized by ISAA.

Gyms Outmoded

The writer remembers when it was quite a battle to secure the construction of a gymnasium in the school for learning. The first assembly hall gymnasium was placed in the Armstrong High School and has alone served boys and girls of this school population from 1912 until this year 1937. Now the only schools beyond the elementary schools that do not "rate" a gymnasium constructed for the purposes of physical education and recreation are Phelps and Margaret Washington Vocational School and Shaw. The gymnasium spaces in Shaw are so cut-up with dangerous edges and obstructions for running plays or games, and with ceilings so low or trussed with beams, that only emergency physical education could be engaged there. Phelps and Margaret Washington needed gymnasiums badly. Cardoza, Francis, and Browne have each one gymnasium only which must be used on a part-time basis. Garnett-Patterson had two splendid gyms, but needed some equipment.

> Randall and Terrell had double gym spaces convertible into a large gym. Browne and Armstrong had new gyms.[15]

E. B. continued to outline deficiencies in the third article:

> The Armstrong gym is entirely too small, but it has a splendid service unit. Dunbar gyms need a lot of remodeling to fit them for modern programs and to suit wider use of the school plant. There is much need for a gymnasium in Division 10 to 13 that has the capacity for spectators at large games similar to several of the gyms constructed for Division 1 to 9. So called assembly hall gyms have been so respected because of light printed walls and unprotected windows that ball games are ruled out of most of them. The name ought to be changed or the walls adjusted for gymnasium purposes. School grounds of the playfield type are very inadequate for colored children. This is due largely to the fact that our junior and senior high schools are located in congested older sections of the city where homes are not only on streets but in slum alleys and courts. The high cost of ground inhibits the purchase of adequate play space. Unfortunately, also, there is only one large athletic field for three senior high schools. One ample stadium. We need to catch up in this regard.[16]

Access to pools during this era and even today inhibits many African Americans from learning how to swim. In 2022, according to *USA Swimming News*, 64 percent of African American children do not know how to swim. In 1937, access was probably lower, and the percentage of African American nonswimmers was probably much higher. Often public money was used to build pools in White areas, but few or non were built in areas where African Americans lived and had access to. In E. B.'s fifth article about the committee's proceedings, he addressed the pool issue:

> **SWIMMING POOLS**
>
> In the matter of swimming pools, there are two public pools for colored swimmers and two for white swimmers. These pools were erected near recreation areas, following the fight some years ago by Representative

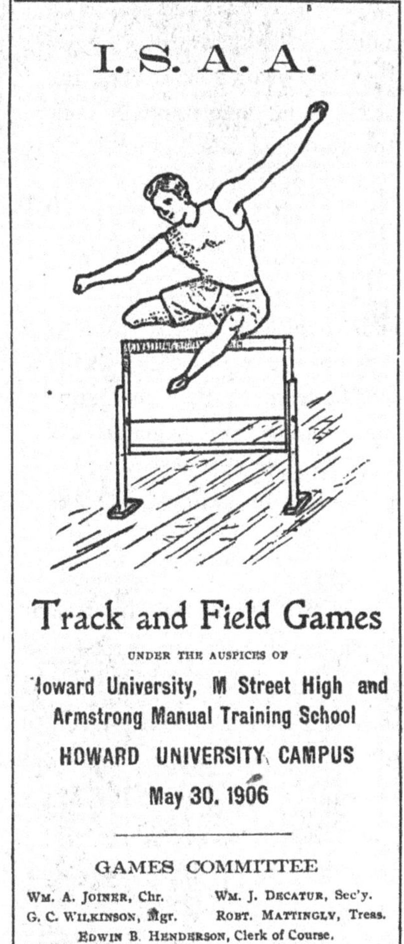

I. S. A. A.

Track and Field Games

UNDER THE AUSPICES OF

Howard University, M Street High and Armstrong Manual Training School

HOWARD UNIVERSITY CAMPUS

May 30, 1906

GAMES COMMITTEE

Wm. A. Joiner, Chr. Wm. J. Decatur, Sec'y.
G. C. Wilkinson, Mgr. Robt. Mattingly, Treas.
Edwin B. Henderson, Clerk of Course.

Officials

Referee—Mr. G. C. Wilkinson, M St. H. S.
Starter—W. T. S Jackson, M. St. H. S.
Clerk of Course—E. B. Henderson, Athletic Instructor, P. S.

Track Judges: Chas. Cooke, H. U.; James Walker, D. C. N. G.; Robt. N. Mattingly, A. M. T. S.
Field Judges: W. J. DeCatur, H. U.; Haley G. Douglass, M St. H. S.; Thos Johnson, Y. M. C. A.
Timers: Dwight Holmes, B. H. S.; Jos. Allen, M St. H. S.; W. B Hartgrove, A. M. T. S.
Scorer—Prof. Wm. A. Joiner, H. U.
Inspectors: A. J. Savoy, P. S.; W. Dodson, A. M. T. S.; A. H. Glenn, M. St. H. S.; Walter Dyson, H. U.
Marshalls: B. Washington, A. M. T. S.; . Freeman, H. U.
Announcer—Joseph Mason, H. U.
Assistants to Officials: Merrian Hayson. Capt. Robt. Taylor. Capt. Thos. Green. Percy Webster. Lieutenant Sevellon Savoy. Lieutenant Brooks Captain Gordan. Joseph Mason. Chas. Moore.

Order of Events

1 100 yard dash—Graded Schools, Trial Heats.
2 " " Semi Finals.
3 " " Inter-Scholastic, Trial Heats.
4 " " Semi Finals.
5 " " Open, Trial Heats.
6 " " Semi Finals.
7 120 yard Hurdle Race, open, Trial Heats.
8 220 yard Dash, open, Trial Heats.
9 220 yard Hurdle Race, open, Trial Heats
10 " shot put, 12 lb. open.
11 1 Mile Run. open.
12 100 yard Dash, Graded Schools. Finals.
13 120 yard Hurdle Race, Finals.
14 High Jump, open.
15 Pole Vault.
16 Broad Jump.
17 100 yard Dash, Inter-Scholastic. Finals.
18 100 yard Dash, open. Finals.
19 220 yard Dash, open. Semi-Finals.
20 880 yard Run, open.
21 220 yard Dash. Final.
22 220 yard Hurdle Race. Final.
23 Basket Ball. M St. H. S. vs. A. M. T. S.
24 Inter-Scholastic Relay, one mile.
25 12 lb. Hammer throw, open.
26 Potato Race.
27 440 yard Run, open.
28 1 Mile Relay Run, open.

NOTICE

No person will be allowed on or within the track except officials and actual competitors, and as soon as their event is over will kindly leave the inclosure at once. The marshal will see that this rule is strictly enforced.

The track measures five laps to the mile. Pistol will be fired at beginning of last lap of mile and last relay.

First track meet program for the ISAA, 1906.
COURTESY OF HENDERSON FAMILY COLLECTION

Nadden and colored Citizens to maintain swimming in the Tidal Basin for both races. When the water pollution necessitated other swimming facilities, Francis Pool was the first built. For a while it was a popular diversion. Later Banneker was built and it attracted more people, including many who formerly traveled to Francis. Takoma and Eckington and a newly built pool in Anacostia are pools to serve White

> swimmers. The 49 pools indoor and outdoor were operated by private clubs, Commercial enterprises, playgrounds, welfare agencies, colleges, and public schools, only seven were listed for colored swimmers. The National Capital Park Pools were excellent in design and in their servicing units. Dunbar and Howard pools are fair in size. Others for colored swimmers are less in size and general development.

Pools Lose Money

> It is interesting to note that every public pool with the exception of McKinley in 1932, and Takoma in 1935, operate at a loss. One of the major criticisms of outdoor pools lies in the season of the year. Swimming should be possible year around and could be if the larger schools had pools built for winter use. Despite the losses in operation involved, there should have been increased opportunities for swimming by the less privileged part of the population.[17]

Through the work of the Recreation Committee, it was possible to bring all the resources together and create a vast coordinated program to promote recreation for all the citizens of Washington, DC, making once restricted and limited venues, many of which had been designated "for Whites only," accessible to Blacks. This was a game changer that helped bring about equal access to facilities, ushering in a golden era for African American athletics in the District of Columbia. This New Deal targeted Washington, DC; brought together all the resources into one agency; and thus helped to develop athletes like Elgin Baylor of the Los Angeles Lakers, Maury Wills of the Los Angeles Dodgers, Dave Bing of the Detroit Pistons, John Thompson of the Boston Celtics and Georgetown fame, and many others.

E. B. would hold a position on this committee until his retirement in 1954. These appointments raised E. B.'s status from a physical education teacher and department head in the local Washington, DC, Colored schools to a national adviser and consultant with departments in the federal government.

10

Building the Framework for Organized Athletics

The Inter-Scholastic Athletic Association (ISAA), the First African American Athletic League

As E. B. went through his teaching duties, settled in, and got to know the lay of the land, he was able to make many professional connections with those he encountered. When he went to the schools, he met the principals. He made a point to meet school board members of the Colored and White schools and express to them the importance of physical education and creating opportunities for youth to participate in athletics as an impetus for public health initiatives. He found several school board members, teachers, and principals who were in favor of creating a framework for introducing organized athletics to the boys in the schools. He also met some who weren't interested in providing the Colored schools with equal facilities for athletics, principally because of the expenditure of money.

E. B. reached out to African Americans who oversaw physical education and athletic directors in Baltimore and other cities in the Mid-Atlantic. What he found was that they, too, suffered from problems with effectively involving youth in physical activities and athletics. He found that there were several reasons, particularly in the southern states, where the school boards, as well as the sanctioning organizations like the Amateur Athletic Union (AAU) and the National Collegiate Athletic

Association (NCAA, coincidentally established the same year as the ISAA), did not want to fund gymnasiums or equipment for African American youth to participate in athletics. He also found that these same organizations and institutions were not willing to recognize or sanction African American teams that were already involved in athletic competition. And most importantly, these sanctioning bodies were unwilling to allow competition between youth from White schools, colleges, and athletic clubs and African American schools, colleges, and athletic clubs. Not in the South!

Therefore, in 1906, it was necessary to create the Inter-Scholastic Athletic Association of Middle Atlantic States to provide organized athletics to African Americans. This league would sanction, provide funding, and organize competitions. The 1910 *Spalding Official Handbook of the Inter-Scholastic Athletic Association* states,

> The Association bearing this name (ISAA), though a comparatively recent organization, is beginning to be recognized as a power for good in the athletics of the schools and colleges for colored youth throughout the Middle Atlantic States.
>
> Several conditions led to the formation of this organization. Among them was the fact that under the conditions in the Middle and Southern sections, where the existence of separate institutions for the colored race is made necessary, the pupils of such institutions are brought into competition with the representatives of the surrounding schools in the athletic meets under the A.A.U. and similar organizations.
>
> Another reason was that the students at these schools are all of very modest means, many of them earning their way through school, and are therefore, unable to raise large guarantees required to arrange games with the more distant Northern schools and colleges who would be willing to play them.
>
> Add to the two mentioned reasons the fact that in the institutions for the education of colored youth, athletics receive little or no aid from the institutional treasury, and that there are very few alumni who are able to give any considerable sums for such purposes, and it is easy to see that athletics under these conditions must live a precarious existence.[1]

E. B. called for a meeting of a few "public-spirited men" in the public schools and universities of Washington and Baltimore who would remedy the lack of opportunities for African American youth in organized athletics. The meeting took place at Howard University. In attendance were W. J. DeCatur and W. A. Joiner of Howard University; Garnet C. Wilkinson of M Street High School; Robert Mattingly of Armstrong Technical High School; E. B. Henderson, physical training instructor in the DC Colored schools; and Ralph Cook of the Baltimore high schools.[2]

These gentlemen determined that an organization was needed to expand the opportunities for African American youth. At that time, the only sports available for students were baseball and football, and they were not conducted in an organized fashion under the current rules of the AAU or other sanctioning organizations. They also discussed that, by only offering baseball and football, only a few at each school were reaping the benefits from such exercise and outdoor sports, while most students were unable to participate in athletics, so additional offerings were needed to allow more students to benefit from healthful activity.[3]

In 1906, these men established the Inter-Scholastic Athletic Association, an organization that would expand athletic opportunities for the youth of the African American communities in Washington and Baltimore and the states of the greater Mid-Atlantic region. Howard University was to become the center of athletic life for the organization. A committee was formed to petition the university's board of trustees for their permission and funds to build a track and hold a track meet, which would be the organization's first sanctioned competition.[4]

The university allowed the petitioners to lay the track, provided that the two instructors employed by the university would take personal responsibility. The estimated cost to lay the track was $400; however, the university would not provide the funding, so the funds would have to be raised elsewhere. The members of the association pooled their own money to foot the bill for the track construction, with no assurance of repayment. A Games Committee was created to officiate the event, adding new members to the association. Volunteers from the high schools participated in building the track oval but hired labor that was necessary to complete the job. Embers from the school furnaces and other sources were laid for the quarter-mile track on the land provided by the university. The teachers from several schools provided the money for prizes and medals, which came to the additional sum of $120.[5]

To get ready for the meets, teams were trained by E. B. in the Washington Colored high schools; by Joiner and DeCatur at Howard; and by Cook and Smith in the Baltimore high schools. The first track meet of African American participants sanctioned by an African American athletic league took place on May 30, 1906, on the campus of Howard University in Washington, DC. The event brought out the largest crowd that had ever gathered on its campus. Between seventy-five and one hundred young men competed in the event. The teams competing were from "Howard, M Street High, Armstrong Tech, Baltimore High, Wilmington High, Baltimore YMCA, Washington YMCA, as well as several local athletic clubs."[6]

Many of those in attendance had never seen an organized track meet. The audience was also treated to an exhibition game of basketball between Armstrong and M Street High Schools.[7] E. B. had been teaching the fundamentals of basketball to boys since he had returned from the Dudley Sargent School of Physical Training. For most in attendance, this would be the first time they would see the sport being played. This exhibition planted the seeds that helped create the desire for a basketball season the following year.[8]

The gross receipts from entrance fees and attendance were almost enough to wipe out the indebtedness the members of the association had pooled together for building the track and promoting and putting on the event, which was a welcomed relief. The event was a resounding success and proved that athletics would be a popular draw in the future for spectators and fans in the African American community in Washington, DC, and in the nation.[9]

The Olympian Athletic League (OAL) of New York (1907)

Around this same time, two hundred miles to the north, in New York City, physical culture was also beginning to form. In New York, the schools were not segregated like they were in Washington, DC. Just like in Washington, basketball was becoming popular in New York City, and there were men like E. B. who wanted to establish organizations to promote physical culture and activities for the African American population there. E. B. established the ISAA in 1906. One year later, the Black New York club teams established a league of their own, the OAL, to organize and control their own teams.[10] It wouldn't be long before these two leagues would compete against each other for a national title.

(Washington) Public School Athletic League (PSAL, 1910)

As the lead instructor in the Washington, DC, Colored School System and a leading voice in physical training, athletics, and recreation in the city, E. B. was always about providing fair and equitable opportunities for youth. His first responsibility was to the students in the schools, and as such, he did everything he could think of to increase opportunities in athletic participation. After several years of growth for the ISAA, E. B. saw there was a need for a league that focused on the needs of school-age children in Washington schools. Having children competing against adults was not equitable or fair, so he organized the Public Schools Athletic League (PSAL) for African American students.

As secretary of the PSAL, E. B. wrote,

> In June 1910, Assistant Superintendent of Schools Roscoe C. Bruce talked to your secretary and Mr. G. C. Wilkinson with regard to the formation of a P.S.A.L in the schools. With the permission and aid of Mr. Bruce and the Assistant Director of Physical Training, Miss Anita J. Turner, work was begun on a constitution and plan of activities. The constitution, by-laws, and plan of work were submitted to the Athletic Committee of the Board of Education. Permission was then granted your secretary to organize the P.S.A.L.[11]

E. B. further stated as a rationale,

> That scholarship, discipline, and attendance can be improved through the proper handling of the means afforded by the rules and activities of the P.S.A.L is no untried theory, but is a practical fact that has been

> demonstrated here in many instances during the past year, and has been proven beyond question in New York, Cincinnati, New Orleans, Seattle, Troy, Newark, and many other cities, where a P.S.A.L exist.[12]

In 1910, the PSAL in Washington, DC, was the first student athletic league for African American students in the country. The students in White Washington, DC, schools had not yet created a league for their students—not until years later, following the example set by E. B.[13]

In 1903, Dr. Luther H. Gulick, a prominent physical educator, had organized the PSAL of Greater New York and was its first secretary.[14] E. B. was aware of Gulick's work; he was also familiar with Gulick from his days at Harvard University, where Gulick was one of the instructors at the Dudley Sargent School of Physical Training. The professional associations that E. B. made during his stint at Harvard gave him an understanding of what might be accomplished among his own race during the days of strict segregation in the early twentieth century.

By establishing the PSAL in the Colored schools, the school board would now allocate funds to build playgrounds and gymnasiums for those schools in Washington, DC. In 1911, the ISAA and PSAL, along with the Teachers Benefit Athletic Association sponsored an indoor track meet that was one of the first large cooperative events including both entities.[15] A 1954 article from the *Washington Afro-American Magazine* reflected on the event:

> [T]he ISAA along with the PSAL and the Teachers Benefit AA (Athletic Association) sponsored a mammoth Indoor Meet at the old convention Hall in Washington. The meet was a gala occasion. Howard Drew, the best sprinter in the nation, was a star attraction.
>
> Many boys who later became famous in track and field began their career that night. One such was Dr. Binga Dismond who became the fastest 440-yard runner in the country.
>
> Following the organization of the ISAA, we organized the DC Public School Athletic League, and aided, through our publication of

the ISAA Handbook of 1910 and 1911, in the formation of the CIAA and the NCIAA.

Later such athletic controls spread to the South, West, and southwest as athletics grew in colored colleges and high schools.[16]

11

Eastern Board of Officials (EBO)

Rules and Refs

EVEN BEFORE THE FIRST SANCTIONED CONTEST TOOK PLACE, E. B. believed that, in order to have African Americans participate in organized sports, there needed to be structure and rules on the courts, fields, and tracks that would govern the contest. Therefore, referees, umpires, timekeepers, statisticians, and more needed to know and enforce the rules in competition for the various sports offered. Although there was resistance at first, the training of competent Black officials proved to be the key for African Americans playing organized sports in the nation's capital.

E. B. started an athletic league to provide equal opportunity to participate in athletics and establish fairness in the competition between teams. In the fall of 1905, he called a meeting at the home of Garnet C. Wilkinson, then football coach at M Street High School. Others in attendance were Merton Robinson, A. Kiger Savoy, Benjamin Washington, Haley Douglass, and William Beckett of Baltimore. These athletic visionaries had the forethought to organize themselves and study the rules of different sports to officiate before they officially formed their league. Led by E. B., these men were successful in bringing a structured, quality athletic program to African American youth of the city. E. B. personally officiated with each of these men in a variety of sports—track and field, basketball, soccer, football, and boxing—and Benjamin Washington's tenure of active officiating in football rivaled E. B.'s. For the first event of the Inter-Scholastic Athletic Association (ISAA), a track and field meet, on May 30, 1906, they established a Games Committee. Personnel needed for every scholastic track meet was shared in rule 1 of the 1910 *Spalding Official Handbook of the Inter-Scholastic Athletic Association of Middle Atlantic States*:

OFFICIALS

Every meeting of the Interscholastic Athletic Association shall be under the control of the following officials:

A Games Committee

One Director

One Assistant Director

One Referee

Three or more Judges at Finish

One Chief Field Judge

Four or more Field Judges

One Recorder of Times

Three or more Inspectors

Three Timekeepers

One Starter

One Clerk of the Course with assistants

One Announcer

One Chief Scorer with assistants

Marshall with assistants

One Official Reporter[1]

At this first ISAA track meet, held on the campus of Howard University, there were 150 contestants and more than 3,000 spectators, E. B. served as clerk of the course, and in ensuing meets, he worked as starter.

But some of the officiating was suspect, even by the White officials, as E. B. found out riding up to a football game as the only Black official in an early contest:

> In the beginning of intercollegiate contests there were few trained (Black) officials. In major football games white officials were used. Even in our first indoor track meet several of the key officials were white men.
>
> In my first Lincoln-Howard game three officials were white men. Howard selected me and a former pitcher on the Washington Ball club. Lincoln selected one from Princeton and another from Haverford. . . .
>
> Riding up on the train with the white officials from Washington, he asked me how I was intending to run the game. Asking what he meant, he said, "Well for every penalty called against Howard, I'm calling one of the same yardage on the next play against Lincoln."
>
> Needless to say, this was a shock to a young idealist. Because this became the pattern of play, the captains of the two teams asked me to

Eastern Board of Officials, first established by E. B. Henderson in 1905 before the first athletic event organized by the Inter-Scholastic Athletic Association. This was the first African American organization to train referees for African American competitions during the era of segregation.
COURTESY OF HENDERSON FAMILY COLLECTION, USED IN THE NEGRO IN SPORTS

> try to do something about it. They did and had the officials agree to call the game just as they would any other.[2]

There were other challenges. For example, as Black officials, they were not respected or taken seriously, whereas White officials were. E. B. continued,

> There were many heads of institutions that did not believe colored players would respect colored officials, even the colored head coaches of some colleges. The late Major Moten, following a game at Hampton congratulated us for being able to run a game with the full respect of the players.
>
> When H.U. athletic authorities decided to use all colored officials in the Lincoln-Howard Classic, we put in a bill for our services identical to the compensation paid former white officials.
>
> Prof. Kelly Miller of H.U.'s athletic committee opposed it by saying this was more money than he got paid for two weeks' work. The question was not raised when the fee was paid to the white officials. There was a time when we would work a game gratis, or for two complimentary passes. My first fee was $5. Later I received fees ranging from $15 to, on one occasion, $100.[3]

As the interest and opportunities in athletics grew, the Eastern Board of Officials split into several auxiliaries to accommodate the growth. It became necessary to create separate officiating entities by region, under the official umbrella of the Affiliated Board of Officials:

> The Eastern Board is the oldest organized officials' group in African American conferences. It originated about 1905 with small discussion groups that met prior to football games with G. C. Wilkinson. . . . At first it took in the officials of several states. It is now a local board. From this group was initiated the organization of the Affiliated Board of Officials which comprises the Middle Atlantic, the Baltimore, the Piedmont, the West Virginia, the Eastern and the Virginia boards. The Affiliated Board is recognized as spokesman for the group of local boards by the Colored Intercollegiate Athletic Association. Over two-thirds of the present membership of the Eastern Board, which

> number more than thirty members, are directors or teachers of physical education, athletics, or recreation. Not only is football an interest of the group, but various sections of the Board specialize in study and officiate in baseball, softball, basketball, boxing, handball, swimming, track and field, tennis, and other sports.[4]

The two sports available to students at the time were football and baseball. Of these, football required the most coordination of personnel and rules knowledge. Beginning around 1908, Garnet Wilkinson, A. Kiger Savoy, Haley Douglass, and E. B. began rules study with the intent of obtaining certification from the national governing rules body to officiate football. In 1911, these men attained their certification yet were not listed along with White officials in the annual Spalding football manual that year. In his book *The Negro in Sports*, E. B. cites one member of the original group for his contribution in officiating football: "Garnet Wilkinson, as a football referee, established a high standard, and exerted more influence on the game than any one individual connected with it."[5]

Both Garnet Wilkinson and E. B. had a lasting impact on the quality of officiating in football by the men of the board. The most succinct description of the board's performance on the gridiron was stated by a man whom E. B. described as "that splendid official," whom E. B. recommended for the position of the first commissioner of officials for the Colored Intercollegiate Athletic Association (CIAA), and who would die in a plane crash fifteen years later, during World War II, while serving his country at the Tuskegee Army Air Field as director of the grounds crew. At the 1930 EBO banquet, Major Harold Martin, then head football coach at Virginia State College, commended the EBO, characterizing them as "men thoroughly familiar with the rules and unafraid to enforce them; neutral in their attitudes; thoroughly honest and approachable; properly equipped, alert and whose general demeanor is one of the belief of honorable intent on the part of the players."[6]

E. B. served in an active capacity into his old age. In 1933, he officiated two games on Thanksgiving:

> While some football officials were bemoaning the fact that Thanksgiving Day found them without an assignment, Dr. E. B. Henderson, of this city, found himself with two Turkey Day assignments on hand.
>
> Regularly scheduled in the afternoon to serve as an umpire in the Morgan-Virginia State game in Baltimore, Dr. Henderson was advanced to the post of referee when Dr. Joseph Trigg, the original referee, reported that he could not serve. Hardly had this change been consummated than Dr. Henderson was confronted by a delegate requesting that he also serve as a referee in the Howard-Lincoln game in Atlantic City on Thanksgiving night. . . .
>
> The game in Baltimore was over at 3:15, having started at 1 p.m., and the Atlantic City game was scheduled to start promptly at 8:30 p.m. This allowed a margin of five hours, 15 minutes in which to get to the shore. A fast car with a chauffeur awaited Dr. Henderson at the close of the Baltimore game, and with his wife and children he was whisked away to Atlantic City, arriving in time to refresh himself before game time.[7]

What makes this doubly a testament to E. B.'s resolve and dedication was that he was seventy years old at the time, and Thanksgiving was his birthday.

E. B. spent almost fifty years serving as an official with various officiating organizations until his retirement from the schools in 1954. His passion for rules and records is evident in *The Negro in Sports* and the *Spalding Official Handbooks*. His work in the field helped to legitimize African American referees and officials. Several officials in the EBO joined the ranks of the professional leagues. The first and most well-known official from the Eastern Board to officiate an NFL game was Johnny Grier, starting in 1988. On November 23, 2020, the first all-Black crew took the field to officiate a contest between the Los Angeles Rams and the Tampa Bay Buccaneers.

The CIAA used the Eastern Board of Officials to officiate their athletic contest. In 1983, E. B. was posthumously inducted into the CIAA Hall of Fame as an official.

12

Basketball Games Begin in Washington (1907)

In the time between basketball's invention by Dr. James Naismith in 1891 and its introduction to the public in 1904 at the St. Louis World's Fair and, shortly afterward, the 1904 St. Louis Summer Olympics, very few African American males had been introduced to the sport.[1] Two years later, the Inter-Scholastic Athletic Association introduced basketball to an African American audience with a game at Howard University played in conjunction with the association's track meet.

There was an appetite for more basketball and sports in general:

> Athletic clubs of young men began to form all over the city and ask for the privilege of playing under the protection of the Association, which requests were always granted when possible; thus, what may be properly termed wild-cat athletics began to give way to organized control and the high ideals of the manly sports were held before both public and participants.[2]

E. B. began introducing the fundamentals of basketball into the physical education curriculum in 1904, shortly after returning from Harvard. He would gather the boys in the small armory in the basement of M Street High School. The sport was already being taught by E. B.'s mentor, Miss Anita Turner, who was teaching basketball to girls in her physical education classes in the Washington Colored schools and at Normal School

No. 2. However, boys were not being trained to play basketball. At first, because it was taught to only girls, many boys perceived basketball as a "sissy" sport or a sport meant to be played by and for girls.[3]

> Basketball was not a popular sport for boys in 1906. The boys preferred the major sports of the day, such as baseball and football. All this was about to change. Boys being boys, the game took on a rougher, more competitive tone upon its introduction. The mix of sweat and testosterone meant more rough play and fouling, whereas the girls were more into the pure fundamentals. At Harvard's Dudley Sargent School, EB learned the fundamentals of the game and quickly became a devotee of the sport because of its delicate mix of brains, brawn, and teamwork. He remembered, "Since basketball was unknown I took over the task of teaching the game, organizing teams, training officials, and promoting

E. B. teaching basketball in his EBO jacket.
COURTESY OF HENDERSON FAMILY COLLECTION

> games. Around 1905 and 1906, I had six basketball teams playing in True Reformer's Hall at 12th and U Sts.[4]

One evening shortly after Christmas in 1906, E. B. and his future brother-in-law Ben Brownley walked into the gymnasium of Washington's all-White Central Young Men's Christian Association. As they walked on the court and through the aisle to their seats, they seemed oblivious to the stares of the other spectators who were also there to enjoy the game. E. B. and Brownley were unaware and unsuspecting of what would happen next. Although most of Washington, DC, was staunchly segregated, E. B. believed that a religious organization like the YMCA would be more tolerant to two clean-cut, young, Christian gentlemen who happened to be of a different race and that they would be accepted if they showed up to observe a game of basketball. Only a week earlier in this very gymnasium, thousands of men of both races had joined hands to sing hymns and embrace the ideals of love, brotherhood, and equality. William Jennings Bryan, the Democratic presidential nominee, expressed the biblical quote "Love thy neighbor as thyself."

There was no love to be found in the Central YMCA that night. Several members of the YMCA complained of "uninvited Blacks invading the club." In this environment and on this night, race would become obviously more important than religion to these Christian gentlemen. The YMCA's athletic director C. Edward Beckett, in the racially explicit language of this period, yelled at E. B. and his guest that they were not wanted or allowed there and that they should leave and never return to the Washington YMCA again.

The two men were evicted, bolting into the cold winter night, and E. B. was rightly upset at their treatment. As they left the Central YMCA, E. B. was determined that Mr. Beckett would not have the last word, and he knew then that, by creating the basketball league and a tournament at True Reformers Hall, he would be able to remedy the injustice he had just experienced. A successful league of his own and a tournament would mark the beginning of Black basketball in Washington and the nation as a whole. If African Americans were not afforded the pleasure of sitting and enjoying a game of basketball in the Central YMCA of Washington, DC, then they would have to start a YMCA, and a league, of their own.[5]

THE TWELFTH STREET YMCA (1908)

E. B. was humiliated by his experience at the White Central YMCA. He was not accustomed to defeat or being subjugated, so he expressed to Jesse Moorland how he was determined to build a Black branch of the YMCA. E. B. vigorously threw himself into the efforts to create the Twelfth Street YMCA.

In 1922, E. B. coached the Washington Colored Schools Championship Dunbar High School basketball team. This team included renowned blood scientist Dr. Charles Drew, in front.

COURTESY OF ADDISON SCURLOCK PHOTOGRAPHY, LIBRARY OF CONGRESS/NATIONAL ARCHIVES

The idea of African Americans having their own YMCA in Washington, DC, goes back to before the Civil War. Anthony Bowen, a formerly enslaved man from Prince George's County, Maryland, purchased his own freedom at the age of twenty-five. He then made good by starting a couple of churches where he would teach young and old to read. He was known for harboring runaway enslaved people on the Underground Railroad. While working at the US Patent Office, Bowen met William Langdon, who became the founder of the downtown Central YMCA, however African Americans were not allowed at that facility. In 1853, Bowen started a Black YMCA, but it struggled. For thirty-eight years, there was not a permanent building, and when it did finally get one, within a few years, it lost the building and was once again without a home.

Shortly after E. B. started his professional career in Washington, a group of Christian men started making serious plans for a permanent home for an African American YMCA in Washington, DC. Large contributions from major philanthropists John D. Rockefeller and Julius Rosenwald were secured to build a structure designed by William Sidney Pittman, the son-in-law of Booker T. Washington. E. B. became a chairman of one of the committees raising money for the new YMCA, receiving a $10 gold piece for raising the largest solicited amount of money to support the new YMCA.

The total cost of the structure was $100,000, and E. B. was busy helping to raise money for the new YMCA because of what it would mean for athletics, as well as generally for Washington, DC. In 1908, President Teddy Roosevelt gave a speech and was there for laying the cornerstone of the new YMCA. E. B. and Roosevelt were both Harvard men, and it is not inconceivable that the two may have met at the ceremony.

In 1911, President William Howard Taft gave an address at the Howard Theater as the final push to secure the funds for the new YMCA. The new African American YMCA facility was finally completed in 1912. It was a full-service YMCA facility, including reception rooms, offices, fifty-four sleeping rooms, a gymnasium, a heated pool with showers and locker facilities, a barbershop, a Turkish bath (steam room), a bowling alley, a reading room, a social room, and a home parlor with an open fireplace.[6] Many who stayed there were a Who's Who of future famous members of the Harlem Renaissance, from Langston Hughes to Charles Drew. It was a marvelous structure and a great resource for the community, not far from U Street, with the True Reformer's Hall just up the street, at Twelfth and U Streets NW.

Shortly after Roosevelt laid the cornerstone in 1908, E. B. organized a team under the banner of the Twelfth Street YMCA. It would be several years before they could practice and play at the YMCA facility, but even so, they named the team the Washington Twelfth-Streeters. E. B. was most interested in the YMCA because of its association with athletics, but he also supported the YMCA as a member of its board of directors and, for a time, conducted Bible study with the young men living there.

13

Bringing Home the Title

Colored Basketball World Championship (1908)

THE TITLE OF WORLD CHAMPION HAS ALWAYS BEEN ONE OF ULTIMATE esteem in the sporting world. The year 1908 would be big in sports, particularly for African Americans. The pugilistic sport of boxing was probably the oldest and most renowned sports contest of its day, almost as big as baseball in the minds of most Americans. The Heavyweight Championship of the World was, and is, the most coveted title in the world of sports, and in 1908, African Americans would have a hero to celebrate—Jack Johnson. Jack Johnson was a different kind of heavyweight fighter. In this time, most heavyweight fighters stood toe-to-toe and slugged it out. Johnson was a skilled boxer who moved and blocked punches. Some said that you couldn't hit him. He fought more like a middle- or lighter-weight boxer. That December, Jack Johnson defeated Canadian Tommy Burns in Australia to become the first African American to win the coveted title of Heavyweight Boxing World Champion. It would be the first time since John L. Sullivan in 1878, when he refused to fight Peter Jackson (a Black boxer), that a White world champion agreed to fight a Black contender.[1]

Also in 1908, there was great anticipation of a match between the two areas of the country where basketball had become popular. The table was set; basketball was catching on in the African American communities of New York and the Mid-Atlantic states. Washington had several teams in their league, but the Washington Twelfth-Streeters from the

Twelfth Street YMCA were the team that would dominate DC basketball for years. This team was coached and captained by E. B. In New York, there were three dominant club teams: the Smart Set Athletic Club, the Alpha Physical Culture Club, and the St. Christopher Club. Philadelphia had the Stentonworth Athletic Club, and Baltimore had the Wissahickon Athletic Club (though they did not have many indoor playing spaces) and the Dunbar Athletic Club. Pittsburgh basketball was about to take off in a big way with Cumberland Posey's Monticello and Leondi Big Five teams.

The question that began to be tossed around was "Who's the best?" A competition was in order, and it would be known as the Colored Basketball World Championship.[2] According to E. B.,

> Big time basketball began with the inception of inner-city games among the club teams of Brooklyn, New York City and Washington, DC. The meeting of the Smart Set Club, the Metropolitan champion (Olympian League) and the winning team of the Inter-scholastic Athletic Association of Washington, DC, in 1908 was the first important inner-city game. The Washington team, the Crescent Athletic Club, was defeated, in Washington and in Brooklyn. In 1909, the writer [EB] organized and was captain of the Washington Young Men's Christian Association team which defeated in Washington and New York all of its opponents including Alpha, the Smart Set, and St. Christopher clubs. For two years (1909–10, 1910–11) the Washington "Y" team was undefeated.[3]

In Washington, in the tournament that played under the Inter-Scholastic Athletic Association, the younger school teams were outclassed by the older players from the Crescent Athletic Club, so the Crescents, as the winner of the competition between all the Washington teams, had the honor of competing against the winner of all the Olympian Athletic League teams of New York City. The Smart Set Athletic Club of Brooklyn defeated St. Christopher Athletic Club, the Physical Culture Athletic Club, and others and was the champion of their league.

The game was set to be played for the Colored basketball world championship for the 1908 season. There would be two games played: one in

Washington Y. M. C. A., National Champions, '09-'10
Seated—Gray, Oliver, Henderson, Clifford, Curtis. Standing—Chestnut, Nixon, Anderson, Johnson.

The undefeated 1909–1910 Washington Twelfth-Streeters from the Twelfth Street YMCA, the national champions or, as they were called, the Colored Basketball World Champions.
COURTESY OF HENDERSON FAMILY COLLECTION; ADDISON SCURLOCK PHOTOGRAPHER, NATIONAL ARCHIVES, LIBRARY OF CONGRESS

front of the Washington fans and one in front of the fans in New York City. The Smart Set outclassed the Washington team in both contests. So for the time being, New York City was considered to have the best teams in the nation, if not the world, or at least among the African American basketball teams at that time.[4]

This didn't sit well with E. B. Shortly after the outcome, he organized a team in Washington under the auspices of the Twelfth Street YMCA. The structure that would become the Twelfth Street YMCA was not yet finished, but in E. B.'s mind, that did not matter. What did matter was building a team that would be able to compete against the New York teams and bring home the title for Washington, particularly his league, the Inter-Scholastic Athletic Association. Two years in a row, the Smart

Set of Brooklyn had dominated the championship series between the two cities. E. B. wanted to make sure there would not be a third year.

Early on, E. B. began to solicit players for his team. He chose them from the teams who participated the year before leading up to playoff between the Crescents Club and the Smart Set. Among the players he chose was Ed Gray, with whom he had played on the Spartans several years earlier in the Basketball Carnival at the True Reformers Hall. Gray had matriculated to Amherst College for his freshman year, where he played on their football and track teams. He returned to Washington to attend Howard University in his second year, where he played football and led Howard to an undefeated season that year. Now back in Washington, he was available to play with the Twelfth-Streeters.[5]

E. B. also recruited Arthur Leo "Buck" Curtis, whose father was a doctor at Freedmen's Hospital in Washington, as forward. F. A. Taylor was another Howard University student who played football earlier that year and was said to have an unstoppable demeanor. Henry F. Nixon, the business manager for the Howard University student newspaper and a former player on the Howard prep squad, was known to be a reliable forward. Maurice Clifford was another forward who was a teacher at Armstrong Tech and had previously played for the Howard University Medics. E. B., with his knowledge of the game and leadership ability, would round out the squad playing center. Although E. B. was not a big man, he was known to be one of the best at center because, at this time in the game, the center controlled the tempo, much like the point guards of today. But also, after each point, there was a jump ball at center court.[6]

To everyone's surprise, E. B. recruited Hudson Oliver to play for the Twelfth-Streeters. Hudson, or Huddie, as he was known, wanted to become a doctor, so naturally he enrolled in medical school at Howard University. Huddie was the Smart Set's best player and had played the previous two years for them when they won back-to-back Colored basketball world championships. How fortuitous for E. B.'s new team to gain the talent and someone knowledgeable of the teams of New York City—specifically from the team that was likely to be their opponent in next year's championship game. This was a real game changer![7]

E. B. was a one-man band. In addition to his teaching duties, he scheduled the basketball games through the Inter-Scholastic Athletic Association's Games Committee. He also coached and played with the Twelfth-Streeters and heavily promoted the sport. And finally, he promoted and chronicled the contest in local media and the *Howard University Journal.*

The basketball season began on Christmas Eve at True Reformer's Hall in Washington with a contest between the Alpha Physical Culture Club squad from the Olympian Athletic League of New York City and the Washington Twelfth-Streeters. The Twelfth-Streeters were far superior to the school teams and the Crescent Athletic Club that had played against the Smart Set and lost the year before.

This game was witnessed by more than six hundred of the city's well-heeled citizens. The *New York Age* sent a journalist to cover the game. Both teams began with "rough play," with lots of fouls called. Play seesawed back and forth until Twelfth-Streeter Buck Curtis sustained a head injury. When play resumed, the Twelfth-Streeters scored four in a row and built a 17–6 lead at halftime. The second half was more of the same, with E. B. scoring four goals, and Huddie several more. The final score of the contest was 32–15. The *Washington Evening Star* said the event was the "cleanest and best exhibition of basketball by a local colored team to date." It was the *Evening Star* reporter's opinion that the New York team seemed so much slower than the Washington Twelfth-Streeters.[8]

In those days, basketball games were a social event and a competition between cities. It was customary for the hosting team to pay all expenses of the visiting team, including transportation, lodging, meals, and socials between the competing teams. Although the game was competitive, the host team was obligated to be a cordial host, and under amateur rules, the emphasis was on good, clean sports and sportsmanship. After the game, Washington's most popular band, the Lyric Orchestra, performed into the night to the crowd of fans who attended the game, as well as many who came afterward for the party. And before the opposing teams were taken to Union Station to return to New York, there was a farewell reception to thank them, whether they had won or lost, for coming to

Washington to participate in good, clean sports and giving the fans of Washington an entertaining affair.[9]

The Washington Twelfth-Streeters would continue their winning ways in both Washington and New York. They defeated the Smart Set of Brooklyn on February 16 at the True Reformer's Hall, 24–15, and the manager of the Smart Set was none too happy about that. Mr. J. Hoffman Wood and his team had been the Colored basketball champions two years in a row and were not looking forward to relinquishing the title to Washington.[10]

On March 30, 1910, the Washington YMCA team would meet the St. Christopher team in the True Reformer's Hall in Washington in front of eight hundred fans. St. Christopher had a strong team. The contest was fairly even during the first half, which ended with a score of 15–9 in favor of the Twelfth-Streeters. But in the second half, the superior conditioning and speedy play of the home team made all the difference, and the Twelfth-Streeters won, 44–15. This was another thrilling victory for Washington, which was just one game away from taking home the Colored Basketball World Championship for the 1909–1910 basketball season.[11]

But something unusual was about to happen. The championship was the next day, where the Smart Set of Brooklyn planned a sport extravaganza, the Indoor Athletic Carnival, Basketball Tournament and Assembly. The Twelfth-Streeters played and defeated the St. Christopher Club and were now expected to travel overnight to New York to play the Smart Set for the championship on March 31. The game was played in front of three thousand fans who gathered in Brooklyn's Fourteenth Regiment Armory. Those who attended were a Who's Who of New Yorkers. Before the contest, a track meet was held as part of the carnival. Among those events was a 1-mile run and a 440-yard dash on the armory's second-floor track. Music was played throughout the event by the twenty-five-piece Excelsior Military Brass Band. There was dancing before, during, and after the contest.[12]

Once the game had begun, everyone settled in to watch what turned out to be a very competitive match. There was very fast play by both teams. The Smart Set was ahead at the half, 14–10. In the second half, though, the Twelfth-Streeters outplayed the Brooklyn team. Bob Kuska describes the contest:

> [I]n the second half, the 12th Streeters caught fire. With Henderson in his pillow-sized knee and elbow pads barking signals to this teammates, the YMCA ran the home team off its on offense and "covered with lightning speed" under its own basket. The YMCA cagers passed the ball from spot to spot, setting up open shots that pulled them ahead of their hosts. Smart Set bounced in a free throw and a lucky shot from the field to move within three points of its opponents late in the game. But the Washingtonians wouldn't buckle. As the final seconds ticketed away and the 12th Streeters clung to their 20–17 lead, the packed house "cheered the YMCA lads to the echo" for their outstanding second half performance and unbeaten season.
>
> At the final whistle, YMCA fans streamed onto the court, hoisting their exhausted heroes onto their shoulders, and parading them across the hall. Smart Set coach J. Hoffman Woods forced his way through the crowd, motioning to the jubilant Ed Henderson. Woods shoved the game trophy into Henderson's hands, saying there would be no formal presentation of the trophy later that evening.[13]

Woods was not happy with the outcome of the game. It surely was a hard pill to swallow when the upstart YMCA team beat them. This was particularly true because it was likely a calculated strategy to schedule the championship game the day after the game in Washington against St. Christopher. But it is a testament to the conditioning of the Twelfth Streeters, and to E. B., as their physical trainer, that they still came out on top. The Washington team defeated all the teams of the Olympian Athletic League of New York City and were crowned the Colored basketball world champions, becoming the first undisputed champions in Black basketball.

To kick off the 1910–1911 basketball season, a contest was scheduled between the Washington Twelfth-Streeters and the Alpha Physical Culture Athletic Club at the Manhattan Casino in New York City. But there were other events in E. B.'s life that would make this trip one of great joy for him and Nell: E. B. had received another raise in the school system after being charged with establishing the first Public School Athletic League (PSAL) in a segregated school division and was now making double what he was making when he first started teaching, so now they felt they could afford to wed. After a long courtship, on Christmas Eve in 1910, they were married in Washington at Nell's church, the Fifteenth Street Presbyterian Church. And because the host team paid for travel and lodging, they decided to make this trip to New York City their honeymoon and take a few extra days to enjoy New York after the big game.[14]

On a cold Christmas Eve in New York City, the Manhattan Casino was packed with two thousand screaming spectators cheering for the hometown team, in their blue jerseys with the big cursive letter *A* across their chests. The Alphas dominated the first half largely because their center, Big Babe Thomas, was having his way with E. B. at center court on every jump ball, which meant that the Alphas would be able to dominate the tip, the ball, the clock, and the scoreboard. E. B. had no legs this night.

Halfway through the second half, realizing that Thomas was the better man that night, E. B. had an idea. He would stay on the court as a guard and have one of the forwards, the taller, less-experienced George Gilmore, play center. It was risky because under the rules and strategies in basketball in 1910, the center jumped the ball at tip-offs after every basket and was the playmaker who ran the offense, much like a point guard does today. Gilmore controlled the tip-offs, while E. B. and Huddie distributed the ball, thus creating the first point-guard position. This strategy worked and turned the game around in the Twelfth-Streeters' favor. When the final whistle was blown, the visiting team escaped from the jaws of defeat and captured the win, 24–19.[15]

Back in the teams' dressing room, the players were overjoyed with their victory. But then a more somber note overtook the gathering. E. B. took this moment to let the team know that he would be retiring from the team. He had made a promise to Nell that, once they were married, he would no longer actively play in competitive basketball—partly because of her concern for his safety but also because she would have to give up teaching, something she loved, after they were married. Therefore, E. B. would have to sacrifice something he loved, as well.

E. B. had brought the team together, but now that he was to leave, there were questions about the future of the Twelfth-Streeters. However, the answer was quickly apparent because more than half the team were enrolled at Howard University. Oliver, Gray, Gilmore, Nixon, and Curtis could be absorbed into the varsity team at Howard. This seemed to be the best solution, they thought, and would make Howard's team the one to beat in the upcoming season. They would be the favorite to win the title in the 1910–1911 season, and that is exactly what happened.[16]

14

E. B. Henderson's Early Published Works

Spalding Official Handbook (1910–1913)

E. B.'s active mind would not allow him to sit idly by and do nothing. After finishing his classes at the various schools where he taught in the mornings, he had time to himself before the recreational activities he was responsible for conducting as an employee of the Recreation Department. He recalled,

> I was living in Falls Church in 1910 following marriage which was about nine miles from my office. I was forced to remain in Washington, DC for four hours in mid-day when there were no recreational activities scheduled. I began to write stories of athletics and secured the help of the Spalding Sporting Goods Company to write one of their manuals about the work in Washington, DC, and Negroes in athletics. I wrote articles and wrote to Negro coaches and beginning directors in the South. I wrote ghost articles for several ISAA [Inter-Scholastic Athletic Association] members and published records, and pictures went to me from the Southern schools. This was the first book on athletics by Negroes.[1]

In the fall of 1909, E. B. began writing letters to James E. Sullivan of the American Sports Publishing Company, who published the Spalding handbooks and manuals. Mr. Sullivan was one of the highest-profile members of the sports and recreation establishment at that time. Many people associated with the Spalding and American Sports Publishing

Company were also associated with the Dudley Sargent School of Physical Training at Harvard; E. B. was very familiar with them, and they with him, and they were aware of the good work he was doing in Washington. The handbooks produced by the Spalding Sport Equipment Company were produced by the American Sports Publishing Company. Several of those associated with the American Sports Publishing Company had been instructors E. B. had studied under in the summer program. E. B. was interested in showcasing the exploits of African Americans' participation in sports and the movement by Blacks to actively promote athletics in schools, colleges, and social organizations in the African American communities around the country. These annual handbooks are believed to be the first chronicling of African Americans participating in sports. E. B.'s booklets are the first to have pictures of Black teams and their records in a Spalding publication.

On October 16, 1909, E. B. received a most agreeable response from Mr. Sullivan:

> Mr. E. B. Henderson,
>
> 1919 11th Street, NW
>
> Washington, DC
>
> Dear Sir:
>
> Yours of the 15th received and noted. Of course, we will help out. As a matter of fact, if you want us to publish your book, we will publish it for you and it won't cost you a cent. We will give you as many copies as you can distribute. You retain your name as editor, and we will publish it for you. I know A. G. Spalding & Bros., are interested in your work, and will gladly pay all the bills. Not make it a Spalding book, or offer it for sale, but make it just your own book edited by you.
>
> Yours truly,
>
> J. E. Sullivan, President[2]

A couple weeks later, Mr. Sullivan wrote,

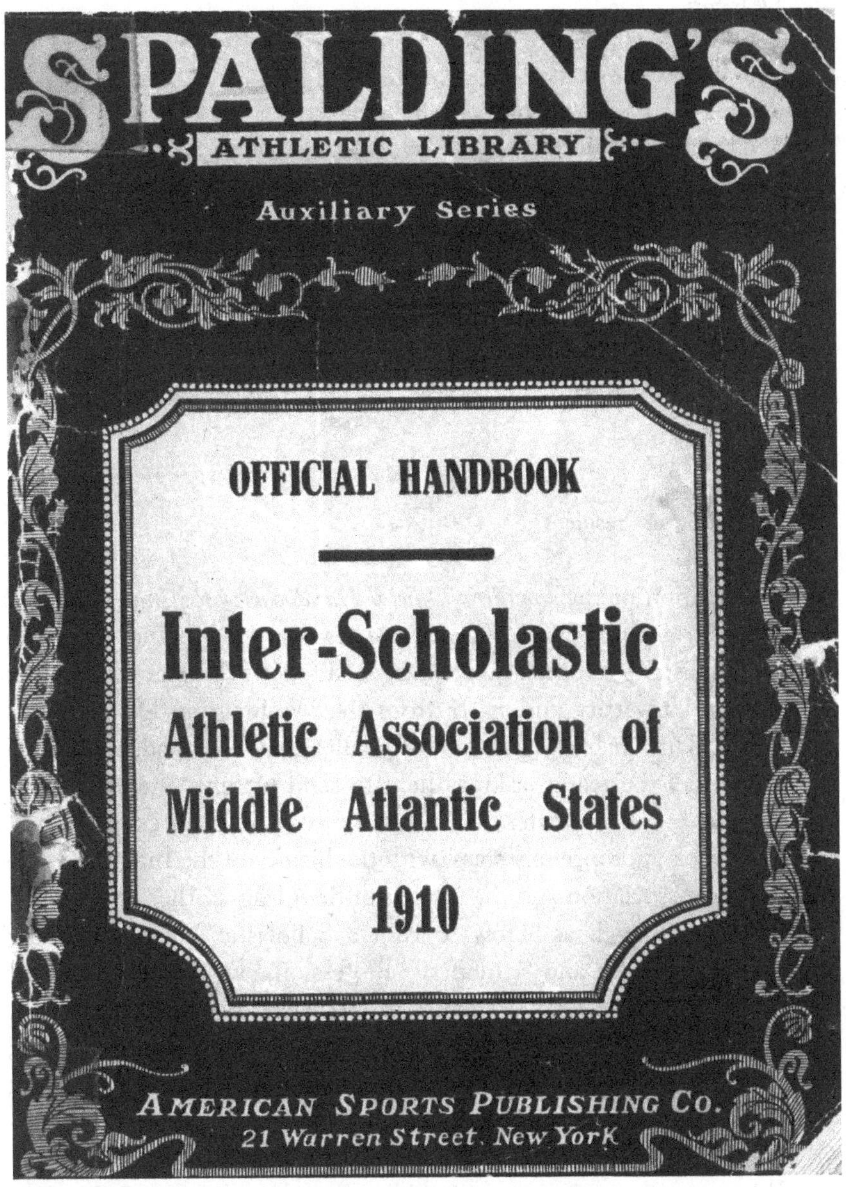

Spalding Official Handbook of the Inter-Scholastic Athletic Association of Middle Atlantic States, published 1910–1913.

COURTESY OF HENDERSON FAMILY COLLECTION

Dear Sir:

Your communication of the 23rd to hand and noted. Get up the dummy and send it on, and we will do the rest.

I note yours in reference to the A.A.U. [Amateur Athletic Association], and your Association, and I can assure you the A.A.U. would naturally feel that it is to the best interest of amateur sport to have your association succeed and become national in character and have control over your own schools. But on what lines an alliance could be entered into, of course I do not know. What are your ideas? For instance, to have an alliance, an association must govern, and usually is an association national in character.

Yours truly,

J. E. Sullivan, President[3]

The first edition of the *Spalding Official Handbook of the Inter-Scholastic Athletic Association of Middle Atlantic States* was sent to the American Sports Publishing Company. It was coedited by William A. Joiner of Howard University and E. B. from the Washington, DC, Colored schools. This first year was particularly challenging. They had to communicate with all the teams, asking them to send pictures and articles on their teams, as well as rosters, scores, and records of their competitions. The handbook appropriately starts with the history of the Inter-Scholastic Athletic Association and the officers of their league. There were many how-to articles, such as "How to Run a Scholastic Meet," "Training the Body for Health and Athletics," "Professional vs. Amateur Sports," "Ethics in Athletics," and "Athletics in Colleges." Because it was their handbook, the ISAA included their financial statement for 1906–1908; constitution; bylaws; laws of athletics; and, last but not least, a photo of the Washington Twelfth-Streeters holding the basketball saying "1909–10 Champs."[4]

This was a very impressive publication that the association put together, but it was painfully obvious why it, as Mr. Sullivan said, "won't cost . . . a cent." The first nineteen pages were devoted to Spalding and the publisher's information, and the last thirty-eight pages were devoted to advertisements for Spalding's sporting equipment. So in addition to chronicling the history of organized athletics in the African American community, it was a promotional and advertising tool for Spalding. It was a win-win for all concerned.

The next year's edition was several pages longer because there were more teams participating and sending in their pictures and records. Joiner was now at Wilberforce University in Ohio. There was a report by the general manager, written by E. B. It touted the news of the first African American school athletic league in Washington, DC, as well as articles on "Training Hints" and "Athletic Courtesy."[5]

Each year, the handbook was getting larger and larger. More teams and more leagues were forming to accommodate athletics for more youths and athletes. A movement was taking hold in African American communities around the country.

The third year (1912) of the *Official Handbook*, William Joiner was no longer coeditor, and Garnet C. Wilkinson took his place alongside E. B. The big news in 1912 was the establishment of the Colored Intercollegiate Athletic Association (CIAA), the first college athletic league for Historically Black Colleges and Universities (HBCUs). New articles included a list of associations and leagues, and the new CIAA constitution and bylaws were printed in this edition.[6]

The 1913 edition of the *Official Handbook* had ballooned to 220 pages. In the short span of four years, participation in athletics had soared. There were now more teams and leagues than anyone would have imagined only a few years previously. Teams were sending in their photos and information about what was going on around the country, wanting to be published in this groundbreaking publication. New in this year's edition was a format for creating league constitutions and an all-star college football team listing, and more leagues were using the handbook to print their official league constitutions and bylaws.[7]

E. B., as well as the members of the Inter-Scholastic Athletic Association, were anticipating another year of publishing their handbook in 1914, when they received some disturbing news from their publisher. This letter of October 30, 1914, was not from the usual Mr. Sullivan:

Mr. E. B. Henderson

M Street High School

Washington, DC

Dear Mr. Henderson:

We are in receipt of the copy and pictures for your interscholastic handbook but regret to say that owing to general business conditions, especially in England, where Spalding have a number of stores and factories, we do not feel that we would be justified in expending the amount of money that it annually takes to produce the Handbook.

We are very sorry to disappoint you, as we took as much pride almost as you did yourself in the book and appreciated the very thorough and complete manner in which the pictures and data were collected and prepared. In view of the fact that cost of the book makes serious inroads in the appropriation that A. C. Spalding & Bros. allows us to publish these books we would desire to suspend the publication of it for this year at least and know that you will make allowance for the unusual circumstances that have arisen this year, which import us to take this action.

We will send the pictures and manuscript back to you via express prepaid.

If we can be of any service to you at any time we shall be very pleased to hear from you.

Very truly yours,

American Sports Publishing Company

This was the last known communication from Spalding. Apparently, although not expressed directly, the clouds of war in Europe precipitated the discontinuance of the publication. But the advancement of African American participation in sports was not something that could or would be stopped. The groundwork had been laid; the infrastructure had been built. E. B.'s whirlwind of activity had paid off in dividends that would benefit his race and the profession of physical education for years to come. According to Leon Coursey, "The Inter-scholastic Athletic Association Handbook had the distinction of being the first book that was ever written by a Black man which dealt specifically with Black athletics."[8]

A Bold Prediction: *Crisis Magazine* (1911)

In 1911, E. B.'s body of work since his days at Harvard University's Dudley Sargent School of Physical Training created a reputation for him. There was another Harvard University man whom E. B. had the pleasure of meeting and convincing to write an article for his journal. Dr. W. E. B. Du Bois had distinguished himself as the first African American to earn a PhD at Harvard University. In 1905, Dr. Du Bois founded the Niagara Movement, whose mission was to organize against and hopefully defeat the *Plessy v. Ferguson* verdict passed down by the US Supreme Court, which had made racial segregation the law of the land in the United States. Because of Du Bois's involvement in the Niagara Movement, he was asked to become one of the founding members of the National Association for the Advancement of Colored People (NAACP) in 1909.[9]

Dr. Du Bois was the editor of the organization's monthly journal, *The Crisis Magazine*, which began in 1910. On the cover of the summer edition in July 1911 was the Black world record holder for the quarter-mile race, the late John B. Taylor, who had competed in the 1908 Summer Olympics and whose record was still unbroken. Also published in this edition was the photo of the 1909–1910 Colored basketball world champions, the Washington Twelfth-Streeters. E. B. also published an article, "The Colored College Athlete," that held a bold statement: "When competent physical directors and equal training facilities are afforded the colored youth, the white athlete will find an equal or superior in nearly every line of athletic endeavor."[10] He goes on, "The native muscular development and vitality of the Negro of the South, if directed in channels of athletic activities would lower many records, now standing, and our leaders should grasp the situation and develop agencies to conserve

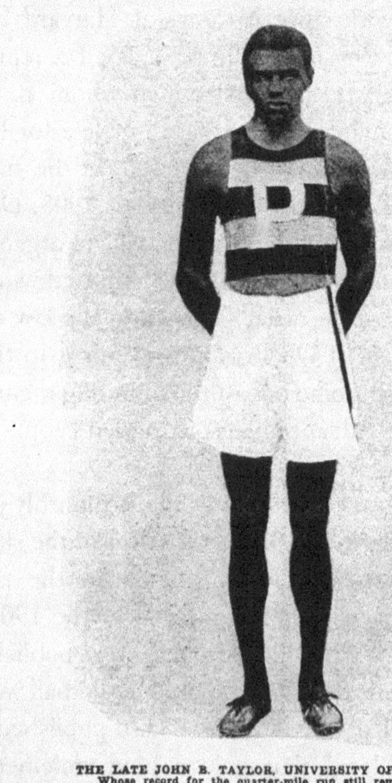

VACATION NUMBER

THE CRISIS

A RECORD OF THE DARKER RACES

Volume Two — JULY, 1911 — Number Three

THE LATE JOHN B. TAYLOR, UNIVERSITY OF PENNSYLVANIA
Whose record for the quarter-mile run still remains untouched

ONE DOLLAR A YEAR — TEN CENTS A COPY

FAMOUS COLORED ATHLETES

E. B. Henderson publishes an article in *The Crisis* entitled "The Colored College Athlete."

COURTESY OF HENDERSON FAMILY COLLECTION; NAACP THE CRISIS, *JULY 1911, LIBRARY OF CONGRESS/NATIONAL ARCHIVES* the vital forces of the race."[11] E. B. predicted, especially in basketball, that African American athletes would dominate the sport once given a chance to compete.

E. B. was advocating for integrated competition in sports. He wanted to break down the color barrier that denied Blacks a chance to compete and prove themselves against Whites in athletic competitions. This is what E. B. would fight for most of his professional life, mostly against the AAU and their edict in the southern United States, where Blacks were not allowed to compete against Whites. This battle endured into the 1940s, when, under pressure, the AAU finally capitulated and allowed the Golden Gloves boxers to compete against each other in the DC Armory. Then, of course, there was Jackie Robinson, who broke the color barrier in America's pastime, baseball.

15

The Hendersons Move to Falls Church, Virginia

The Suburban Life

After E. B.'s last game against the Smart Set of Brooklyn, he and Nell moved to rural Falls Church, Virginia, where E. B.'s parents and grandmother were living. E. B. convinced Nell that it would be better to raise a family away from the hustle and bustle of city life, in a less crowded and slower-paced environment. From his summers growing up and visiting his grandmother in Falls Church, E. B. was a lover of nature and outdoor activities, and Eliza was a great influence in his younger years. How he was ever able to convince the more urbane and socialite Nell to move to the country and in the house with his parents and grandmother is a mystery, but like everything else, it was likely carefully thought over and discussed beforehand.

Falls Church was a small town approximately six miles from the Washington, DC, border. It was considered a bedroom community of Washington, with an electric trolley line that traveled into the city on the hour. This style of living was quieter, less stressful, and more conducive to raising children. The electric trolley lines brought the suburban lifestyle into the metropolitan DC area.

E. B.'s grandmother Eliza was now almost sixty-five years old and unable to take care of herself very well, let alone tend to her store next to the old Falls Church. Therefore, E. B.'s parents, William and Louisa, tended to Eliza and kept her store in order. William also worked for the Federal Office of Printing and Engraving in the city and caught the trolley line into town each day. Louisa tended to her mother-in-law's health needs, then headed next door to the store to run the business. E. B. traveled into Washington on the trolley line each day and continued teaching and coaching, but his days of playing were over.

Nell had visited Falls Church many times with E. B. during their six-year courtship, so she was very familiar with his parents and grandmother. But it must have been a huge adjustment from living in Washington, with all the activities at her fingertips. Still, she did not complain. She kept herself busy helping Eliza, doing chores, and playing piano at the Second Baptist Church near town. She continued to claim the Fifteenth Street Presbyterian Church in Washington as hers and would go to church with her mother occasionally on Sundays. The people in the

The home Edwin and Mary Ellen Henderson built in Falls Church, Virginia, in 1913.
COURTESY OF HENDERSON FAMILY COLLECTION

Falls Church Black community were all very nice and accepting of her because of the status of E. B.'s family in the small town. Still, from time to time, she felt bored.

Eliza was a very smart and savvy businesswoman. After taking over the Falls Church store from Frederick Foote Jr. and building her own store, she bought a piece of property where the Falls Church tobacco barns once stood. Soon thereafter, with the proceeds from her business, she bought another piece of property that had once belonged to her aunt Harriet Foote Turner, who had seven acres in the vicinity. She consolidated almost another three acres near her home. Eliza passed less than a year after E. B. and Nell moved to Falls Church, leaving the house and her other properties to William and Louisa. She was buried in the Galloway United Methodist Church cemetery with a large headstone.

Shortly after Eliza's death, E. B. and Nell offered to buy from his parents one and a half acres of the land Eliza had purchased. There they would build their home and start a family. E. B. and Nell had eyed a house, model 225, in the Sears and Roebuck catalogue that they wished to buy through mail order. The one-and-a-half-story bungalow was large enough to have gatherings and bedrooms enough for a child or two. After purchasing the land from E. B.'s father, they began to make payments on the house. It cost $1,400, but they wanted another $400 worth of extras. Their dream for home ownership was about to begin.

Trouble in Paradise

The village of Falls Church, unlike most communities in Virginia, had a biracial Home Guard. The Home Guard was established usually by towns sympathetic to the Confederacy during the war to protect the community while the men went off to fight. Falls Church was a community of Union sympathizers and was occupied by the Union for most of the Civil War, but from time to time, Confederates intruded the community.

One morning in early 1912, as E. B. reached the trolley station, he found his father sitting on the curb near the East Falls Church trolley station. William had to be at work earlier than E. B., so it was troubling to see that he was still at the station. His father had been assaulted and pulled from the train by one of the Home Guardsmen when a White woman wanted to enter the trolley by the rear doors, the doors where African Americans were forced to enter so they didn't have to walk through the White customers at the front to get to their seats in the rear.[1]

E. B. was angry and felt this injustice must be addressed. He filed suit against the Home Guardsman who had manhandled his father and pulled him from the train. A bystander was willing to be a witness for William in the case, Joseph DePutron, an upstanding citizen of Falls Church who had a law practice in Washington, DC. He had seen William being pulled from the trolley and was also incensed over the incident.[2]

The situation was very intense. On the day of the trial, one side of the courtroom was filled with members of the Home Guard, supporting the accused Home Guardsman. On the other side were members of Falls Church's African American community, who were there to support William Henderson. The main witness for the plaintiff was Mr. DePutron. The judge in the case ruled in favor of William Henderson and charged the Home Guardsman to pay $20 and court costs. The Black folks in the courtroom cheered after the judge's verdict. The Home Guard were outraged and left the courtroom angrily.[3]

The next day, as E. B. and others approached the East Falls Church trolley station, they could see hanging from a light post an effigy of Mr. DePutron, even though William's race was really at the core of the matter. In the very near future, this would be apparent. Moving to the country presented issues other than a change in proximity, especially if you were Black. But for now, all anyone could do was take down the effigy and continue life as usual.[4] Afterward, E. B. bought a car and began to drive into Washington.

The Joy of Home Ownership

The Henderson household was blessed with a son, Edwin, born on September 27, 1912. He was born at Freedmen's Hospital in Washington, DC. E. B. and Nell were still living with his parents, and the addition of their newborn was even more motivation to move into their own home. The couple had been making payments on the Sears kit home and doing their due diligence to make the move once the baby was born.

In the early fall of 1913, model 225 from the Sears and Roebuck catalogue arrived at the East Falls Church train station. A truck brought all the pieces for the house to their lot on Fairfax Courthouse Road, to the lot E. B. purchased from his parents. Building a house would be a monumental task. E. B. was going to need some help.

Luckily, there was a family of builders just down the street, the Tinners. The patriarch of the family, Charles Tinner, had ten children. He had been a member of the Home Guard during the Civil War and had purchased several acres at the top of a hill looking in both directions. Tinner was interested in this spot because he would be able to see who was coming and would be able to protect his family from harm, if need be. Tinner gave a plot of land to each of his ten children so they could build a home on what is still known as Tinner Hill in Falls Church.

Mr. Tinner instilled in his children self-sufficiency. By owning their own land and being able to build their own homes, they would not have to depend on others for their livelihoods. All the Tinner men were carpenters, well diggers, masons, or some other occupation in the building industry. One of his children, Joseph Tinner, was a sought-after stone mason in Falls Church.

Although E. B. was handy with a hammer and saw and did as much of the work to build his house as he could, some things were better left to professionals. E. B. was a teacher, and he had a lot going on in Washington with teaching, the league, coaching, and refereeing, so he solicited the Tinner family to help build his new Sears kit house. Before the cold of the winter months set in, E. B., Nell, and little Edwin settled into their new, warm home.

The Night Farmer

The *B* in E. B.'s name is for *Bancroft*, literally, "from the bean field." He would do a little farming as a child when he came to visit his grandmother during the summer, but no one knows why he got that name. Shortly after buying his lot, E. B. was approached by Captain Norman about purchasing his farm that was on the same spot as the headquarters of Camp Alger.[5]

Camp Alger was land chosen by Secretary of War Russell A. Alger. It was established May 18, 1898, to train soldiers for the Spanish–American

War, and 35,000 troops that constituted the Second Army Corps, under the command of Major General William Graham, were stationed there.

The troops stationed at Camp Alger were from the Eighth Ohio Infantry Regiment and the Ninth Ohio Volunteer Infantry Battalion, an African American regiment under the command of Major Charles Young, the second African American to graduate from West Point Military Academy (the same Major Young whom E. B. witnessed a White soldier refusing to salute).[6] Many troops disembarked at the East Falls Church station, while an equal number were dropped off at the Dunn Loring train station.[7] Camp Alger was short-lived because of an outbreak of typhoid fever due to a scarcity of water and the want of bathing facilities; the camp was shut down in late September 1898.[8] Captain Norman purchased the land once it was abandoned by the army.

Being a country boy at heart, E. B. recalled around 1915,

> I entreated Garnet C. Wilkinson and three other teachers, and we scraped together enough for a down payment. Sam Compton and I lived on the farm. Wilkinson spent his summers there since he was a principal of a high school.
>
> It was hard work trying to farm and teach school. I was known as a nighttime farmer. We had horses, cows, a grand orchard and raised garden and the usual farm crops. But we were always strapped for money with which to pay the note and renew loans.
>
> It is my regret that we could not keep the big farm which is now the beautiful National Cemetery and Park on the Lee Highway.[9]

Although the farming didn't work out, E. B. enjoyed his home in Falls Church, where he would retire after a hard day's work in the city. It was a place where he could come for rest and solitude, a place where his ancestors were from. It's quite possible he was living on land where his Native ancestors had once walked, a place where his enslaved ancestors toiled and sweated to enrich someone else's family. Falls Church was as good a place as any to stake a claim. But soon he would find his true calling and the reason he was brought to this place. There was a storm brewing. Falls Church was where his skill set and connections would prove necessary to combat injustice.

E. B.'s formal portrait for the Public School of the District of Columbia, from which he retired in 1954 after fifty years of service.
COURTESY OF HENDERSON FAMILY COLLECTION, ALSO DISTRICT OF COLUMBIA COLORED SCHOOLS

16

Protest in Virginia

The NAACP's First Rural Branch

On March 12, 1912, the Virginia General Assembly enacted legislation enabling towns and cities to adopt ordinances providing for the separation of the races. In the winter of 1914, Mayor John B. Herndon reported to the town council of Falls Church that a Black person had moved to West Falls Church and suggested the council adopt a segregation ordinance. The ordinance was drafted but did not pass. At the next meeting, the council learned that there was a state law that allowed local jurisdictions "to provide for designation by cities and towns of segregation districts for residence of White and Colored persons."[1]

E. B. later recalled, "Disturbed by this action, I called together some of the leading Colored citizens. We met at the home of Mr. Joseph B Tinner."[2] Seven men from the community joined E. B. and Tinner. Tinner would be the president, And E. B. would be secretary, for two reasons: (1) he was the best person to prepare the correspondence going out, and (2) he was already a member of the Washington branch of the National Association for the Advancement of Colored People (NAACP). The president and secretary "consulted with Attorney Jacob DePutron to draw up a resolution of protest to present at the Council Meeting."[3] They decided their organization would be named the Colored Citizens Protective League (CCPL).

There were three districts in Falls Church. The West End of Falls Church, where the Blacks lived, was in the third district which, "[a]ccording to the census taken by the segregation committee, instructed by the town as of January 15th, 1915, this district having a population of 1212 Whites and 113 Colored residents [was] declared a district of White persons."[4] Districts 1 and 2 would also be designated as Whites only. They created a fourth district for Colored only. Blacks who already lived in Whites-only districts could remain, but if they wanted to sell, they would only be able to sell to a White person. Due to hostilities toward Blacks because of this action taken by the town council, chances were that other residents in the district would force them out.

The CCPL wrote letters to all the members of the town council, as well as Falls Church businesses and churches, asking how they stood on the issue of the ordinance and segregation of residential district by race. Tinner and E. B. voiced their petition against the town council position at the meeting on January 11, but the council passed the ordinance by a vote of 4–1.[5]

On January 18, the CCPL met at the home of E. B. and Nell. These men understood that protesting the actions of the town council possibly put their lives and the lives of their families in jeopardy. Reports were made on discussions members had with Mr. DePutron; Father Van Ingleham of the Catholic Church, who disavowed the rumor that the Catholics were in favor of segregation; and Councilmen Harmon and Nourse. Also approved was the decision to send a letter to Dr. W. E. B. DuBois asking to form a branch of the NAACP in Falls Church. E. B. was familiar with Dr. DuBois from his contributing articles to *The Crisis* and his membership with the branch in Washington. The letter, dated January 20, 1915, expressed concern for the group's safety but also said that they would be happy to provide resources to the committee there to help them fight.[6]

Meanwhile a referendum was scheduled for May 25, 1915. In addition to voting to elect three town council members, the flyer said,

Citizens Meeting

I am instructed by the council to invite all citizens of the Town at the Council Rooms on Tuesday, May 25, 1915, at 8 p.m.

To express, by ballot, their choice, from among the qualified voters of the Town, for the three members of the Council to be voted for at the election.

Other Questions

The Council has also instructed me to give notice that at the election on June 8, 1915, 1 p.m. to sunset, a separate ballot will be provided and every resident tax payer is requested to come to the polls and express by ballot, approval of two questions pending in the council, as follows, viz:

First: Segregation of the races within the Town. Yes or No

Second: Change of charter so as to give the council authority to increase the maximum rate of taxation in the Town twenty cents on $100. Yes or No.[7]

The referendum passed!

Now that the citizens of the town of Falls Church had spoken on the issue, on June 28, 1915, the Falls Church Town Council accepted the boundaries for the districts formed to separate the Whites from the Colored section of Falls Church. Thirty-two percent of the population of Falls Church was African American and would be confined to about 5 percent of the land.[8]

After the referendum and the city's adoption of the boundaries, the CCPL hired attorneys Thomas Jones and Walter Oliver, the latter a former member of the legislature, to file suit against the town of Falls Church, *E. B. Henderson et. al. Petitioners v. The Town of Falls Church, VA, Defendant.* E. B. invited Judge Thornton of the circuit court of Fairfax County to Falls Church to view the district the town had created. Judge Thornton decided "to hold his determination in abeyance until after the decision on a similar case currently before the United States Supreme Court was decided."[9] Judge Thornton was referencing *Warley v. Buchannan*, which was argued in the US Supreme Court on November 5, 1917. The Supreme Court declared that such laws were unconstitutional.[10]

TOWN ELECTION!

As provided in the charter of the Town of Falls Church, the annual election for

THREE MEMBERS OF THE TOWN COUNCIL

will be held

TUESDAY JUNE 8th, 1915, AT THE COUNCIL ROOM

BETWEEN THE HOURS OF 1 P. M. AND SUNSET.

All voters of the Town who have qualified themselves to vote by paying the required State capitation tax six months prior to June 8th, 1915, and are registered upon the registration books of the Town, are entitled to vote at this election.

The terms of W. T. Westcott, first ward; Dr. J. B. Gould, second ward; and Dr. R. Munson, third ward, expire this year.

CITIZENS MEETING

I am instructed by the Council to invite all citizens of the Town to meet at the Council Rooms on

Tuesday, May 25, 1915, at 8 P. M.

to express, by ballot, their choice, from among the qualified voters of the Town, for the three members of the Council to be voted for at the election.

OTHER QUESTIONS

The Council has also instructed me to give notice that at the election on June 8, 1915, 1 p. m. to sunset, a separate ballot box will be provided and every resident tax payer is requested to come to the polls and express by ballot, approval or disapproval of two questions pending in the council, as follows, viz:

First: Seggregation of the races within the Town. Yes or No.

Second. Change of charter so as to give the council authority to increase the maximum rate of taxation in the Town twenty cents on $100. Yes or No. (Present fixed maximum rate is sixty cents and ten cents additional for High School, if the school board so requests.)

ROAD DAY

Council considered the proclamation of the Governor regarding "Road Day" and designated Tuesday, June 1st as "Road Day" for the Corporation and every male citizen of the Town is requested to work on the streets of the Town that day or furnish a substitute. Such work to be done under the direction of the road board in each ward.

JOHN G. HERNDON, Mayor.

REGISTRATION OF TOWN VOTERS

The undersigned Registrar for the Town, hereby notifies all voters who have [illegible] istered for town elections, that the registration books are open at any time from now [illegible] 7 P. M. [illegible] 1915 and that I will register any voter who has resided in the Town for one [illegible] the books of the registrar for the county and that I will be at the [illegible] June 1st 1915 from 1 to 7 P. M. when the books will be cl[illegible]

GEO. W. [illegible]AWXHURST,

[illegible] and Ex-Off

Referendum to segregate the town of Falls Church. E. B. and Nell would have had to sell their home to a White family and move the Colored section of town. This injustice led to a protest launched by the Colored Citizens Protective League, which evolved into the first rural branch of the NAACP in the United States.

COURTESY OF HENDERSON FAMILY COLLECTION

E. B, Mary Ellen, and sons James and Edwin in 1922.
COURTESY OF HENDERSON FAMILY COLLECTION, ALSO SEEN IN THE WASHINGTON AFRO, *1954*

This decision made Falls Church's ordinance null and void. However, the town never rescinded their ordinance, not even when became a city in 1948. But in 1998, thanks to the creation of the Tinner Hill Heritage Foundation, which was established to research, preserve, and present the history of the efforts of the Colored Citizen's Protective League and the Falls Church NAACP, then mayor David Snyder and the city council retroactively officially rescinded the law and granted a full apology to the citizens of Falls Church City.[11]

The decision by the Supreme Court was a great victory for the CCPL and the African American citizens of Falls Church. Now that this was behind the group, they turned their attention to forming a rural branch of the NAACP. The problem was that the NAACP bylaws required a minimum of fifty persons signing up in order to form a charter. That was not always possible in smaller rural communities where segregation was particularly strong, lawlessness and vigilante groups like the KKK might be more active, and people were putting their lives and livelihoods on the line. So E. B. wrote a letter to his friend Dr. Francis Cardoza, president of the Baltimore branch of the NAACP, who had been the principal of M Street High School in the late 1800s. The CCPL submitted an application to form a branch in Falls Church, and on June 28, 1918, a charter was given by the National NAACP for the "Falls Church and Vicinity NAACP." They became the first rural branch of the National Association for the Advancement of Colored People in the United States.[12]

There was a problem with the naming of the branch because it didn't represent the other local jurisdictions of Fairfax, Alexandria, Arlington, Vienna, Centerville, and others, which caused some resentment. But E. B. and the branch made it clear that they were there to represent all the Colored people of Fairfax County and Northern Virginia because they were the only affiliate of the organization in the area at that time. The small local branch would officially receive a charter to become the Fairfax County branch in 1944.[13]

> The CCPL and the Falls Church NAACP were very active in bringing other communities and jurisdictions into the fold of the NAACP. There were several "vicinity" branches established between 1918 and 1923, in Arlington, Alexandria, and Leesburg. But in the 1940s, the National NAACP sought to change the names and give new charters to county branches. EB submitted many articles about the NAACP and social justice activities in Northern Virginia to the *Washington Bee*, a Black newspaper in Washington. In October 15, 1921, one article stated, "Now that the Leesburg Branch of the N.A.A.C.P. is in existence, the officials of the Fairfax County Branch are busy planning for the organization of the Arlington County Branch of the Association."[14]

Another article from July 23, 1921, shows how successful the young branch was in bringing members to the fold:

> The National Association for the Advancement of Colored People has selected Mr. E. B. Henderson of Falls Church as a district organizer in Virginia. The Fairfax County branch of which Mr. Henderson is secretary and drive colonel exceeded the allotted quota of 400 members by more than 100. New branches will be organized in Loudoun County, Arlington County, and Leesburg this summer.[15]

In 1918, the issues of serious concern included segregation and inequality in the schools and restrictions on transportation and voting rights. The branch's Transportation Committee was important to the mobility of Blacks and their ability to travel to work and for leisure. Much like anywhere else in the South, in both Virginia and DC, African Americans were forced to sit in the rear sections of the buses and trolleys. Eventually the DC buses would allow seating anywhere, but E. B. was forced off the bus once because he refused to move to the rear after crossing the Francis Scott Key Bridge between Georgetown and Arlington.[16] This would continue until *Morgan v. Virginia*, the US Supreme Court case that outlawed discrimination in interstate transportation years later.[17]

Another committee for voting rights addressed poll taxes and women suffrage, which would not happen until 1920. The Poll Tax, or Capitation Tax, as it was named officially, was collected each year by the jurisdiction's treasurer from all African Americans who wanted to register to vote. The tax was usually around $1.50 per year. To be able to vote, an African American had to show proof of payment of the tax for each year leading up to a scheduled election. If you didn't pay or couldn't show proof, you were denied participation in an election.[18] Another method of exclusion for African Americans was the infamous Literacy Test. The test was supposed to be based on questions about the Constitution, but at the discretion of the voting clerks, who were all White in most states, a test taker could pass or fail based on race. Whites did not have to take the test because of the Grandfather Clause, another Jim Crow–era law to suppress voters. It didn't matter what your answer was; your application for voter registration was always filed in the trash.[19]

Of all the committees, the Education Committee had the strongest emphasis by the NAACP in Fairfax County. It was led by Nell, who was well known to the Fairfax County School Board because of her courageous advocacy for the educational needs of African American students. Ollie Tinner was another leading member of this committee. She was a shop teacher at the John R. Francis Jr. High School on the edge of Georgetown at Twenty-Fifth and N Streets NW, Washington. Being a Tinner, he was involved in the NAACP, just like the rest of his family in Falls Church. The Education Committee would have bake sales or other fundraisers and then go to the Fairfax Board of Education and give them the money toward their new school or new books or coal for the potbelly stoves. But there was never any real movement on providing for African American students, until Nell came up with a disparity study.[20] When E. B. asked the school board about money for a new school for the Black population in Falls Church and Fairfax County in general, one member actually said, "We have to take care of our White students first."[21]

AFRICAN AMERICAN EDUCATION IN FAIRFAX COUNTY, VIRGINIA

One of the most common desires of African Americans was to learn to read so that they could study the Bible. During the antebellum period, it was illegal in slave states like Virginia to teach any African American to read and write prior to emancipation from slavery. The masses of African Americans were hungry and thirsty for reading and writing, and it was all the more desirable because it had been kept from them. But even after emancipation, threats and intimidation of those who taught African Americans to read and write were commonplace.

The first known incidence of African Americans being taught to read and write in Columbia was when John Read and his daughter Betsy started a school around 1863–1864 at a small structure next to the Falls Church Baptist Church, which at that time was next to the Falls Church Episcopal Church. Read was a lay minister of the Baptist Church and had been corresponding with Emily Howland of the Friends Aid Society in Philadelphia about starting a school, and he asked for their support. This school attracted more than sixty students. There were so many Blacks eager to learn that half the class would sit while the other half would stand, and then at some convenient time, they would change places and continue with the lessons. Afraid of being found out, the school discontinued meeting all together and started meeting in smaller groups instead. Betsy would go to their houses to teach. Even though they thought they were careful, eventually they were found out, which led to the abduction of John Read in 1864.[22]

With the aid of the Freedmen's Bureau,

> By December 1866, there were eight Black schools in Fairfax County, most of them supported and staffed by the Friends Aid Society of Philadelphia. Though the malicious burning up of a school in the vicinity of Frying Pan and the breaking up of one near Lewinsville somewhat discouraged Blacks the number of students in schools was steadily increasing.[23]

The Falls Church Colored School was established with the help of the Friends' Aid Society of Philadelphia around 1888 on land donated by James Lee, an early Black landowner, along Annandale Road, where most African Americans lived after slavery ended. This effort was aided by a former Union officer, Colonel John Crocker. It wasn't a very sound structure, as none of the Colored schools were at that time. During World War I, the school was shut down because they could not find a teacher.[24]

Before the beginning of the 1919–1920 school year, members of the community asked Nell if she would reopen the shuttered Falls Church Colored School. The salaries for teachers were meager, and the Colored teachers made even less than White teachers. Under these conditions, it was harder to attract teachers to Fairfax County. Nell had not seriously considered ever teaching again since retiring from the DC Colored schools when she married E. B. Nell told them she had just had a baby, her second son, and she couldn't. But when they said that they would find someone to babysit James, she agreed.[25]

The Colored schools in Virginia were very different from the Colored schools in DC. In DC, there was a commitment to educating African American youth; not so in Virginia. Not too long before, it was a crime to teach Black people to read and write. And in Fairfax County and most of Virginia as a whole, there were no schools above the seventh grade for African American youth, except for vocational schools for trades.

The lack of equitable funding was an issue; Black schools were not being funded as a priority. The Colored schools got the hand-me-downs from the White schools. In Falls Church, the school for White children was a two-story brick building with indoor plumbing, central heat, and a classroom for every grade. The Falls Church Colored School, which

Nell had just reopened, was a two-room schoolhouse with clapboard exterior, no running water, heat provided by a potbelly stove in the center of the room, and pit toilets outside (outhouses). Water was brought from a neighbor's well for the children to drink. And unlike schools for Whites, the Colored schools didn't have a separate teacher and room for each grade. There was a kindergarten through third-grade class and a fourth- through seventh-grade class. Lola Saunders taught the lower grades, while Nell taught the upper grades. Nell would be affectionately named Miss Nellie by her students and members of the community.[26]

The student instruction books were hand-me-downs from the White schools and were out of date. Even more dastardly, the White students knew their books would be given to the Black students after they were done with them, so some books had expletives and racial insults in them or pages torn out so certain information or concepts were missing from their instruction. To Nell, this was an injustice and not something she would stand for; she would get books from the DC schools. But she also went in front of the school board and advocated for better schools in Fairfax County.

Threats, Hate Mail, and Burning Crosses

The Hendersons lived under constant pressure from those who wanted to keep the status quo of racial subjugation and intimidation. In the early 1920s, a cross was burned on E. B. and Nell's lawn. Menacing phone calls were a problem. E. B. and Nell had the telephone operator not send calls to the house after a certain hour, and when phone calls came directly to the house, they got an unlisted number. There was a constant stream of hate mail coming to the house and mailbox. E. B. once stated, "My wife has shared this work and also the constant threats made upon our lives through telephone calls and anonymous letters. I have nearly 100 such letters."[27] There was a lady, also named Henderson, in Falls Church who also had the first initial *E* in her name. Her daughter allegedly would open the mail, read it, and say, "He don't need to see that!"[28] She then would tear up the hateful correspondence.

In the midst of a campaign over a transportation issue, E. B. received the following piece of mail:

Professor:

Some night when you are peacefully dreaming in your downey couch of the charming BABOONS you have been instructing, and sniffing in the delightful odor exuding from their bodies, you will be rudely awakened by GHOSTS standing on either side of your couch and after you have been gagged, you will be borne to a tree nearby, tied, stripped and given thirty lashes on your ETHIOPIAN back, and left to be found by some passer-by.

We are for law and order just so long as you aforesaid ETHIOPIANS behave, but when you thrust yourselves on your superiors, the white people, your doom is sealed.

You had better consult with your advisers, the W. & Va. Railraod officials, and say to them that you will not be their cats-paw.

A word to the wise is sufficient.

(Signed) K.K.K.

KKK letter written to E. B.

COURTESY OF 1965, HENDERSON, HISTORY OF FAIRFAX BRANCH OF THE NAACP

Professor:

Some night when you are peacefully dreaming in your downey couch of charming BABOONS you have been instructing and sniffing in the delightful odor exuding from their bodies, you will be rudely awakened by GHOSTS standing on either side of your couch and after you have been gagged, you will be borne to a tree nearby, tied, stripped, and given thirty lashes on your ETHIOPIAN back, and left to be found by some passer-by.

We are for law and order just so long as you aforesaid ETHIOPIANS behave, but when you thrust yourselves on your superiors, the white people, your doom is sealed.

You had better consult with your advisers, the W. & Va. Railroad officials, and say to them that you will not be their cats-paw.

A word to the wise is sufficient.

(Signed) K.K.K.[29]

EMINENT DOMAIN: LEE HIGHWAY

Around 1921, in celebrations to honor America's Civil War, there was a movement to create a highway from coast to coast to honor Confederate general Robert E. Lee. Such memorials, statues, and name changes were prevalent in the United States around this time frame. The United Daughters of the Confederacy built statues to honor soldiers of the Confederate troops in every Southern town, as well as some Northern ones.

In 1921, the Falls Church NAACP called a "mass meeting" to talk about the proposal to cut a highway through Arlington and Falls Church heading west:

Mass Meeting!

October 17, 1921

All citizens of Arlington and Fairfax Counties who are interested in the building of *Lee Highway*, through Cherrydale, Falls Church and Merrifield to Fairfax, are urged to attend a public meeting to be held

At

Odd Fellows Hall

West Broad Street

Falls Church, Virginia[30]

It was customary in this country for local, state, and federal governments to use eminent domain to take land from private citizens for projects that were to the advantage of the "public good." Unfortunately, Black landowners were given less consideration than White landowners. Traditionally, roads have been cut through swarths of African American land, and this was about to happen in Falls Church. The African American citizens of Falls Church and Arlington put up a protest, to no avail. The Lee Highway Association was to build a highway from coast to coast to honor General Robert E. Lee, the commander of all Confederate soldiers, who fought to keep African American people enslaved. If Lee had been successful, E. B.'s family would still be enslaved.

In Falls Church, the highway cut through the African American community, including E. B. and Nell's land. Their house was on one side of the highway, and the barn and garden were on the other. After the road was built, the cow got out and was hit by a car, and the Hendersons had to pay for the repairs of the person's automobile. E. B. would eventually sell the acre on the other side of the road.[31]

Cross Burning

One evening not long after the letter from the KKK, Nell was home with their sons when she heard men gathering outside their home. When they entered the yard, she gathered the boys and slid quietly into the crawlspace under the house. She could hear the men calling for her husband to come outside and then the commotion of the men hastily digging a hole and lighting the cross. After a short while, E. B. drove up and found Nell and the boys under the house, shivering.[32] At this point, E. B. had enough:

> Not only have I a large collection of anonymous letters but so virulent were the telephone calls to my home all through the night dating back in 1915 that my phone was unlisted from that time until 1964.
>
> One time when the KKK was parading regularly throughout Arlington County and our NAACP was making headlines, I was threatened so much that I went to Superintendent Kelly of the Washington Police and asked permission to carry a pistol in my car. This he granted and told me to "Kill any of the God-damned KKK people" who bother me on my ride to and from Washington.[33]

Picture taken at Second Baptist Church in Falls Church. Third from the right is Charles Hamilton Houston. Henderson belonged to both the Fairfax County and Washington, DC, NAACP, holding committee chairs in both simultaneously.
COURTESY OF HENDERSON FAMILY COLLECTION

Clearly, Nell, like E. B., was fearless against racial hatred and inequality. A lesser woman might have picked up and left in the face of the threats against her life. She was a tough lady, and that's what E. B. needed. The two of them were a dynamic duo in the fight for racial justice in Washington and Virginia.

"SEPARATE AND UNEQUAL"

In 1867, a man named James Lee, a free man of color, bought property along Shreve Road (now Annandale Road) from Colonel John Crocker. The land had once been part of the Dulaney Plantation, a one-hundred-acre farm before the Civil War. James Lee was sequestered by Confederate troops to build the fortifications in Centreville for the Battle of Manassas. His brother Charles Lee joined the US Colored troops. James saw how the schools for Blacks were relegated to churches, and he felt that they should have a schoolhouse, so he gave the land for the school around 1888.

Nellie taught and was principal at the Falls Church Colored School beginning in 1919. She and Ollie Tinner were very familiar figures at Fairfax County School Board meetings, as they continued to advocate for a new school and better conditions generally for Black schools in the Fairfax County Public School District. It became clear that what they were doing was not working, so Nell and the NAACP came up with a different strategy.

Using the Fairfax County Public School budget for 1938, Nell analyzed their spending and initiated a disparity study. Her study, "Our Disgrace and Shame," really caused a stir in both Black and White communities. It illuminated how the school board had been spending most of the taxpayers' dollars to build and fund education for White students, whereas Black students were getting the crumbs: 97.4 cents of every dollar in the budget went to White schools, leaving only 2.6 cents of every dollar to educate Black students. There were new schools for White students, while Black students remained in their shabby one-, two-, and three-room schoolhouses. New books went to White schools, while the Black students would get the hand-me-down books White schools were discarding.[34] Her study was shared nationally by the NAACP and published in prominent local and regional newspapers.

OUR DISGRACE AND SHAME

SCHOOL FACILITIES FOR NEGRO CHILDREN IN FAIRFAX COUNTY

WHITE SCHOOLS

1 All brick or stone, except 4 wooden buildings
2 Have running water, janitorial service, inside toilets, central heating
3 Children ride in heated busses.

NEGRO SCHOOLS

1 One to three room wooden buildings
2 All have outside "pit" toilets for teachers and children, no running water; all stoves in the rooms
3 No janitorial service—teachers do all cleaning, haul water, make fires
4 Three schools have no water on premises
5 Some children walk from 4 to 6 miles to school
6 Buses are old and rickety and are not heated.

HOW SCHOOL FUNDS ARE SHARED

In 1935 the School Board sought a grant of $153,022.50 from PWA and a bond issue (which was defeated) to raise $187,027.50. Of this total of $340,050.00 it was proposed to spend for:

WHITE SCHOOLS	$330,750—97.4 per cent
COLORED SCHOOLS	9,000— 2.6 per cent

In 1935 this county owed the State Literary Fund $188,739.32 (all of which had been spent on white schools). In that year the colored population of the county was 19 per cent.

The 1945-46 PROPOSED budget provided among other items:

FOR WHITE SCHOOLS		FOR COLORED SCHOOLS
Administration	$18,380	0
Operation of School Plant (Salary of janitor, light, telephone and fuel)	80,350	?
Capital Outlay	$745,000	$45,000

The following proposed expenditures of a proposed loan from the State Literary fund were approved:

WHITE SCHOOLS	COLORED SCHOOLS
$50,000 for Herndon High School	0
$40,000 for 2 classrooms, wash room and cafeteria at Vienna	0
$20,000 for 2 classrooms at Lincolnia	0
$10,000 to complete 2 classrooms at Groveton	0
$40,000 additional was secured to add elementary rooms to Madison School	

Nell Henderson's disparity study.

COURTESY OF HENDERSON HISTORY OF FAIRFAX BRANCH OF THE NAACP, *1965*

In 1945, an article reported that Nell would be retiring from the school that had been built partly through the efforts of a Friends organization fifty-seven years ago. However, in the 1940s, the widow of the school's founder officially bequeathed the land to Fairfax County Public Schools to build the first modern school for African Americans in Fairfax County, a school with running water, indoor toilets, central heat, a cafeteria, a teacher, a classroom for every grade, and (one additional ask of Nell) an auditorium. When she heard about the Fairfax County School Board plans to build a new school on the site of the Falls Church Colored School, she changed her mind about retiring. After the school opened, Nell would stay as principal for one more year, and she retired at the end of the school year in 1949. She was a pillar of the community and admired by all.[35]

Brown v. Board Meets "Massive Resistance"

E. B. retired in 1954 from the Washington, DC, Colored schools with great accolades from all his colleagues. The following year, E. B. was elected president of the Virginia State NAACP. The *Brown v. Board of Education* decision that struck down *Plessy v. Ferguson* was just a few months old, and the mandate was to desegregate "with all deliberate speed."[36] Virginia, unlike most states, had seven lawyers working cases in the state because Governor Harry Byrd vowed to put up "massive resistance" to desegregate and to defy the Supreme Court's decision. Leading the team for Virginia were two dynamic lawyers, Oliver Hill and Spotswood Robinson III. They were both involved in the earliest case in the NAACP's effort to desegregate public schools.

The first challenge in the courts was *Davis v. County School Board of Prince Edward County, Virginia* (Farmville).[37] The Robert Russa Moton High School in Farmville was desperately overcrowded. It was designed for 250 students, but the student population had grown to almost 500. Teachers were holding classes in "tar paper shacks" on the property. Sixteen-year-old Barbara Rose Johns organized and led the students on a walkout and two-week strike over the overcrowded and inferior facilities. Before the walkout, the students caused a distraction to make the principal leave campus. They marched downtown to Farmville First Baptist Church, where they held a rally, and they boycotted classes and solicited the help of the NAACP to sue for their right to a public education.

Rather than capitulate to the demands of the courts or the NAACP, Prince Edward County shut down, ending public education, and providing scholarships for the White students to attend a private academy. In 1955, when E. B. was president of the Virginia NAACP, the effects of this case were still apparent. The lawyers for the NAACP won case after case, but every time, the Harry Byrd machine would move the goalpost and throw up another roadblock.[38]

This fight would last through the 1950s. Even after *Brown v. Board of Education*, the public reaction dragged on for years. After E. B.'s two-year term as president, he returned to Fairfax County to fight for desegregation in the local schools there. Meanwhile, in 1958, the state legislature formed the Thomson Committee to conduct hearings that some said were designed to outlaw the NAACP activities in Virginia.[39]

E. B. remembered,

> Following my address before the state legislature I was called before the Thompson committee when it came to Northern Virginia. One of the preliminary questions asked of me was, "Dr. Henderson, what is your race?" To this I replied, "This calls for some consideration. One of my great-grandfathers was an Indian. My father's father was Portuguese, and my mother's father was one of the highly respected white citizens in Williamsburg, Virginia. Her mother was this gentleman's slave. Now, which race should I subscribe to?" No further questions were asked of me.[40]

Luther Jackson High School, the First Black High School in Fairfax County

In 1954, Luther Jackson High School opened to much fanfare, and rightfully so. It was the first high school in Fairfax County that African American students could attend. Ironically, Luther Jackson was a segregated high school opening the same year as *Brown v. Board of Education*. As was the tradition in Virginia, Fairfax County did not support education beyond the seventh grade for African Americans. If you wanted to continue with your education before Luther Jackson opened, you could either travel east to Washington to attend the academically superior Washington Colored schools or travel west to Manassas Industrial School to learn a trade.

Manassas Industrial School had started out as Manassas Industrial School for Colored Youth, or the Jennie Dean School. Attending Manassas School meant catching a rickety, hand-me-down bus provided by the Fairfax County Schools for a two-hour bus ride each way. Students would rise before sun-up to catch the bus and often returned home after the sun set that evening, making attending school a full-day ordeal. According to some of the students, the bus would often break down and leave them stranded on the highway.[41]

Jennie Dean was an African American woman who wanted to build a school for Black children to learn trades, much like how Booker T. Washington started Tuskegee Institute in Alabama. She had adopted his philosophy of education and economic uplift. With her efforts, she attracted financial support from philanthropists like Emily Howland and Andrew Carnegie, and Frederick Douglass spoke at the opening of the school in 1894. After Jennie Dean's death, support for the school faltered, and the state stepped in, making it a regional school that supported the youth of Arlington, Fairfax, Fauquier, Page, Rappahannock, Shenandoah, Warren, and Loudoun Counties and the city of Alexandria in Northern Virginia.[42]

> In the late 1940s and early 1950s, the African American community was fed up with the lack of a secondary school for them in Fairfax County, so the community came together and demanded change: "As in other counties, the leaders, with the dynamic support of the people in Fairfax County, confronted school, and other community officials for a new look at the schools, the construction of a new in-county school plant."[43]

E. B. was one of the driving forces behind this effort:

> The NAACP, led by Dr. Edwin B. Henderson, Rev. Milton Sheppard, and others, was very active in the movement to build a new high school. Dr. Henderson produced a flyer that was distributed by the NAACP detailing the disparities in funding between black and white schools. . . . [A]ccording to Henderson, the NAACP devoted much of its time toward education issues.[44]

Mary Ellen Henderson in 1950, upon her retirement from teaching.
COURTESY OF HENDERSON COLLECTION

The superintendent of the Fairfax County Schools, Mr. W. T. Woodson, did not want to work with the NAACP, but the countywide Fairfax Colored Citizens Association and the NAACP worked hand in hand.

The NAACP took action in the courts to pressure the schools, which eventually forced Woodson and the board of education to capitulate and make the necessary changes. An interracial committee was formed to work with citizens and the school administration. A letter from the Fairfax NAACP to the school board stated,

> The Executive Committee of this organization questioned the status of plans for the proposed high school for Black children. . . .
>
> The conditions of travel, time consumed, and generally unfavorable conditions at the Regional High School are causing numbers of drop-outs. . . . The Board directed the Superintendent to reply advising that funds were included for the purchase of a site and the erection of a high school for Colored pupils in Fairfax County in the bond issue.[45]

The February 1951 Fairfax County School Board meeting reached an agreement to build a high school for its African American students, Luther Jackson High School. The school board decided they would need at least fifteen acres to build a high school that was on par with the White schools in the county. The school board considered four possible sites: (1) John S. Barbour's property for $1,200 per acre; (2) Wilson Farr's property, but he could not be contacted because he had gone to Florida; (3) the property of Ashby Graham, who had twenty-five acres, but it lacked sewer facilities, and he strongly opposed the school board's proposal and decided he would develop it himself; and (4) a fifteen-acre site in Merrifield on property belonging to Ottomarius Enid Stone Faison, an African American woman. The Colored Citizen's Association sent a letter to the school board expressing their preference for either the Graham property in Fairfax or the property in Merrifield.[46]

Mrs. Faison was a widow who had acquired the land in her husband's will. She was represented by Mr. Ollie and Guy Tinner. The school board wrote up a proposal to buy her land, but she wasn't interested, probably due to the low bid they offered her. Seeing the offer as an insult, she refused to respond to it. When she did not respond, the school board wrote a resolution and "acted to acquire this site by condemnation," using the county's power of eminent domain to take the land and giving Mrs. Faison the meager compensation of $533.33 per acre.[47]

Their offer was less than half of what they offered John Barbour. Additionally, they did not give her any right of refusal as they did with Wilson Farr or Ashby Graham. She obviously did not want to sell her property. When Wilson Farr didn't respond, they didn't take his land by eminent domain. Even so, on July 19, 1951, the Fairfax School Board executed a resolution to take her fifteen-acre property for $8,000.[48] Although the opening of the first high school in Fairfax County for African American students was a marvelous accomplishment and was met with great fanfare, the method in which they acquired the land to build the new high school was less than honorable.

Final Push to Desegregate Fairfax County Schools

In 1959, twenty-six African American children applied to be admitted to all-White schools. When the school board denied their admission, the Fairfax NAACP sued on behalf of the students in federal district court. Fairfax County Public Schools had proposed a plan to gradually integrate one grade a year until all K–12 grades were integrated, which would have taken thirteen years. Federal district judge Albert V. Bryan issued a decision ordering the county school board to admit some but not all the "Negro children" to the schools to which they had applied.[49]

By then, the number of students who had applied increased to thirty. Of those, twenty-seven had formerly attended all Black schools and would now be able to integrate the all-White Fairfax County Public Schools in the 1960–1961 school year, which grew: ninety-three Black students attended formerly all-White schools in 1961–1962; 214 Black students, in 1962–1963; and more than four hundred Black students, in 1963–1964.[50]

In the 1965–1966 school year, the Fairfax County Public School system finally saw the futility of delaying the inevitable and became totally desegregated.[51] It had taken twelve long years (1954–1966) to complete the desegregation of the public schools in Virginia, which was a long way from what the Supreme Court had mandated. When the schools finally integrated, all the Black elementary schools were closed except one, Louise Archer Elementary School in Vienna. It was believed the Black schools were closed because they were in Black neighborhoods, and White parents were afraid and thus were not going to send their children into those neighborhoods. The James Lee Elementary School in Falls Church was once again shuttered, only to be opened again years later as a community center in the African American enclave along Annandale Road in Falls Church.

Although we applaud the landmark decision of *Brown v. Board of Education*, integration of the public schools was a double-edged sword for African Americans. No longer needing to fund two schools, one to teach Blacks and one to teach Whites, was of great advantage to the school board's building and maintaining facilities. But almost all the elementary schools in Black neighborhoods were closed when the school system desegregated. And although Blacks were able to go to supposedly better schools and facilities, a majority of the teachers in the Black schools were no longer needed and were not rehired. Some believed the teachers in the Black neighborhood schools were more nurturing, caring, and empathetic to the needs of their Black students and were more knowledgeable. But when Black students transferred to the formerly all-White schools, many of their teachers were White and no longer gave them the nurturing they received in the Colored schools.

Many programs and assemblies conducted in the Colored schools, like where Nell Henderson was principal, were to motivate and support students with the knowledge of others who looked like them and who had overcome great obstacles to achieve great things. These kinds of programs were no longer important in the integrated school curriculum. Textbooks never adequately included African American history or their accomplishments, but in the former Colored schools, this omission was supplemented by teachers' lesson plans. However, in the new environment that African American students in Fairfax County would find themselves, this was not so. Over the years, this would have a negative effect on African American student development in the United States.[52]

Dr. W. E. B. Du Bois believed that Black people needed their own schools. In an essay from the 1935 *Journal of Negro Education*, he states,

> "Does the Negro need separate schools?" His answer was an emphatic "God knows it does." Du Bois' attitude toward racially segregated schools was emphatic: as long as whites believed in inferiority of black people, black children and young adults were better off in separate schools and universities. . . . Separate schools held the promise of a better education only if the community believed in and invested in their schools and their teachers. With sufficient resources and support, black children and college students, Du Bois believed, had a better chance of flourishing in separate schools where they would learn about black history and culture, be taught by teachers who empathized with them and believed in them, and be sheltered from discrimination, abuse, and neglect in classrooms and schools controlled by whites.[53]
>
> Du Bois goes on to say, "I have long been convinced . . . that the Negroes in public schools in Harlem are not getting an education that is in any sense comparable in efficiency, discipline, and human development with that which Negroes are getting in the separate public schools of Washington, DC."[54]

> This is why EB's bold statement in 1911 was so important: "When competent physical directors and equal training facilities are afforded the colored youth, the white athlete will find an equal or superior in nearly every line of athletic endeavor."[55]

E. B. wasn't only speaking in terms of athletics but rather every aspect of academic, intellectual, social, and professional endeavor.

Even in light of these facts, the Fairfax County Public Schools and the much smaller Falls Church City Public Schools are considered among the best in the country. In 2005, the Falls Church City Public Schools named their new middle school in honor of Nell, the Mary Ellen Henderson Middle School, a testament to her leadership in education in Northern Virginia.

E. B. served on several NAACP committees and executive board positions in Fairfax County, in Virginia, and in Washington, often simultaneously. In 1955, members of the Fairfax branch nominated him for the Spingarn Medal. Even though he was considered, and deservedly so, he did not receive it, and it probably wasn't that important to him anyway.

17

Protest in the Nation's Capital

Rosa Parks's act of resistance by refusing to give up her seat on a Montgomery, Alabama, city bus in late 1955 is generally credited as the start of the modern civil rights struggle. But her act was not created in a vacuum. She was inspired to resist because of what happened to a teenage boy in Money, Mississippi, a few months before and his mother's bold decision to show the world the brutal reality of Southern cruelty in America. Shackled by Jim Crow segregation, African American lives were marginalized by the denial of civil and human rights, combined with acts of cruelty and brutality. Although Blacks were emancipated, they were not truly free. In Martin Luther King Jr.'s "I Have a Dream Speech," he said,

> Five score years ago, a great American, in whose symbolic shadow we stand today, signed the Emancipation Proclamation. This momentous decree came as a great beacon light of hope to millions of Negro slaves who had been seared in the flames of withering injustice. It came as a joyous daybreak to end the long night of their captivity.
>
> But 100 years later, the Negro still is not free.[1]

Resistance to oppression has taken many forms over the four hundred years since slaves were brought to these shores. Each generation found a way to fight back against the denial of their humanity. And each generation stood on the shoulders of those who came before them.

During E. B.'s lifetime, the model for resistance was to use the laws, amendments to the Constitution, and legal address through the courts to gain those civil and human rights that had been denied through Black Codes and Jim Crow laws in Southern states. E. B. used the power of the pen; he wrote letters, organized protests, and filed court cases to bring down the barriers of segregation in his advocacy for civil rights for African Americans in Virginia, and his strategies worked. E. B. would use many of these same strategies to combat segregation in the nation's capital.

The Washington Branch of the NAACP

E. B. and Nell joined the Washington branch of the NAACP years before they initiated the Falls Church/Fairfax County branch after they moved to Virginia. Living in Virginia but working in DC, E. B. was active in both branches and for many years held positions on executive committees for both branches simultaneously.

Nell grew up attending the Fifteenth Street Presbyterian Church, whose pastor was Francis Grimke, the brother of Archibald Grimke, who founded the Washington branch of the NAACP in 1912. The Fifteenth Street Presbyterian Church had always been one of social activism, going back to African American abolitionist Henry Highland Garnett.

The NAACP was started after a group of White and Jewish progressives were appalled when a White mob attacked the African American community in Springfield, Illinois, Abraham Lincoln's hometown, on Lincoln's birthday in 1908. The group of progressives decided to create an organization to address the violence and injustice directed at African Americans in the United States. Among those who responded to the call were Mary White Ovington, Henry Moskowitz, William English Walling, and Oswald Garrison Villard. This early group also included African Americans W. E. B. Du Bois of the Niagara Movement; Archibald Grimke of the National Council of Colored People; Mary Church Terrell, founder of the National Association of Colored Women; and Ida B. Wells, the journalist who exposed how the sinister strategy behind lynching was used to intimidate and keep the average African American subordinate.[2]

E. B. attended the 1921 NAACP national convention in Detroit, where he met Mary White Ovington, James Weldon Johnson, Walter White, and President Moorfield Story, a White lawyer from Boston. At this event, E. B. was asked by Ms. Ovington to take a more national role, but he declined, choosing to stay in his more local advocacy work and his profession in the Washington and Northern Virginia area.[3] Much of E. B.'s time and energy was spent in service to civil rights and the pursuit of justice. He was instrumental in starting the Falls Church and Vicinity branch, which was the first rural branch in the United States, and helped to develop strategies used around the country.

In 1955, after the Supreme Court decision in *Brown v. Board of Education*, E. B. was elected president of the Virginia Council of NAACPs (the state branch) to fight "massive resistance" to bring desegregation to the schools in Virginia. From 1955 through 1958, E. B. worked with lawyers Oliver Hill and Spottswood Robinson to overcome the "Harry Byrd machine" and to open up the school districts that had closed rather than desegregate their schools.[4]

In his final years, after moving to Tuskegee, Alabama, E. B. helped establish the Macon County branch of the NAACP. In total, he was an active member of the NAACP for sixty-five years.

Protesting the Uline Arena and AAU Golden Gloves

From late 1941 to 1960, and before the DC National Armory, the Uline Arena was the largest venue for indoor sports and entertainment (seating nine thousand). It was named for Michael Uline, a Dutch immigrant who had made his ice business into an entertainment empire in Washington, DC. It was the scene of many competitive and aesthetic events, such as wrestling, boxing, basketball, ice hockey, and the Ice Capades, as well as political events. In 1960, it became the Washington Coliseum, and the Beatles' first concert in the United States in 1964 was held there.[5]

In 1941, the Amateur Athletic Union (AAU) was the oldest and largest promoter and organizer of amateur sports and still is to this day. E. B. was involved with the local branch of the AAU because he wanted to improve and broaden recreational activities and athletics for African American youths in Washington, DC. Annually the AAU, in conjunction with the local police department, put on the Golden Gloves boxing tournament. But Washington, DC, had a policy of not allowing Blacks to box against Whites in the competition, even though in other places it was not an issue. This was also the case for professional boxing until late in 1941, when Joe Louis fought Buddy Bear in Griffith Stadium.[6]

The local AAU branch wrote on the back of every sanctioned amateur event, "Promotion would be suspended and denied future permits if promoters permitted mixed boxing." This did not sit well with E. B., who decided he would protest what he saw as an injustice. E. B. had always wanted African Americans to be able to compete against their White counterparts so that the false ideology of White supremacy would be dismantled.[7]

> EB had protested about the injustice in not allowing Blacks to compete against Whites in the Golden Gloves events for many years, but this time he went a step further. EB wrote a letter to Eugene Myers, the president of the *Washington Post*, asking him to no longer promote or sponsor the boxing tournament at the Uline Arena. Additionally, EB wrote to Mrs. Eleanor Patterson, the owner of the *Washington Times-Herald*, asking her to do the same. The *Washington Post* issued a statement: "Mr. Myers issued a statement that the Post would no longer sponsor or support the boxing tournament so long as black young men were denied."[8] Soon after, the *Times-Herald* also withdrew their support for the same reason. Additionally, EB would organize a protest to the discriminating policy and picket lines in front of the Uline Arena. EB recalled, "I was approached by some of the promoters, who made money out of the games, asking me would I let them go for one season more. I refused to let up the picket lines. Mrs. Patterson withdrew her support when the two boys from the YMCA's boxing team entered suit against the AAU."[9]

Unfortunately, the suit did not come to trial until after the national Golden Gloves was completed in Boston, Massachusetts. The lower court ruled the case was moot, but Henderson and the attorneys sent the case up to the court of appeals. Upon hearing the case there, the three judges "castigated" the AAU and remanded the case back to the lower courts for trial on the merits of the issue. E. B. stated,

> [R]epresentatives of the AAU were ready to vote to lift its sanctioning edict in boxing and track and promised if we would lift the case out of court, they would do so.
>
> With the advice of our lawyers, we withdrew the case in a way that we might re-enter, and the AAU has since raised no barrier to inter-racial boxing and track, and recently (1954), lifted the bars against racial weight lifting, judo, and wrestling.
>
> Needless to say, these results made it possible for our boys to measure their abilities against any and all, and did a lot to raise the level of respect of all citizens in our community.[10]

This was a big win that would pave the way for interracial competitions, particularly in Southern states, where segregation was enforced. Now the AAU would not be able to stand in the way of interracial competitions anymore. But E. B.'s differences with the Uline Arena were not over. The arena also had discriminatory policies for admission of African Americans to some events held there. Michael Uline objected to allowing African Americans to the Ice Capades events, because

> [he] did not want the black people to attend events where the participants were in bathing attire and where the audience was more or less a "social" group.
>
> The protest brought together the NAACP's Committee on Recreation, of which E B was the Chairman, and the 12th Street YMCA to bring pressure on Uline to change his policy.
>
> Neither rain nor snow lessened our ardor. After about a year of declining patronage, Mr. Uline called a press conference and announced from then on there would be no limitations in attendance.[11]

Committee against Segregation in the Nation's Capital: The Marian Anderson Concert

The NAACP, when starting a protest over a specific concern, would start a Citizen's Committee to publicize and mobilize citizens in the particular effort. The Committee against Segregation in the Nation's Capital was established in the late 1930s as a group in the Washington NAACP to strategically desegregate entertainment in Washington, DC. Two of the most successful campaigns were protesting segregation at Constitution Hall and the National Theatre. When it was first established, E. B. was elected vice chair of the committee, but after the chairman, who was a lawyer, was called away for a case in Tennessee, E. B. became the chairman. With E. B. as chairman, the committee began to strategize how it would proceed.[12]

Most White theaters would not allow Blacks to be seated. Many theaters and other entertainment venues relegated African Americans to the balconies, or as Charles Douglass, Frederick Douglass's son, called them, the "Jim Crow seats."[13] At that time, Charles called for a boycott of the White theaters and implored, "Build your own theaters as you do your churches. . . . Are we forever to be dependent upon Whites for theaters, hotels, cafes, and stores of all descriptions?"[14]

In 1931, Roland Hayes was contracted to give a concert at Constitution Hall and had given friends tickets to attend his performance, but upon arrival, they were turned away. When he heard that his friends were not allowed to be seated, he refused to perform until they were allowed in the hall. This caused some commotion, but his friends were seated some thirty minutes later, and he came onstage and performed his concert. After this incident, the governors of the Daughters of the American Revolution (DAR), who owned Constitution Hall, refused to engage or contract another Black singer.[15]

Marian Anderson was invited to perform at the White House in 1935. Starting in 1936, Ms. Anderson sang an annual concert to benefit the Howard University School of Music. It had become such a draw that Howard University could not find a venue large enough for her to perform. In January 1939, Howard University petitioned the DAR to use Constitution Hall for Ms. Anderson's concert because at that time it was the largest auditorium in Washington. The DAR refused to allow her to perform at Constitution Hall, largely because it would have made a mockery of their all-White audience policy.[16]

The Washington NAACP created the Marian Anderson Citizens Committee (MACC) to address this affront. Eleanor Roosevelt, a member of the DAR, was appalled by the organization's refusal and ultimately protested by relinquishing her membership. This would up the ante on the upcoming NAACP protest.[17] E. B. said,

> I was in the company very frequently of Mrs. Eleanor Roosevelt, the wife of President Franklin Roosevelt, and we would meet at the YWCA, and she was very helpful in the many fights for equality that we had, and when I was treasurer of the War Worker's Association during the Second World War she invited me to the White House on several occasions.[18]

E. B. was also friends with Secretary of the Interior Harold L. Ickes due to their association with the Washington Recreation Committee, on which they both served. But it was at the request of Mrs. Roosevelt and the Marian Anderson Citizens Committee that Secretary Ickes made the arrangements for Ms. Anderson to sing on the steps of the Lincoln Memorial on Easter Sunday in 1939 in front of 75,000 people, who braved the chilly morning air that day.[19]

The success of the event infamously highlighted the hypocrisy of the Daughters of the American Revolution's policy of segregation, as E. B. noted in a letter to the editor the week after Ms. Anderson's landmark performance. Several years later, Marian Anderson was invited to perform at Constitution Hall.

PROTESTING THE NATIONAL THEATRE

Some, like the famous Washington actress Helen Hayes, felt that the National Theatre had long held an ironic name because it was not welcoming to all its citizens. She would later refuse to perform at the National Theatre because of its segregation policy.[20]

In 1916 and again in the 1920s, the National Theatre would be in the spotlight of protest because of its booking of D. W. Griffith's infamous *Birth of a Nation*, first entitled *The Clansman*, which glorified the KKK

E. B. at the White House with President Truman and the 1948 Women's Olympic track team.
COURTESY OF HENDERSON FAMILY COLLECTION

and demonized Black people. The NAACP picketed both times it was shown at the National Theatre.[21]

In 1933, *The Green Pastures*, with an all-Black cast, opened at the National Theatre to an all-White segregated audience. The NAACP protested and pressured the production to withdraw from the National Theatre entirely; instead, the theater compromised, and Blacks were allowed to attend two all-Black special performances.[22]

In 1936, the National Theatre put on the performance of George Gershwin's classic American opera *Porgy and Bess*, which featured a predominately Black cast. The American Federation of Teachers; the AFL-CIO; the Theatre Guild; and Todd Duncan, who created the roll of Porgy and was a professor of music at Howard University pressured the National Theatre to relax its segregation policy, which it did for this work. Duncan was instrumental in the strike that led to the brief relaxation of the strict segregation rule at the theater.[23]

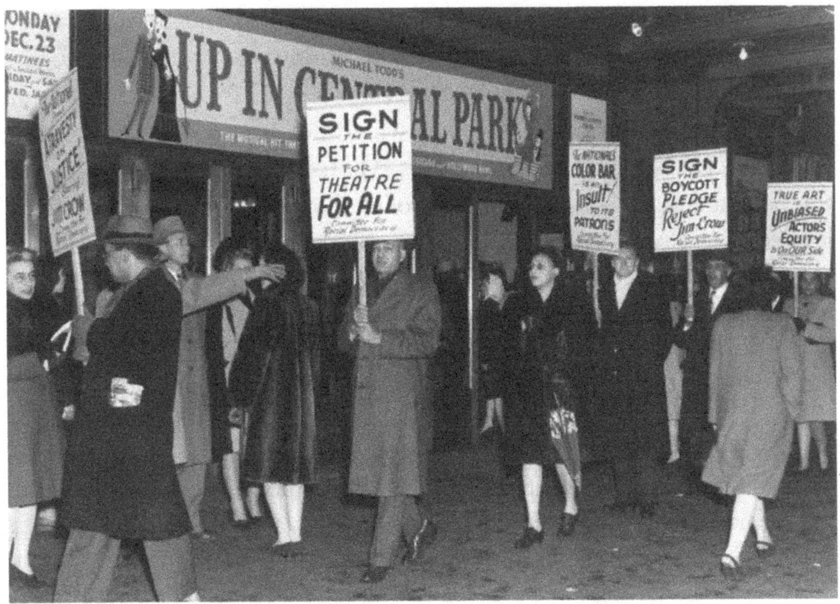

E. B., rear in line, holding a picket sign in front of the National Theatre.
COURTESY OF MOORLAND SPINGARN RESEARCH CENTER, HOWARD UNIVERSITY ARCHIVES, HOWARD UNIVERSITY, WASHINGTON, DC

The Washington NAACP felt that an effort was needed after the production of *Porgy and Bess*. In the mid-1940s, the Committee against Segregation in the Nation's Capital created a splinter group, the Committee for Racial Democracy, which organized the effort against the National Theatre. After a teacher from Dunbar High School had been refused seating upon presenting his ticket, the NAACP started to use the National Theatre's refund policy as a protest strategy.[24] The theater changed their policy and included on the back of each ticket "We reserve the right to seat only those whom we like" and claimed that they were the "victims of a scam designed to diminish their profits."[25]

In 1947, the strategy was to build a case against the National Theatre in the courts. The Committee for Racial Democracy demanded the theater rescind their policy and threatened legal action. Picket lines commenced outside the theater during the production of the play *Blossom Time*. President Harry Truman and his wife, supposedly unknowingly, crossed the picket line to see the play at the National Theatre. This caused some outrage, particularly in the Black community. Helen Hayes, vice president of the Actors Equity Association (AEA), signed a petition circulated by AEA announcing they would not appear onstage until the polices were changed. In April 1947, AEA, the Dramatists Guild, and the Screen Actors Guild adopted a policy that union members would no longer be allowed to perform in segregated houses. E. B. explained,

> Many White persons worked with us. I went to New York on one occasion and met with the President of Actor's Equity and Mr. Mark Connally, and the NAACP Secretary, Walter White, in the home of Mrs. Cornelia Otis Skinner. We secured the active support of the Actors Guild who then said that they would refuse to play where there was segregation. Later I purchased a ticket and presented it at the door of the National Theatre and was refused. We then filed a suit with the help of NAACP lawyers. Before the case was adjudicated, however, the owner, Heilman, gave up the National Theatre as a legitimate theater and turned it into a moving picture house.[26]

Washington now was without a major theatrical venue for productions. Helen Hayes decided to perform at a smaller local theater in Montgomery County, outside Washington. After the event she wrote a letter to the editor of the *Washington Post*, praising the integrated audience of more than 9,100, saying, "DC residents were ready for integrated theatres."[27]

Coursey sums up E. B.'s pragmatic strategies very succinctly:

> Again, Edwin Bancroft Henderson's success and ultimately some benefit or reward of equity for all the people of Washington, DC lie in his uncanny capacity for persevering, organizing, leading, administrating while under pressure. It is evident that another aspect of Edwin Bancroft Henderson's success is inherent in his ability to think critically and deal directly with the problems and not be misled by its many symptoms. Case in point would be his creating and securing the previously mentioned agreement from the Actors' Guild and the initiation of the various court cases.[28]

"CENTRAL FOR CARDOZO": A COMMUNITY COLLABORATION

Francis Cardozo High School opened in 1933 for African American students in a building that had been vacated by the Business High School for White students at the intersection of Ninth Street and Rhode Island Avenue NW in Washington, DC; it was totally inadequate for a regular full-service high school. There was no outdoor space for sports, recreation, or physical education activities, and it had a small gymnasium that was only half the size of a regular gymnasium. Francis Cardozo, the clergyman, politician, and former principal of Preparatory High School for Colored Youth, deserved better, and so did the students who went to the school named in his honor.[29]

In 1949, it was very apparent that the Black population was growing while the White population was moving out of Washington, DC, to communities that were being built just beyond the city's borders. Forty-one organizations from the African American community came together to protest and advocate for the relief of the Black students at overcrowded Francis Cardozo High School. Their truly illuminating twenty-one-page document showed that allocations for schools that taught Black students did not increase as the Black population increased, whereas schools built to teach White students received larger allocations for better facilities.[30]

The White student population was dwindling. The huge high schools that the Washington, DC, school board had built since the First World War were becoming underpopulated due to White Flight. Many White parents were now sending their children to affluent private schools within the city limits, as well. The result was schools like Central High School, designed to accommodate 2,400 students, had an enrollment of only 822. Additionally, no high school for Black students had been built since the First World War, but six new high schools were built for White students during this same period.[31]

> Classes for the 1,796 students at Cardozo were done in shifts to accommodate all the students. The cafeteria only held 248 students at a time, approximately one-seventh of the student population. The gymnasium was only half the size of a regulation high school gym, while the recommendation for a high school was two gymnasiums. Cardozo High

> School's land consisted of less than an acre, whereas the recommendation for a high school its size was twenty, and the White high schools in DC averaged more than ten acres per campus.[32] On page 4 of the document in bold letters, it said, "Why should Negro children share inadequate facilities when available empty pupil stations are available in other district high schools?"[33]

Another issue was that all the Black high schools were in a small cluster in the city, but the White high schools were spread throughout so that Black students had to travel farther distances than their White counterparts to get to their schools. In addition, the price of a new high school was between $3.5 million and $6 million, and the federal government was not willing to out lay that kind of money to build a high school for Black students. The 822 White students could easily have been transferred and absorbed into the also underpopulated high schools in the city, like Roosevelt, Eastern, or McKinley Tech, all of which had vacancies of more than 1,000 each.

The petition ends with a bold demand in bold letters:

> 6,000 empty seats in seven high schools for whites means an unjust waste of millions of dollars of the taxpayer's money—while Negro students at Cardozo are presently threatened with a loss of accreditation.
>
> The board of education must act uniformally for all children in the District of Columbia. We strongly urge—without reservation or equivocation—that the board of education transfer Central High School Plant to house Cardozo children.[34]

There were 10,000 signatures on the petition. E. B. represented the Washington NAACP, among the list of forty-one agencies and groups. What was truly amazing about this document was its statistical analysis, demography, and cost analysis, which left little doubt that the decision to turn over the school was the right one. The school board capitulated and turned over the Central High School campus to the students at Cardozo, starting in the 1949–1950 school year.[35]

Yet, many of the students from the White Central High School did not leave happily or quietly. Even though the White students were angry, the inequality was obvious and could not continue. Transferring a palatial high school for Whites to Black students in the nation's capital was a huge triumph.

Forcing the Washington Redskins to Integrate

After the 1920s, the NFL was segregated until after World War II. Then, just like baseball's Jackie Robinson, NFL teams began to reintegrate the game, but the Washington football team refused, and Blacks protested. The atmosphere was tense in Washington. In 1961, the Washington Redskins were the only team in professional football that had not selected or traded for an African American player to their roster. In fact, Stewart Udall, secretary of the interior, more than once called the Washington Redskins, the Washington "Paleskins."[36]

Their flamboyant owner, George Preston Marshall, a showman and brilliant promoter, blatantly vowed that he would not pick an African American football player for his team. To add insult to injury, he had not fielded a competitive team for years. The Washington Redskins only won one game in 1960 and had a string of losing seasons going back to the end of World War II. So why not integrate? The Washington Redskins were the southernmost team in the National Football League (NFL), and their fan base was the Southern United States. At this time, there were no teams in Georgia, Florida, Tennessee, or Texas. Dixie was played at halftime, and their fans identified with the Southern custom of segregation.

The population of Washington, DC, in 1961 was slightly favoring African Americans and growing. The Black majority was not happy with their football team. Their games were played at the Griffith Stadium at the corner of Seventh and U Street NW, right next to Howard University, a majority-Black section of town, so White fans had to travel into a Black section of Washington from the suburbs to see the Washington Redskins play their home games.

The federal government built a new stadium for them on land owned by the Department of the Interior, on the eastern side of Washington, just west of the Anacostia River. But the government had the upper hand, and there were rules that the team would have to abide by if they wanted to play there. Upon completion of the Washington Stadium (later named RFK Stadium in honor of Robert Kennedy), the Redskins signed a thirty-year lease to play there. In March 1961, Secretary Udall warned the Redskins that they would not be able to move into the shiny new stadium unless they complied with federal guidelines, which were nondiscriminatory; they had to desegregate the team.[37]

> Meanwhile, there were protests by African Americans civil rights groups and sportswriters. The sportswriter for the *Washington Afro American*, Sam Lacy, was calling for a boycott, and he had a weekly column to give voice to his protest. Marshall was a known racist and segregationist, and he was not going to give in to a showdown in Washington, DC. At the lead, once again, was EB: "E. B. Henderson urged blacks and whites to boycott all Redskin games until the team integrated its roster. If Africans Americans and 'our liberal friends stay away until the Redskins cease to be all-white, Mr. Marshall will eventually become a true American.'"[38]

Thomas Smith frames it as such:

> While baseball, as the then-more-popular sport, drew most of their attention, Black journalists also pushed hard for reintegration, as they put it, of professional football. Having achieved that goal in the years after World War II, several writers were incensed that the last team to desegregate was located in the democratic capital of the United States. Journalist Sam Lacy, L. I. Brockenbury, and Brad Pye, as well as Washington community leaders E. B. Henderson and Lawrence Oxley, spearheaded the Black effort to integrate the Washington Redskins.[39]

This "showdown" was well suited to E. B.'s strengths, combining both athletics and civil rights:

> Henderson devoted himself to combating what he called "racial fascism." Henderson insisted that the best way to achieve racial tolerance was through interracial sports competition. "More than any other factor it is the field of competitive sports that American youth learns the true spirit of America." He once wrote "Millions of people on Saturdays and

> Sundays as spectators of major college and professional football learn vicariously the lessons of tolerance and fair play."[40]

Additionally, E. B.'s friend, sportswriter for the *Washington Post* Shirley Povich, who deplored racial injustice, had an ongoing feud with Marshall for many years and was a very strong advocate for the change. He demanded that Marshall capitulate and draft a Black football player.

Begrudgingly, the Washington Redskins drafted Heisman Trophy winner Ernie Davis and then traded him to the Cleveland Browns for Bobby Mitchell, who became the first Black Washington Redskin in the 1962 football season.

The March on Washington

The March on Washington for Jobs and Freedom was more of a demonstration than a protest. Dr. Martin Luther King Jr. said at the beginning of his famous "I Have a Dream" speech, "I am happy to join with you today in what will go down in history as the greatest demonstration for freedom in the history of our nation."[41]

The year 1963 was most tumultuous in the struggle for civil rights in America. The "Birmingham Manifesto" landed Dr. King in jail.[42] On "D-Day," one thousand students ditched classes and marched two by two out of Sixteenth Street Baptist Church, enduring fire hoses, police dogs, arrest, and other tactics by Birmingham's commissioner of public safety Bull Connor. Dr. King wrote his "Letter from a Birmingham Jail," one of his most illuminating writings in response to eight Southern White religious leaders calling his tactics "unwise and untimely." In June, President John F. Kennedy, for the first time, condemned segregation and announced his intention to pass a civil rights bill.[43] The next day, Medgar Evers was murdered by Byron De La Beckwith. There was a reckoning afoot.

A. Philip Randolph and Bayard Rustin organized the March on Washington. This was not the first time they had proposed a March on Washington. Randolph had a long history of being able to mobilize people in protest during his time as a leader for civil and labor rights.[44] As a friend and associate of Randolph from his days writing a monthly column in the *Messenger* in the 1920s, E. B. was front and center when Dr. King gave his famous "I Have a Dream" speech at the Lincoln Memorial on August 28, 1963.

E. B.'s long career protesting for social justice in Washington would soon come to a close, and upon retiring, he would receive a hero's farewell. But he still wrote letters to the editor that many in Washington looked forward to reading on a weekly, if not daily, basis. Getting older meant his legs and voice might have been a little shakier, but his thought-provoking pen would still inform people of the issues of the day.

18

The Rise of Professional Sports in Washington, DC

Horse Racing in the District of Columbia

GOING BACK TO COLONIAL DAYS, THE SPORT OF AMERICA'S WEALTHY IN the Washington area was horse racing. It was believed that American horse racing was born in Georgetown when a purse of 25 pounds was offered on a May 30, 1769, race.[1]

The Washington Jockey Club was founded in 1797, and its first racetrack was only blocks away from the White House, extending from Seventeenth to Twentieth Streets, NW, where the Eisenhower Executive Office Building is today.[2] In 1802, the initial horse racetrack was relocated from within sight of the White House to the Holmead Farm, where Meridian Hill is today. The track extended from Fourteenth to Sixteenth Streets NW, just south of Columbia Road NW. Here the Washington Jockey Club built a one-mile oval track. In 1834, the Washington Jockey Club hosted the first steeplechase in the United States. Two other tracks that existed in Washington were the Crystal Springs, later known as Brightwood Trotting Park, and the Piney Branch Race Course, located at what is now the Carter Baron, along Colorado and Sixteenth Streets NW.[3]

The horse track at Benning Road in the Deanwood community was first established in 1876 and opened as a public track in 1890. Some of the early races included the Willard Hotel Handicap, the Grand

Consolation, the Dixie, and the Vestal Stakes. The opening day of the track brought a meager crowd of two thousand, but it gained in popularity and soon attracted a mixed crowd that rivaled all the other tracks of its day. Among those who frequented the track was Teddy Roosevelt's daughter Alice.[4]

African Americans were known for being some of the best trainers of horses and jockeys in the country until around 1902:

> Black horsemen played a vital role in shaping early American turf history, and the Kentucky Derby is no exception. The history of the Kentucky Derby and Black horsemen are intertwined. The Derby and Churchill Downs owe a great deal to those who helped shape America's greatest race. Thirteen of the 15 riders in the first Derby were Black, and Black reinsmen won 15 of the Derby's first 28 runnings.[5]

The first Kentucky Derby in 1875 was won by a Black jockey named Oliver Lewis. Lewis was followed by William Walker (1877); George Garrett Lewis (1880); Babe Hurd (1882); and probably the greatest of all the Black jockeys, Isaac Murphy, who won three Kentucky Derbies, in 1884, 1890, and 1891. Two other Black jockeys won two derbies, Willie Simms (1896, 1898) and Jimmy Winkfield (1901, 1902).[6] However, after Winkfield's win in 1902, there was a concerted effort to eliminate African American jockeys in horse racing thanks to Jim Crow segregation at the Kentucky Derby, as well as in other professional sports.[7]

Blacks in Baseball in Washington, DC

In 1839, baseball was invented by Abner Doubleday in Cooperstown, New York, though this is often disputed. The sport became very popular shortly after the Civil War. Teams were popping up everywhere, especially in the Northeast and Mid-Atlantic states. In Washington, DC, a Black team, the Washington Mutuals, was established, and the first recorded game took place on July 19, 1867. Frederick Douglass's sons Fred and Charles both played on the Mutuals, and their father was an avid fan of the game, often traveling to see them play.

E. B. wrote an article in the June 24, 1950, issue of the *Baltimore Afro-American* about the Washington Mutuals regarding a discovery of the team's records. Mrs. Catherine "Kitty" Bruce, the daughter of the club's secretary, Charles Bruce, gave E. B. a handbill advertising the game, the recorded scores, and a letter to the editor of a Philadelphia paper protesting the Philadelphia team which falsely claimed a victory in the contest against the Washington Mutuals. E. B. wrote,

> One of the most interesting of sports documents to come to light has fallen into my hands. It is the score book of the Washington Mutuals baseball team, with scores recorded of games played by this club from July 19, 1867 until 1875. This team appeared two years after the civil war ended consisting of some of the famous men of Reconstruction Days. Many of these players had been born as free men, others were freedmen. Two of the players throughout this period were sons of Frederick Douglass who was the great factor in abolishing slavery. These two players were Fred and Charles, better known as Major Charles Douglass. Because of the popularity of the team in the cities of the East, Hon. Frederick Douglass followed them all over the circuit in which they played. Others of repute on the "Mutuals" were: Major "Chris" Fleetwood; Pliny Locke, father of Dr. Allan Locke of Howard University; and Judge Molineaux whose father was Abram Molineaux Hewlett, recognized as the first physical director in the gymnasium built for college physical education in the United States, at Harvard University where he remained for ten years.[8]

E. B. ended his article, "It's a long way from the Mutuals, a member of the National Association, to Jackie Robinson, et al. playing on the Brooklyn Dodgers, but baseball was as American to negroes in 1867, as it is today. We often fail to look back when we cheer our heroes of today."[9]

The first Black professional baseball league, the Negro National League, was established in 1920. Starting in 1940, the Homestead Grays, a Negro League team out of Pittsburgh, began to play half their games in Griffith Stadium in Washington, DC.[10] Over the next three years, between 1942 and 1945, Satchel Paige's team, the Kansas City Monarchs, and Josh Gibson's Homestead Grays played before mostly capacity crowds that practically doubled the attendance of the Washington Senators baseball team of the White American League. The matchup between the Negro league's best pitcher and its best hitter kept the fans coming to see the games at Griffith Stadium, much to the delight of Clark Griffith, the owner of the Senators and the stadium:

> At that time, the Negro leagues were among the most lucrative black-owned businesses in the United States, in large part because of rivalries such as the Homestead Grays versus the Monarchs, which continued to bring in massive crowds during World War II. Washingtonian Sam Lacy aided in the increased exposure of black baseball players, as he routinely took a sledgehammer to racism and segregation of the sport. . . . [T]he first black member of the Baseball Writers Association of America and the man who chronicled Jackie Robinson's integration of MLB, Lacy worked for the *Washington Tribune*, *Chicago Defender* and *Baltimore Afro-American* and brought greater awareness to achievements of African Americans in sports.[11]

Over the course of forty years, the Negro leagues took on various configurations until they ultimately disintegrated when the color barrier was broken. After Jackie Robinson successfully integrated Major League Baseball, more and more teams began to add Black players to their rosters, and the talented players began to jump ship to the White major league teams until it was unsustainable for the Negro leagues to survive. The Washington Senators were not one of those White Major League teams to add a Black player to its roster until most other teams had already done so. In 1951, the Homestead Grays disbanded, leaving the growing Black population of Washington, DC, without a team to cheer for.

Recreational Opportunities for African Americans

In the early twentieth century, the Great Migration began to encourage African Americans still located in the Jim Crow South to hop on trains to the urban industrial centers in the North. In places like New York City, Chicago, Detroit, and Cleveland, companies placed advertisements in the Negro press for jobs that offered aspiration of a lifestyle free from the segregation, discrimination, and hostilities in the post–Civil War southern states. Although the northern cities did not technically adhere to the rules of Jim Crow segregation, Black people still experienced second-class citizenship regarding where they could live and the jobs they could hold.

During the first mass migration of enslaved African Americans, Washington, DC, held the greatest promise for a good life. In 1900, it had the largest percentage of African Americans in the United States. There was a very active social, entertainment, recreational, and intellectual scene in Washington for Black people. In addition, there was a well-established upper-middle class that took full advantage of their status as the "Black bourgeoise." Washington was not an industrial city, but it was the seat of the federal government, offering many good-paying jobs and appointments with both the municipal and federal governments.[12] This group of prominent Blacks were also active in commercial enterprises of the U Street corridor; Georgetown; along the Potomac; Barry Farm; and Deanwood, east of the Anacostia River. Deanwood, in particular, became a lively spot for Washingtonians, both Black and White:

> Although Deanwood is located on the outskirts of Washington, two attractions ensured its popularity: Benning Race Track and Suburban Gardens Amusement Park. Opening in 1890, Benning Race Track operated for nearly 20 years along the Anacostia River between Benning Road and Kenilworth Avenue. . . . The grandstand and clubhouse brought "high society" White folks to Deanwood by the thousands in the early 1900's. . . . Alice Roosevelt, oldest daughter of President Theodore Roosevelt and wife of Nicholas Longworth, Speaker of the House, and other White political "first ladies" of the day were known to spend many of their social hours at Benning Race Track, enjoying the nice breeze and beautiful manicured shoreline of the Anacostia River.[13]

In addition to a racetrack, the first and longest-running African American amusement park was established by a group of Black entrepreneurs, architects, and licensed engineers, such as H. D. Woodson, to create the synergy and community that became Suburban Gardens:

> During legal segregation, Deanwood housed Suburban Gardens, the city's only amusement park. Located at 50th and Hayes Streets, the Black-only operated park encompassed nine acres when it opened in 1921 and swelled to 20 acres before it closed in the 1940's. . . . For ten cents, patrons enjoyed a carousel, dance hall and playground in the early 1920's. Later expansions included a roller coaster, airplane swing, Tilt-a-Whirl, Skee-Ball, miniature railway, shooting gallery and swimming pool. Daredevil shows and circuses also drew large audiences. The park was eventually sold to Abe Lichtman, a Jewish entrepreneur.[14]

The desire to be entertained was always attractive to people who either were celebrating good times or finding relief from bad times. Lichtman owned the Lincoln and Howard Theaters on U Street and was known as a benefactor who financed and supported many African American entrepreneurial endeavors.[15]

As a pioneer, E. B.'s focus was on teaching physical education, promoting amateur athletics, and creating opportunities for recreation and entertainment through sports and sporting events—not for money but for health and recreation. The idea was that professionalism would make the game about the money, and winning at any cost would take the place of sportsmanship and fair play. He felt his role was to promote sports not only for the games' sake but also to develop character and healthy habits and bodies. E. B.'s appointment to the Federal Security Agency to coordinate school, community, city, and federal resources gave him the platform to push for equal facilities for African American youth in Washington, DC:

> Henderson . . . knew that he had to keep pushing for Black athletics to stay up-to-date and competitive. "Let us admit that those who worked for school facilities under a passing dispensation did all they could do under the circumstances," wrote Henderson in 1948. "Tomorrow's schools will require large gymnasia, space for spectators, swimming pools, rooms for apparatus and games, ample locker space, and many acres for athletics for boys and girls." Yet again, Henderson would be correct about the coming trends in sport.[16]

Basketball in Washington after the Twelfth-Streeters: Amateurism's Last Stand

E. B. put amateur athletics for Blacks on a solid footing by establishing athletic leagues that provided opportunities for youth to participate in organized sports, as well as opportunities for entertainment by spectators in Washington to enjoy basketball and other sports. Almost all the sports initiated in Washington were amateur and sanctioned by the Amateur Athletic Union (AAU), the Inter-Scholastic Athletic Association (ISAA), or in the Public Schools Athletic League (PSAL). However, the enthusiasm for athletics generated by those early years of New York City and Washington's intercity athletic competition created the appetite for more sports as entertainment in the early twentieth century. New York took this enthusiasm to another level early on by creating semi-professional and professional basketball teams; these did not develop in Washington, largely due to segregation.[17]

The venues in Washington where basketball could be played were hardly adequate, which led Howard and other Washington teams to schedule their games in the larger arenas in New York. With a much larger population, New York had much larger arenas, a much larger pool of potential players, and was not handcuffed by Jim Crow. The larger cities in the industrial North had no restrictions on race, allowing Blacks and Whites to play with and against each other. This was the kind of competition E. B. had envisioned during his long struggle with Jim Crow in Washington for the day when Black and White athletes could compete against each other equally and on a level playing field.

In Washington, there were few arenas large enough to accommodate crowds, but none of these were available for African Americans to book for their contests. It was an ongoing complaint by New York City teams, who did not want to play in Washington because there wasn't enough money in it for them to make the trip South. In New York, big ballrooms and large armories could accommodate a regulation court and several thousand spectators, allowing for profitable competitions. This difference meant that professional, or "pay-to-play" teams like the New York Rens could develop and thrive in unsegregated Northern cities.[18]

The Central (White) YMCA had a regulation-size basketball court, but Blacks weren't welcomed there. Later, basketball competitions would be held at the Uline Arena, but Michael Uline, the "Ice King," also had a no-Blacks policy for many events in his arena. Basketball for African American teams was relegated to the ballroom of the True Reformers Hall, which did not have enough room for a regulation-size court. (Later, the Twelfth Street YMCA didn't have a regulation-sized basketball court either.) The True Reformers Ballroom on the second floor had support beams within the boundaries of the court that players had to avoid during the game. In the 1920s, the Turner Arena, a huge garage turned into an indoor arena at Fourteenth and W Streets NW, was large enough to accommodate a regulation-size court. However, seating was limited and at best would only accommodate a couple thousand spectators.[19]

The basketball scene in Washington was mainly in the schools, colleges, and club teams at first, but their facilities were still subpar compared to New York City. Armstrong High School was the first Black high school to have a gymnasium with a regulation-size basketball court in the nation, which was helpful for training and made Armstrong one of the strongest high school teams in the country in the early 1900s, but it could only accommodate two thousand spectators, which was hardly adequate.

Early on, there weren't enough high school quints to play against, so Armstrong played a mixture of college teams, like Morgan and Storer Colleges; YMCA teams from Baltimore, Philadelphia, and Pittsburgh; club teams like St. Cyprian AC; and high schools as far north as Wilmington, Delaware, and as far west as Clarksburg, West Virginia.[20]

As the Roaring Twenties rolled along, amateur sports waned, and sports started to take on a new business model: Entertainment value had a dollar sign attached to it. The prevailing ideology could be summed up, "[T]he term 'amateur' meant a trip down memory lane."[21] Professional teams became prevalent with big city teams like Bob Douglas's New York Renaissance and Chicago's Savoy Big Five (the Savoy team later changed its name to the Harlem Globetrotters). These teams became very successful starting in the 1920s and lasting through the Depression, with the Rens disbanding in the late 1940s and the Globetrotters continuing to this day. However, their business model and style of play was markedly different. The Harlem Globetrotters were very talented, entertaining their audiences through comedic acts, or, in other words, clowning on the court. By contrast, the New York Rens didn't take to clowning on the court. They were serious-minded professionals:

> Back in Harlem, Bob Douglas wasn't having none of that. He vehemently opposed clowning—not for money, not for acceptance, nor any other reason. The Renaissance Big Five entertained through their talent, knowledge, and teamwork; the recipe for wins. He believe that their fans "wanted to watch a game of skill and not an exhibit that belonged in a circus sideshow," according to *Amsterdam News* sports columnist Dan Burley. Bob selected his players "strictly on basketball merit," Burley would explain. "They must have height, speed, nerve and the ability to shoot."[22]

There was an effort in the mid 1920s to reignite the glory days of the amateur league. The basketball scene in Washington, DC, transitioned from the Washington Twelfth-Streeters, to the Howard University Big Five, to Armstrong High School, and then to a group of semiprofessional teams during the 1920s. The three dominant Black teams in Washington were the Carlisle Big Five, managed by Ewell Conway; the Alcoes, managed by Henry Hill and later by William Carter; and the Community Yellow Jackets, a former YMCA team that won the city's Black title in 1927, managed by Sam Lacy.[23]

One of their White counterparts in Washington was the Palace Laundry Big Five (sometimes known only as the Palace Big Five, or the Laundrymen). Owned by George Preston Marshall, best known as the owner of the Washington Redskins, the team was sponsored by Palace Laundry, a chain of laundries in Washington. They played at the Arcade at the corner of Fourteenth and Irving Streets NW, whose arena could seat a maximum of four thousand. The Palace Laundry team was a member of the American Basketball League (ABL), which, like all the pro and semipro leagues at this time, prohibited Black teams from joining.[24]

In 1927, there was a last-ditch effort to create a Black amateur league. The Eastern League of Associated Basketball Clubs included several amateur teams from the East Coast and Mid-Atlantic states: (1)

the Vandals of Atlantic City, New Jersey; (2) the Buccaneers of Newark, New Jersey; (3) the Capitol Club of Asbury Park, New Jersey; (4) the Vanguard Postal of Brooklyn, New York; (5) the Monumental Elks of Baltimore, Maryland; (6) the Athenians of Baltimore, Maryland; (7) the Carlisle Field Club of Washington, DC (who replaced the Alcoes of Washington); and (8) Harlem's St. Christopher Red and Black Machine:

> Led by commissioner Andrew F. Jackson, the men behind the Eastern League vowed to restore sobriety to a game they believed had grown drunken and lawless through four seasons of professionalism. . . . The enthusiasm peaked a few weeks later when the Eastern League reached a tentative agreement with a new amateur association in the Midwest, led by the beloved long-jump champion DeHart Hubbard, to play a postseason world series of Black amateur basketball. It was rumored the leagues would merge into the first national Black amateur basketball association, a network that would overshadow the disorganized professional game.[25]

The Eastern League suffered from a number of setbacks that showed it was loosely organized and, in some respects, loosely structured. A week into the Eastern League's existence, the Baltimore Monumental Elks dropped out and were replaced by the Tuxedo Tigers of Orange, New Jersey. Originally the Eastern League announced the Washington team was the Alco Big Fives, but within a week, the shifty Ewell Conway, known for being a "win at any cost" hustler, convinced the Eastern League to make the exchange in favor of his Carlisle Big Five. Actually, the Carlisle Big Five was a semipro team because Conway paid his players. Also, Conway was known for raiding players from other teams for his roster, known as "wildcatting." These tactics were not in compliance with amateurism or the rules of the Eastern League. Conway was the epitome of what amateurism was up against and feared most. Because of his problems playing in segregated Washington and its limiting factors, he saw the Eastern League as a way out of his predicament:

> For Conway, it was the same old problems—no generous owner to pay the bills, subpar facilities for first-rate promotions, meager local competition, skimpy season schedule, and fickle, footloose players.

> The Eastern League seemed to offer Conway a way out of his predicament. The League format, in theory, imposed structure—a full schedule, a championship race, a shared set of rules—and offered the status of belonging to an up-and-coming association. There was also the chance to compete in Harlem and, if all went well, boost his club's reputation on U Street as the slayer of New York's finest amateur teams.[26]

At the commencement of the season, the Carlisle Big Five lost two of its best players, center Slim Henderson and forward Eddie Davis, who had enrolled in college at Virginia Seminary Institute. The Eastern League had instituted a rule, resolution 13, that required all teams to submit a full and final roster by the start of their second game to eliminate wildcatting. Conway decided not to comply and neglected to submit a final roster. Without Henderson and Davis, the contest on December 23 in Harlem against St. Christopher showed how weak the Carlisle Big Five were without their two star players; they lost the contest in a 46–24 rout.[27]

The next games took place during the college winter break. Conway insisted that, although Henderson and Davis played for their college team, they "both still maintained active membership at the Carlisle Big Five."[28] The Vandals of Atlantic City protested both players being allowed to play in the contest. Commissioner Jackson allowed the two players to compete, leading to an embarrassing 42–20, one-sided victory for the home team.[29]

The commissioner's decision to allow Henderson and Davis to play caused an immediate controversy and damaged his integrity and the credibility of the Eastern League. In late January, in an effort to stop the bleeding and to do some damage control, the Eastern League made the Carlisle team forfeit their two previous games and cancelled their game against the Vanguard Postal of Brooklyn just before tip-off. Conway retaliated by attempting to sabotage the league, refusing to play the Vandals in a rematch. But the damage was done, and the writing was on the wall. The Carlisle Field Club withdrew from the league in protest.[30]

> The Eastern League was broken. The appetite for amateur basketball died on the vine. There was an attempt to hold a championship showcasing the winners of the Eastern League, St. Christopher's Red

> and Black Machine, against DeHart Hubbard's Midwestern League Champions, the Cincinnati Comets.[31] However, "for reasons lost in time, the big, face-saving game never happened. Scheduled for March 28th, it appears to have been canceled at the last minute. Likewise, newspapers provide no details about the final moments of the Eastern League. Just as suddenly as it had appeared on the scene the previous Thanksgiving, the league vanished like a cat in the night."[32]

Professional Basketball in Washington: The Washington Bears

The amateur game had become relegated to a training ground for the professional game. One of the problems with the Eastern League was the lack of talented players available to form teams that would attract the crowds to make the league profitable. The professional and semiprofessional game had usurped most, if not all, of the best players. The business model for all the major sports had moved to a professional pay-for-play model. Teams like the New York Renaissance and the Harlem Globetrotters were now the reality in the sport.

In 1941, thirty-plus years after the Washington Twelfth-Streeters' undefeated season that brought the first basketball championship to the nation's capital, another team would come along to claim championship honors in Washington, DC. Professional teams had taken the place of playing simply for the love of the game. As an educator, E. B.'s focus was solidly on scholastic athletics and the development of youth and talent to play at colleges and in the amateur ranks. But the game developed into a business model that compensated the talent on the floor, and rightfully so.[33]

The best team in professional basketball, Black or White, was undoubtedly the New York Renaissance. The Rens were founded in 1923 by the basketball entrepreneur Robert "Bob" Douglas, sometimes referred to as "Smiling" Bob Douglas because of his mild demeanor. But don't let the smile fool you: He was as shrewd a businessman as there came. His team took their name from the Renaissance Casino and Ballroom on 7th Avenue between 137th and 138th Streets in Harlem. Douglas struck a deal to use their ballroom as their home court.

There were several White professional leagues, most of which only lasted a few years until the late 1930s, and none allowed Black teams to join their leagues, so the Black teams played each other on a barnstorming basis. The maximum capacity of the Renaissance Ballroom was about 1,500 spectators, but Douglas, the savvy owner-manager of the team, realized that he could play more games and make more money traveling the country and playing teams with larger arenas. He purchased an REO Speed Wagon bus, affectionately known as the Blue Goose, and exchanged the luxury of Harlem and city life to lead a barnstorming team that traveled the country.

Starting in the late 1930s, gasoline rationing due to the war in Europe began to inhibit traveling on the Blue Goose, making it difficult for Douglas's team to continue barnstorming. On some occasions, the team bus might have to travel four hundred miles to the next game. But as it became more and more difficult to travel, the team's revenue dwindled. Players were not happy, and their usual salaries were in jeopardy. Many started looking elsewhere for opportunities.[34]

The Washington Bruins (Bears)

One of the places they looked was Washington, where sportswriter Sam Lacy had put together a new Black professional team for the 1940–1941 season. "I got the idea because there was nothing for Blacks to do in the winter, particularly on Sundays," he recalled. With the help of two friends, Harold (Hal) Jackson and Art Carter, the Washington Bruins (Bears) were born.[35]

Not long after the idea was hatched, Lacy was called away to Chicago to push and lobby for a Black player in Major League Baseball. (He ultimately was one of the reporters to break the Jackie Robinson story.) In his place, Ewell Conway, the former manager of the Carlisle Big Five, came onboard. Conway, who was a shrewd character, approached Abe Lichtman, who owned the Howard and Lincoln Theaters in the U Street corridor, to sponsor the new team. Lichtman was reluctant at first, feeling he might be hustled again by Conway, but he warmed to the idea, and the team came to be the Washington Lichtman Bears.[36] Most of the Rens jumped ship and swam ashore in Washington. "The Bears were reminiscent of the 1935–1939 Renaissance teams," noted the *Washington Afro-American* of the team that would play until the end of the war in 1945. "As a matter of actuality, there were times when the entire playing five was composed of former Rens."[37]

The team booked the Turner Arena on Fourteenth and W Streets NW in Washington's U Street corridor. The arena was little more than a converted garage that would seat just about two thousand spectators, but the Bears' playing helped to bring the U Street area back to life during in the early 1940s. Broadcaster Hal Jackson became the general manager of the Washington Bears.[38] He was the radio announcer for Howard University Athletics and the Homestead Grays, the team started by early basketball great Cumberland Posey in 1912. Beginning in 1940, the Homestead Grays played half their games in Washington at Griffith Stadium, next to Howard University on Georgia Avenue.[39]

In 1943, the Washington Bears completed an undefeated season, compiling a record of 41–0. The team would go on to win the 1943 World Professional Basketball Championship, defeating the Oshkosh All-Stars, 43–31. The championship was an invitational tournament that began in 1939 for professional teams sponsored by the *Chicago Herald American* newspaper, pitting independent squads against teams from the National Basketball League (NBL), one of the precursors to the National Basketball Association (NBA) of today.[40]

Bringing another basketball championship to Washington made E. B. very proud:

> Applauding the Bears' championship was Ed Henderson. Now in his late fifties—more than thirty years removed from the undefeated 12th Street YMCA team, Henderson was lucky enough to have watched his dream of organized Black athletics come true and mature. Black schools and sports clubs had produced world-class athletes in every major sport and helped to challenge false racial stereotypes.[41]

End of an Era

For a quarter-century, the New York Rens were unquestionably the winningest team in professional basketball. After World War II, when gasoline was no longer being rationed, the Rens were able to reconstitute their players and get back to barnstorming around the country in the Blue Goose. The Washington Lichtman Bears began to decline and eventually folded.

On December 19, 1948, the Rens were "invited" to join the previously all-White National Basketball League (NBL), replacing the Detroit Vagabond Kings and becoming the first all-Black basketball team to play in a White professional league. The NBL was desperate, losing the Minneapolis, Indianapolis, Fort Wayne, and Rochester franchises to the opposing league, the Basketball Association of America (BAA), just prior to the 1948–1949 season. The NBL was in deep trouble. According to Susan Rayl, the foremost scholar on the New York Rens,

> Bob Douglas and the New York Rens were dealt a losing hand. The bankrupt Detroit franchise, the Detroit Vagabond Kings, was the team that Bob and the Rens were dealt. The league chose the city of Dayton for the Rens as home court. Another handicap was having to accept the losing record (2–17) of the Detroit Vagabond Kings, which they had to carry since they came in after the start of the season. With forty games left in their season, they would have had to win almost all forty games to be considered for the playoffs. All of these factors put them in a precarious situation.[42]

Although the Rens had previously drawn big crowds playing in Dayton as a barnstorming team, they found little support from the fans as the local professional team playing at the Dayton Coliseum:

> As a barnstorming team, race was a favorable factor for their success. White fans would come out to see the Rens play against their local all-White team, cheering for their local team to beat the all-Black Rens. But, under their new arrangement, the Rens gathered little support and paltry attendance. The last games of the season were all played on the road in opposing arenas. At times they were used as a draw in double headers, which attracted more fans on opposing courts than they would at their own home court.[43]

To make matters worse, Bob Douglas split his team: half continued barnstorming around the country, while the other half suited up on the court in Dayton. Splitting the team proved to be too much. Douglas was sending many of his best players to play with the more profitable barnstorming team to boost revenue instead of putting the best team on the court of the lingering Dayton NBL team. The Dayton Rens ended the season with a 16–43 record, in last place.[44]

At the end of the season, both the NBL and the Basketball Association of America merged to form the NBA. Both leagues met in separate rooms at the Morrison Hotel in Chicago on July 1, 1949. The BAA was in the driver's seat, being the larger and more profitable league. All the professional teams in both leagues were invited to start the discussions, but of the twenty-one-team circuit, not everyone would make the cut.[45]

It was abundantly clear that the powers that be were in favor of eliminating the Rens. Although the Dayton Rens were unprofitable, every team in both leagues operated at a loss during the 1948–1949 season. Through the month-long negotiations and backroom dealing at the meetings, the final decision was made to cut the Rens.

The New York Renaissance had been a successful sports franchise. They compiled a record of 2,588 wins and 529 losses, averaging 130 games per season.[46] When they came to town, people spent money. They were a revenue generator—not just for themselves but also for the businesses, restaurants, hotels, clubs, and on and on. All the cities and towns that grew up during the Great Migration fed on the revenue-generating sports franchises that came through their towns. But the team had ultimately come to an end.

19

Articles, Letters, and *The Negro in Sports*

Letters and Articles

IT WAS EVIDENT AT AN EARLY AGE THAT E. B. WOULD HAVE A PROCLIVITY toward intellectual pursuits; however, his endeavors were magnified by his energy, persistence, and passion for order and structure in his athletics, social justice, and literature. He was always writing something, whether it was letters, articles, or publications of some sort; he left a truly amazing prolific body of work. His sixth-grade principal, Ms. Julia C. Grant, exposed the horrid conditions at the dilapidated Bowen School to an investigative reporter. The school was closed, leading to the total reconstruction of the physical plant.[1] Although he didn't stay there for long, she left an impression on him, and this may have been where he first learned the power of the pen.

He started his writing by reporting sporting events, and later, he wrote letters to the editor, much like Ms. Grant. He wrote about the crucial issues around him, usually discrimination and denial of basic human rights, sporting events, healthy living, and the dignity and beauty of African Americans and their contributions to society. E. B.'s first writings of note started before he entered M Street High School:

> Perhaps the beginning of my hobby of writing letters to the editor began before I reached high school. After a ball game between my team and an opponent I wrote the results of the game and walked a couple miles to the office of the *Washington Star* newspaper to have it

> published for which I was paid a penny a line. It appeared on the then single sports page. This began my thousands of letters to the editors which I write down until today.[2]

E. B. continued to write for the *Washington Star* from then on. He and a colleague, Curly Byrd, later the president of the University of Maryland, contributed most of the articles to the one-page sports section in those days. Later, he recalled,

> When I refereed a football game or came from a meet, I would usually write it up and send it to the *Star*. These were the days when there was very little in the sports columns of the papers. I also used to select, after the fashion of Walter Camp, an All-American Football Team among the Negroes. This was accepted as our All-American team, and this was published also in both newspapers and in my book.[3]

J. Waldo Fawcett, the associate editor at the *Washington Star*, said in 1954 that E. B. had contributed more letters to the editor of Washington newspapers than any other citizen that he was aware of. During E. B.'s lifetime, he easily had more than four thousand letters to the editor published in newspapers all over the country. He donated a collection of more than one thousand to the archives at the Moorland-Spingarn Research Center at Howard University.[4]

After he retired and moved to live with his son Jimmy in Tuskegee, Alabama, he continued to write letters to the *Washington Post*, the *Birmingham News*, and the *Tuskegee News*. Good habits are hard to break. Through his writing, he created a platform, and people looked forward to his opinions, his insight into the events of the day, and his take on the news. After seeing a letter he had written in the *Washington Post* after he moved to Alabama, one admirer said,

> It was a great pleasure to find you popping up in the pages of the *Washington Post* today. I have missed you. For many years, the letters-to-the-editor signed by E. B. Henderson were among my favorite breakfast table reading.

> Since newspapers do little to nothing to help readers identify the writers of these letters, it came as a surprise to me to discover, finally that you were professionally identified with athletics. It is true that your letters were often on this subject, but they also covered other areas; for quite a while I probably assumed that you were a professor of literature or history or perhaps an exceptionally articulate lawyer, who just happened to be a knowledgeable athletic buff on the side.
>
> I hope I am not insulting an entire community of people when I say that it is extremely rare to encounter any athlete, coach, or athletic director who is not only distinguished by a wide background in the liberal arts but who also handles the English language with clarity, and distinction.
>
> If you ever write letters-to-the-editor nowadays, I wish you would write them to the *Washington Post* so that I can read them. It would be like old home week.
>
> With very best wishes,
>
> Marion Holland[5]

As a correspondent for the National Negro Press Association (NNPA), E. B. contributed articles and letters to the *Washington Star*, the *Washington Post*, the *Washington Times-Herald*, the *Washington Daily News*, the *Washington Tribune*, the *Baltimore Sun*, the *Richmond Times Dispatch*, the *Norfolk Journal and Guide*, the *Washington Afro-American*, the *Baltimore Afro-American*, the *Pittsburgh Courier*, the *Atlanta Daily World*, the *Birmingham World*, the *Florida Sentinel*, the *Ohio State News*, the *Call and Post of Washington, DC*, the *Cleveland Call and Post*, the *Detroit Tribune*, the *Savannah Herald*, the *St. Paul Recorder*, the *Chicago Defender*, and others.[6]

E. B. also mentioned,

> Another man I admired very much was A. Philip Randolph, who is a vice president of the CIO-AFL. He and a friend of his, Chandler Owens, organized and published a magazine called the *Messenger* way back there in the early days when they were fighting the war for labor.

> They paid me—a lot of money then—ten dollars a month to write the athletic story in their magazine.[7]

The *Messenger* started out as a very radical magazine with rather far-left leanings but became a cultural iconic magazine later in the 1920s. They were controversial because they advocated for antilynching, Black labor unionism, and ending Jim Crow segregation. They claimed, "Our aim is to appeal to reason, to lift our pens above the cringing demagogy of the times, and above the cheap peanut politics of the old reactionary Negro leaders."[8] After February 1920, it identified itself as a "Journal of Scientific Radicalism." And in June 1923, it billed itself as the "World's Greatest Negro Monthly," featuring many of the rising Black writers of the Harlem Renaissance.[9] Among them were Langston Hughes, Zora Neal Hurston, Claude McKay, and Arna Bontemps. E. B. was in good company with these contributors, contributing a monthly column on sports, recreation, and healthy living from 1925 to 1928.[10]

The Negro in Sports

By far, E. B.'s greatest writing achievement was *The Negro in Sports* in 1939, revised in 1949. The 1939 publication came out shortly after Joe Louis won the Heavyweight Boxing Championship in 1937. The 1949 publication came out following Jackie Robinson smashing the color barrier in Major League Baseball in 1947. Of the many books written before *The Negro in Sports*, such as Menke's *Encyclopedia of Sports*, John Krout's *Annals of American Sports*, Jennie Holliman's *American Sports*, and Herbert Manchester's *Four Centuries of Sports in America*, none dealt with African American participation in athletics.[11] *The Negro in Sports* was the first book to chronicle the feats, obstacles, and accomplishments of Black athletes. According to Leon Coursey,

> *The Negro in Sports* provides a historical account of Black participation in interscholastic, intercollegiate, and national athletics. This book also provides a historical account of the efforts to organize interscholastic, intercollegiate, and officiating groups. This book reveals many of the

hardships that Black athletes were forced to contend with during their endeavor to participate in athletics.[12]

In 1988, Arthur Ashe published his book on the history of African Americans in athletics, *A Hard Road to Glory*. Ashe was interviewed on the *Today Show* by Bryant Gumbel, who asked, "Why did you choose this topic? I mean it's certainly not one that hasn't been done before."[13] Ashe responded, "That's a good question. The reason is that it has never been done in detail, or very comprehensively. There were two attempts made, one by Dr. Edwin Henderson, who was the first Black publicly appointed official who ran the physical education department for the public schools in the Washington, DC. The Colored public schools."[14] On its face, *The Negro in Sports*, is the primary source from which later authors, like Bob Kuska, Claude Johnson, and Arthur Ashe, gathered much of the

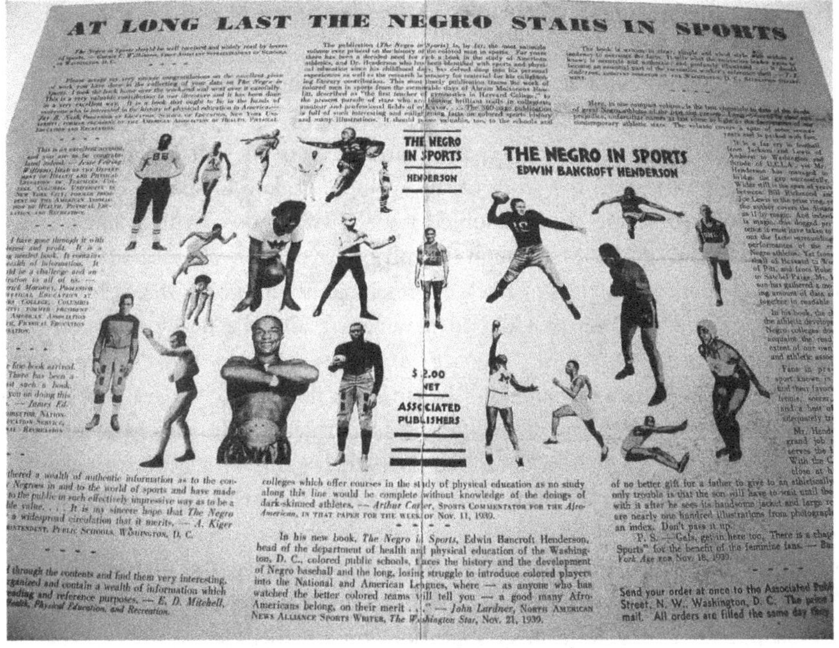

Dust jacket for *The Negro in Sports*, 1939–1949.
COURTESY OF HENDERSON FAMILY COLLECTION

information for their books about the early days of African American participation in athletics.

There weren't many major publishing companies in the late 1800s or early 1900s that African Americans could interest in publishing books, so the "Father of Black History," Dr. Carter G. Woodson, founder of Negro History Week, started Associated Publishers. His Association for the Study of Negro Life and History, an organization to preserve Black history, and Associated Publishers published *The Negro in Sports*. In 1937, at the behest of Dr. Woodson, E. B. wrote the definitive book on African American participation in sports. Woodson had worked in the DC Colored schools during his storied career and was aware of E. B. professionally, as well as his written endeavors. From E. B.'s contributions to the Spalding handbooks, a great amount of work had already been done in creating a book. He spent many hours in the Library of Congress doing research on what he didn't know:

> Since the beginning of my career, I had kept note of performances of our boys in the college arena of sports from the day when only a handful of Colored athletes could be found in all the major colleges about the nation.
>
> Then one day in 1937, Dr. Carter Woodson sent for me and asked me to write the story of the Colored athlete in sports. At first I demurred saying that I doubted my ability at book writing, but he promised to guide me through the intricacies of the work.
>
> I spent many days at the Congressional library going through the few bound volumes of Colored newspapers and the heavy tomes of daily papers.
>
> With masses of material, I began, with the help of Carter Woodson, to write. We had many arguments as to style. He wanted to use only precise English in describing a football game or a boxing event. I insisted this would prove dull reading to those who loved or knew sports.
>
> Eventually, after a lot of proofing and rewriting, the first edition came off the press in 1939. Several thousand copies were sold. In fact, it was the best seller of his publications for a while.[15]

The first run of ten thousand quickly sold out, and a second printing was necessary to meet the demand. *The Negro in Sports* was filled with pictures, bios of the athletes, their official records, and statistics. It was hugely popular because African Americans held their sports heroes in highest esteem and looked up to them for their victory in America's popular pastime, which lifted the spirits of African Americans living under oppressive Jim Crow segregation. The second printing also sold out, so in ten years, a 1949 edition was a welcome idea.

The 1949 *The Negro in Sports* was a much larger book at 500 pages, compared to the 1939 edition's 370. It included all that was in the first edition and updated with all the eventful sports breakthroughs that took place in the 1940s—which was quite significant, particularly with Jackie Robinson breaking the color barrier in Major League Baseball and the reintegration of African Americans in the National Football League.

Following the publication of *The Negro in Sports*, accolades came in from newspaper editors, historians, sportswriters, former students, colleagues, and others who knew E. B., worked with him, or knew of him through his previous writings. Such was the case with Dr. Charles Drew, whom E. B. coached in basketball at Dunbar High School when he won the city championship in 1922. Dr. Drew received a sports scholarship to the University of Massachusetts, Amherst, where he was a four-letter man. After finishing at Amherst, he spent several years at Morgan State, where he revamped their athletic program. But fortunately for us all, he went to medical school at McGill University in Montreal, Canada, and Columbia University, where he would perfect the science that created the first blood bank.

Charles Drew wrote to E. B. on the occasion of the 1939 release of *The Negro in Sports*:

> Dear Mr. Henderson
>
> Through great want of time, I've put off too long congratulating you on the splendid book you got out on Negro athletes. It's a grand job: I want to thank you for autographing a copy of your book that Francis Gregory and my sister sent me for a Christmas present, and express my

appreciation for your generosity in the amount of space you allotted to me.

I doubt if anyone has really told you how big a part you have played in the lives of a lot of the men you wrote about in your book, not so much by the things you've said, or by the things you have done or by the lessons in physical education, but rather by virtue of the things you have stood for and the way you have lived throughout all those years. The big thing that in those days of fallen idols of all types, it is particularly refreshing to know of a few people who we thought were just about tops when we were kids, when looked at in the sober light of more mature years, to find that they still are tops, that they have been consistently through the years, standing for things which they have said other folks should be, that they have tried to do the things which they have said should be attempted, I personally feel a great debt of gratitude to you. Some few always have to set the pace and give the others courage to go on into places which have not been explored. We have so few things to be proud of, that the presentation of so much that is good in one book is sure to have results far beyond your farthest dreams. You have set the pace continually, and we who have had the privilege of coming under your influence cannot but feel just a bit "chesty" when we say, "Mr. Henderson, sure I knew him, he taught me in high school and you bet he's O.K."[16]

Drew went on to say that his work for his PhD in medicine at Columbia was done. Next, he was headed to Howard University Medical School to teach the next generation of Black doctors. In sports metaphor, he spoke about changing the trajectory of Black medicine at Howard by creating intellectual activity and advancing medicine. And he ended, "It should be great sport. If at the end of 25 years I can look back over my steps and feel that I have kept the faith in my sphere of activity in a manner comparable to that in which you have carried on in yours I shall be very happy."[17]

Omega Psi Phi Fraternity

Another organization that offered congratulations on the publication of *The Negro in Sports* was the Omega Psi Phi fraternity. E. B. was a proud member of Omega Psi Phi, and in 1940, he was chosen as Omega Psi Phi's Man of the Year, after the publication of *The Negro in Sports.*

The Omega Psi Phi fraternity is one of the Black Greek fraternities and sororities known as the Divine Nine. The fraternity was established on November 17, 1911, when three undergraduate students (Edgar Amos Love, Oscar James Cooper, and Frank Coleman) and a young Howard University biology professor (Dr. Ernest Just) fellowshipped through the night. The three men and their professor developed the principles around which the fraternity is centered—manhood, scholarship, perseverance, and uplift—and their motto: "Friendship is essential to the soul."[18]

In the spring of 1922, the first graduate chapter of Omega Psi Phi (Alpha Omega chapter) was initiated at Howard University to include many who were beyond the age and experience of the undergraduate. E. B. was interested. Some of these men were returning from World War I, while others were in their professional experience beyond their college years. Several of E. B.'s friends and colleagues were already members of the fraternity, and being an organizational man, he felt the need to be a part of a dynamic group whose principles he built his life around, i.e., *Manhood, Scholarship, Perseverance, and Uplift.* Those who initiated the Alpha Omega chapter of Omega Psi Phi were Cato Adams (E. B.'s best friend), George Brice, Walter Burke, Gordon Houston, Campbell Johnson, Charles Johnson, Charles Marshall Sr., and Garnet Wilkinson.[19]

The official charter was prepared by a father and son team of Omegas: Charles Herbert Marshall Sr., who pledged to join the fraternity under his son, Charles Herbert Marshall Jr. The first group of pledges were Prince Potentilla Barker, William Tecumseh Bradshaw, Roscoe Conklin Brown, Eugene Augustine Clark, John Wesley Cromwell Jr., Colonel West Alexander Hamilton, Edwin Bancroft Henderson, Robert Nathaniel Mattingly, Clyde Cantey McDuffie, Arthur C. Newman, Samuel Wilson Rutherford, Alfred Kyger Savoy, and Walter Smith.[20]

Several of these men were E. B.'s friends and professional colleagues in the public schools, like Adams, Mattingly, McDuffie, Savoy, and Wilkerson. Others worked in government and other professions. There is a literal Who's Who of the many noteworthy members of the Alpha Omega chapter of Omega Psi Phi, many of whom E. B. probably knew, including

- Dr. Ernest Just, biologist, founder
- Clifford Alexander, secretary of the Army;
- Sterling Brown, writer and poet;
- Dr. Montague Cobb, pioneer in physical anatomy, author of *Race and Running*;
- Ambassador Mercer Cook;
- Dr. Charles Drew, inventor of blood plasma, dean of Howard University Medical School;
- Frederick Drew Gregory, astronaut, NASA administrator, Charles Drew's nephew;
- Judge William Hastie;
- Walter Hill, James Nabrit, and Spottswood Robinson, civil rights attorneys for *Brown v. Board of Education*;
- Dr. Benjamin Mays, dean of Howard School of Divinity, mentor to Dr. Martin Luther King Jr.;
- Robert Weaver, first Black US presidential cabinet member, NAACP president; and
- Dr. Carter G. Woodson.

The fraternity's expression of their appreciation for E. B.'s crowning literary achievement, *The Negro in Sports*, meant a lot to him.

The Pigskin Club

Another organization that showered E. B. with praise after the release of *The Negro in Sports* was the Pigskin Club. The Pigskin Club was established by Dr. Charles B. Fisher in 1938 to bring together those who had played sports and understood the benefits of wholesome athletic competition and to honor those involved in football:

Purpose

> [T]hat there be an ever improving relationship between persons interested in the game of football, that there may be given encouragement for good clean sports; that there may be a more perfect understanding among such persons; and that there may be mutual benefit and pleasure derived from such association.

Eligibility for membership

> Satisfactory evidence of having won a letter in college football competition; satisfactory evidence of having made some outstanding contribution to the sport of football.[21]

E. B. helped to organize the Pigskin Club and was proud to be a charter member. To him, the Pigskin Club was a fraternity of sportsmen in the Washington area, and they held a position of very high prestige in Washington circles. Invitations were traditionally sent to all the Heisman Trophy winners. Many of the African American Heisman Trophy winners paid homage to the organization. They held an annual banquet to honor the best players, coaches, and teams of all sports, not just football, in the Washington, DC, metropolitan area. Jim Brown, Ernie Davis, Eddie George, and others graced the dais of the banquet, which E. B. always looked forward to attending. In the 1940 program, he is noted as the "Father of Inter-Scholastic Athletics," probably a more proper title and a greater honor than father or grandfather of Black basketball.

The Black Athlete

Dr. Woodson passed away in 1950, and Dr. Charles Wesley, the past president of Central State College (now University) in Ohio, would take the helm and continue to uphold the Association for the Study of Negro Life and History. Years later, Dr. Wesley's crowning achievement was an encyclopedia set on every aspect of African American life and history. One volume was on Blacks in athletics, so naturally, he approached E. B.

on revising a third edition of *The Negro in Sports*, to be entitled *The Black Athlete*.

However, E. B. was concerned about committing to writing *The Black Athlete* for two reasons: (1) At E. B.'s age, approaching eighty-six years old, he wasn't sure he had the energy to write another book, and (2) "[T]he growth of Black athletes' participation in athletics today is so extensive that it would necessitate an encyclopedia to deal effectively with such a revision."[22] Addressing E. B.'s concerns, Dr. Wesley was able to secure the assistance from the editors of *Sport Magazine* to obtain pictures, official records, and statistics to supplement what E. B. had already written in *The Negro in Sports*. So in his mideighties, E. B. collaborated with the editors of *Sport Magazine*, and in 1969, *The Black Athlete* came off the press and was added to a fifteen-volume encyclopedia set, *The International Library of Negro Life and History*, published by the Association for the Study of African American Life and History (ASALH).

> In 1976, one year before EB passed, the North American Society for Sports History recognized him for his contributions and honored him by making him an honorary president of their organization. His legacy as an author is a major part of his contribution to society and American sports culture. Not only did he lay the groundwork and build the infrastructure for African Americans to participate in athletics, but he also chronicled the participation and progression of African Americans in sports in the early to middle twentieth century. He once prophesied, "If I am remembered for very long after I am gone it will be because I wrote *The Negro in Sports*."[23]

20

Highland Beach, Maryland

E. B. ALWAYS SAID HIS HAPPIEST TIMES WERE WHEN HE WAS AT HIGHland Beach. His love of nature and water lured and invited him to its shores in the Southern Neck, near Annapolis, Maryland. He loved to swim and fish from his earliest days, so he naturally loved the water there. He also enjoying being in the company of African Americans of Washington's elite society, the Black bourgeoisie, which he aspired to become part of one day. From his time at M Street High School, E. B. cultivated friendship with members who clambered to the shores of the Chesapeake Bay, where he would walk long distances for exercise with his friends Milton Francis and Haley Douglass at Highland Beach, the oldest Black resort beach community in the nation, where Black people could buy property and form their own community during Jim Crow segregation. Nell and her family were part of this elite group, as well, so it is easy to see why Highland Beach held a special place in E. B.'s heart, mind, and soul.

Highland Beach has a storied history. In 1892, Major Charles Douglass, son of the famous abolitionist Frederick Douglass, and his family went to Annapolis, Maryland, hoping to spend some time on the shores of the Chesapeake Bay at the Bay Ridge Resort and Amusement Park, just south of Annapolis. Douglass and his family were turned away on account of their race, but upon leaving, they walked across a small railroad bridge. The area just south of the Whites-only resort had a long stretch of beachfront, which Laura Douglass fell in love with. Also with them was their son Haley, who remembered the event in a 1932 court deposition:

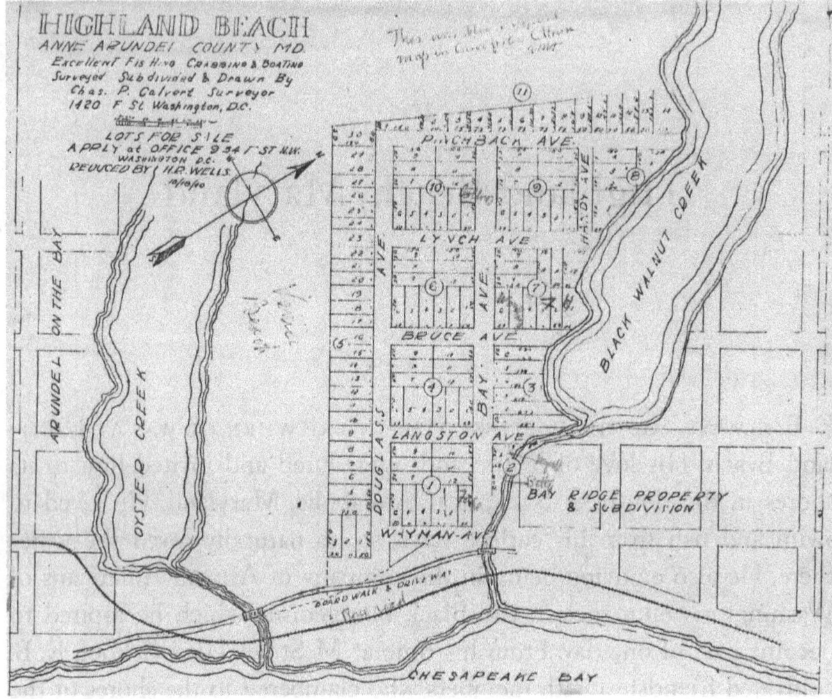

Map of Highland Beach, Annapolis, Maryland, circa 1900.
FROM THE SURVEY OF THE PROPERTY AROUND 1900

> In 1892, Charles R. Douglass and his wife and myself came to Bay Ridge, it was a summer resort adjoining (the future) Highland Beach property. My mother, Laura Douglass, liked the place so well that she tried to find a place where she could board for a few weeks, and so she walked around the beach to the South of Bay Ridge, and was directed by a bus driver to the house of Mrs. [Sarah Anne Brashears] Lane, and it was through Mrs. Lane that she learned of the other thirds of the property belonging to the persons referred to as heirs. My father then made inquiry and learned that the property could be bought, and through an attorney in Annapolis negotiated for the sale of the property.[1]

The Brashears and their heirs owned 48 acres, purchased by William and Charity Brashears from the 366-acre Duvall Plantation in 1858, before slavery was abolished. Their land was bordered on three sides by bodies of water: the Chesapeake Bay to the east and two estuaries, Black Walnut Creek and Oyster Creek, to the north and south, respectively. To the west was a high plateau, or "highland," for which the community garnered its name.[2]

Two Brashears heirs, Daniel Brashears and Georgiana Lane, were interested in selling their portion of the former plantation to Douglass (two-thirds of the forty acres, or twenty-six and two-thirds acres). With the financial assistance of his famous father, Charles was able to purchase the land for $1,000, which was considered overpriced at that time. Charles was an employee of the Pension Office and a federal civil servant, so to avoid any possible problems, conflicts of interest, or impropriety, he placed the deed in the name of his son, Joseph.

Charles had been struck with the bold idea of developing the land into a community where many of his African American friends in Washington could purchase property to get away from the summer heat and hustle of the city and come to an idyllic spot along the Chesapeake Bay. Because they wouldn't be welcomed to such resorts as the Bay Ridge and others owned by Whites, African Americans could own their own place at Highland Beach to rest and frolic in the water during those hot summer days in the city.

Surely this was a risky proposition to purchase the land, and promoting the idea would take much time and energy from Charles. But he quickly went about surveying the land; subdividing into 6 streets, 11 blocks, and 129 lots; and registering it at the Anne Arundel County Courthouse.[3] And thus, Highland Beach was founded in 1893:

> Charles Douglass explains in a letter to his father on May 15, 1893, that he chose the name Highland Beach because "the land at that point is higher than either side of me on the beach." With the exception of Bay Avenue, Douglass drew upon the surnames of famous African American personages of that era to name the streets. Douglass Avenue was named for his famous father Frederick Douglass; Langston Avenue for John Mercer Langston, U.S. congressman from Virginia, founder of the Howard University School of Law, and minister to Haiti; Bruce Avenue for Blanche K. Bruce, U.S. senator from Mississippi; Lynch

The Hendersons' summer cottage, "Loafing Holt," at Highland Beach, Annapolis, Maryland.
COURTESY OF HENDERSON FAMILY COLLECTION

> Avenue for John R. Lynch, U.S. congressman from Mississippi; Pinchback Avenue for Pinckney Benton Stewart (PBS) Pinchback, governor (acting) of Louisiana; and Wayman Avenue for Rev. Alexander Walker Wayman, the influential bishop of the African Methodist Episcopal (AME) Church in Baltimore, and the eulogizer at the funeral of Frederick Douglass.[4]

Milton Francis's father, Dr. John R. Francis, was a doctor in Washington, DC, who owned a private hospital on the edge of Georgetown along Pennsylvania Avenue. Frederick Douglass asked to trade lots with him because he owned the lot next to Black Walnut Creek, and he was afraid that his grandchildren might fall in and drown. So, they traded lots along Highland Beach's Chesapeake Bay waterfront.[5]

> In the beginning, other than the Douglasses, the Terrells (Mary Church Terrell and her husband, Judge Robert H. Terrell), and Dr. John R. Francis, who built their homes early on, most purchasers of lots would engage in summer encampments until they eventually built their summer cottages at Highland Beach. One early cottage was

> built by George Bowen, who had been born into slavery and became a successful restauranteur and caterer in Baltimore. He and his wife, Edna, entertained such guests as Emmitt J. Scott and poet Robert Fearing: "The large cottage became a vacation site for many of the most prominent African Americans of the day. Its impressive list included the likes of Congressman P. B. S Pinchback, Congressman George T. White, poet Paul Lawrence Dunbar, author Charles Waddell Chestnutt, and educator Booker T. Washington, to name a few."[6]

Because of E. B.'s love for the water and nature, he purchased a lot on Bruce Avenue on the shores of Black Walnut Lake in 1907. Shortly thereafter, he became involved with this select group of DC's African American community. After he married Nell, they did little improvements, clearing the land and readying his lot along the lake, but he did not begin building his home until after finishing their home in Falls Church. Still, like other families at the beach, he would camp when the weather wasn't too hot (because of Nell's aversion to hot weather) and enjoyed swimming, fishing, and boating on the lake and the bay. He became quite well known among his peers at Highland Beach.[7]

As time went on, more and more people purchased lots, and it became obvious to many that, as a small African American community, they needed to evolve from a village into a town. When they had enough people to form a nexus, they decided the best way to protect their community and control the development and resources would be to incorporate with the state legislature. The capital of Maryland was there in Annapolis, just a few miles away.

In 1921, a committee was formed, with E. B. as the chairman, to incorporate Highland Beach into the town of Highland Beach. Other members of the committee were Haley Douglass, Milton Francis, Eula Ross Gray, and Osborne Taylor. The committee, led by E. B., marched from Highland Beach to the Maryland State House to officially file to incorporate.[8] As an incorporated town they could "carry out municipal functions such as adopt regulations and ordinances, prescribe penalties and fines, levy and collect taxes, and maintain the public roads. . . . Highland Beach thus became the first African American incorporated town in the state of Maryland."[9] However, Highland Beach was the second African American town in the United States to do so. The bill "appointed Milton A. Francis, Osborne T. Taylor, Edwin B. Henderson, Haley G. Douglass, and Eula Ross Gray as the town's first commissioners until an election could be held in July 1923. Haley G. Douglass, by vote of the commissioners, became the town's first mayor."[10]

Now that Highland Beach had an official status as a town with an official government, there was safety, autonomy, and permanence for this community of African Americans. The following year, 1924, E. B. was elected mayor of Highland Beach. Although he never frayed from leadership or responsibility, he found out that holding public office, being a public servant, and trying to please everyone weas impossible and very frustrating.

He remembered,

> The people wanted improvements and I seemed to have the energy and push to get things done. Here I found the way of an office holder is hard. This was my first lesson in small town politics.
>
> The people wanted electricity brought in and electric lights. This was done but some did not want the lights on the corners where they lived. Lights attracted mosquitoes and at that time the only protection was mosquito netting thrown over the bed at night. You had to duck under quickly. This bit of progress made a few voters sore.
>
> Although Major Douglass had made a good plan and the streets were on the plot, great trees grew up in the center of some of the main streets. Auto-mobiles were beginning to take the place of the horse and buggy.
>
> By vote of the commission body, I was given authority to remove the trees from the middle of the streets. I went to the Beach at Easter, hired farmer Mr. Pinckney and two teams of horses, and rooted up the trees. This made a few more voters angry because certain trees they loved were in front of their homes.
>
> Then, there was a habit of stepping off lots or measuring with a tape. People built on lots by estimation. So, I had the county surveyor come over and survey the streets.

> To the amazement of some and consternation of others, some found parts of their lots in the street. One owner had a fence put in the street to claim possession of certain trees. Well, I made more voters angry and after three years, I gave up the mayoralty and declined to run for re-election.[11]
>
> However, as long as EB spent his summers at Highland Beach, he continued to serve on the board of commissioners and committees for which he had interest in seeing certain projects done, such as the community pier: "I was one of Dr. Hartwell Burrell's Pier Committee which raised over $2,000 to build the pier which affords so much pleasure. I have seen scores of children gain strength and maturity, marry and bring families back to spend summers at the beach."[12]

On the shores of Black Walnut Lake, E. B. built his cottage and spent many summers there raising his two sons. He also was a mentor to many youth throughout the community, engaging with them in summer fun and activities. On Labor Day weekends, he refereed foot races and sporting events on the beach to celebrate the holiday. He was also very engaged with the community, becoming the first president of the Highland Beach Citizens Association.

He and Nell enjoyed socializing with the interesting group of people who populated Highland Beach. Their little cottage at the end of Bruce Avenue, right at the edge of Black Walnut Lake, was named "Loafing Holt" after the poem by Paul Lawrence Dunbar, which to them fit their experience perfectly. On Dunbar's frequent visits to Highland Beach, he often recited his poetry in the evenings around a bonfire on the beach, to the delight of the Highland Beach community. Dunbar was frail and suffered from tuberculosis for many years. In 1898, he married Ruth Alice Moore, and they lived in Washington, DC, where they were members of Washington's social scene. However, neither he nor their marriage would last long enough for them to build a cottage at Highland Beach. Alice left Paul shortly after purchasing their lot, after enduring four years of an abusive marriage.

Later in the 1920s, Richard Ware attempted to build a hotel, two three-story structures, hoping to attract more African American families to vacation at Highland Beach:

> Mrs. Ware had a reputation for being an exceptional cook and the hotel enjoyed considerable success during the 1920's, but was received with some ambivalence by the community. It was regarded by some as a less desirable, more commercial operation than Bowen's, which operated in a more subdued manner as a "guest house." It had a large front porch which served as a dining hall and also where dances were held. The dances took place on Saturday nights, where Dick Hall, a cousin of Mrs. Ware, and his band played and guests performed all of the latest dance steps until the midnight hour. The basement level was called the "Grotto," where there was a pool table, slot machine, and jukebox.[13]

A fire destroyed one of the three-story structures later in the same decade. The Wares continued to operate on a smaller scale for many years, but Highland Beach never became a commercial destination for vacationers. The families who owned property in the community wanted a private retreat for them and their guests, and it has remained that way to this day.

Most activities at the beach revolved around the water, where swimming, fishing, crabbing, boating, canoeing, sailing, speedboat racing, and water skiing were the obvious activities of choice. Some took these activities to an extreme as feats of endurance. E. B. and others in the community challenged themselves and swam seven miles across the Chesapeake Bay to Kent Island on the other shore.

Another popular sport at Highland Beach was tennis. At one time, there were seven tennis courts in Highland Beach. In the 1920s and 1930s, tennis was at a fever pitch, and there was an annual American Tennis Association (ATA) tournament held there. The ATA, which was started in Washington in 1917, was the organization for which African Americans competed during Jim Crow segregation. Its first championship was held in Druid Hill Park in Baltimore and was won by a Highland Beach resident, Mr. Talley Holmes. The ATA tournament in Highland Beach lasted for a week and was interlaced with social events.[14]

As Highland Beach families grew, there was a need for activities for children and residents of all ages. A pavilion was built as a community gathering place for residents and their guests, where Sunday school, bingo, talent shows, dances, movies, and all manner of entertainment was

E. B. was known for spending his evenings at Highland Beach, fishing from the shore while smoking his signature corncob pipe.
COURTESY OF HENDERSON FAMILY COLLECTION

held for everyone from infants to senior citizens. The Highland Beach Pavilion was designed by resident Dr. John E. Washington:

> The pavilion was an eight-sided wood structure, with large-screened windows on each side that opened inward and upward toward the ceiling, supported by ropes and pulleys. Benches were constructed around its inside perimeter. The sophisticated design of the framing of the rafters in the roof allowed for absence of interior supporting beams,

> which resulted in a completely open floor space in its interior that was ideal for the activities it sheltered.[15]

Many of the families of Highland Beach saw the community as a safe, cloistered place where they didn't have to worry about their children being out and about. Many women were teachers who spent the whole summer at the beach with their children. Many young people met and made friends with the children of other elite families at the pavilion, and many families were connected by either blood or marriage. Many friendships forged there lasted a lifetime; some even met their future husbands or wives. E. B. and Nell's son Jimmy married the granddaughter of Dr. John R. Francis.

> Most of the people who could afford a cottage at Highland Beach were highly professional people, doing interesting things in Washington and around the country. During his professional life, EB enjoyed the beach as a respite and place to decompress and relax. In retirement, he was able to spend more time at Highland Beach. Many remember him setting up his bench on the beach at the mouth of Black Walnut Creek and throwing out the lines of his very long surf-fishing poles. He caught more fish and bigger fish than those who preferred to fish from the pier, probably because, at the mouth of the creek, the larger fish would wait for the smaller fish to come out to them. EB would sit there, smoking his characteristic corncob pipe and thinking about days past and projects still ahead. As he recalled, "Some of the happiest times of my life have been spent at Highland Beach despite my civil interest."[16]

21

Sunset

Retiring to Tuskegee

There were many tributes from the various arenas where E. B. spent his career: in the schools, athletic organizations, and the various NAACP branches that he gave his time to. In one tribute from 1974, an engineer for Falls Church said, "Forty years ago, as a young engineer, I surveyed the lands of your mother's estate. You had a better education than I, both academically and in life. In addition, I told my parents you were handsome—a Clark Gable in sepia. Most of all I respected your qualities of heart and mind that made you a man."[1]

Probably the most touching send-off was at a dinner put on by the Fairfax NAACP in 1965, before E. B. and Nell moved from the area to spend more time with their son Jimmy and their grandchildren in Tuskegee, Alabama. The tribute to E. B. was sung to the tune of "I'm Gonna Sit Right Down and Write Myself a Letter" by Fats Waller:

I'm going to sit right down and write the press a letter
And tell them all a thing or two
About democracy
About the NAACP
About our football heroes;
Be they white or Negroes.
I'm going to tell them how the world could be much better
And of the good things men have done;

I'm going to sit right down and write the press a letter
And sign it E. B. Henderson

I'm going to write the *News*, the *Star*, the *Post-Times-Herald*
The *Times Dispatch*, *News-Leader*, too
In letters to "Ye editor"
I'll say what must be said
About events of moment
Make my timely comment;
In times of stress the press will know that they will get a
Statement from my fruitful pen;
I'm going to sit right down and write the press a letter
And sign it E. B. Henderson.

The tribute to Nell went,

School days, school days,
Good old Falls Church school days
We carried the water and fetched the wood
We had a teacher who understood,
All of our needs and what to do
She taught us reading, and numbers too,
She taught us to respect all men
Miss Nellie Henderson!

School days, school days,
Good old James Lee school days
Our teacher helped open wide the door
To all the good things we're living for
All of our teachers we revere
Some of whom were kind and some severe,
But there is one to us most dear
Miss Nellie Henderson![2]

Although there were many testimonials and tributes to E. B. and Nell, too numerous to count or go into here, their service and contributions to the larger metropolitan Washington community were worthy of that and more. They looked forward to their retirement, even though for E. B., retirement did not mean slowing down his mighty pen. He continued to write letters and chapters to books after they moved to Tuskegee.

The growth of the Virginia suburbs after World War II meant it was no longer the quiet village setting the Henderson family enjoyed when they moved there to raise a family in the early twentieth century. Massive new housing developments and Levittown subdivisions were being built with cookie-cutter houses, many of which had covenants that refused to sell to African Americans. Additionally, redlining made it hard for Black people to get FHA loans in traditionally African American neighborhoods.

E. B. and Nell's fiftieth wedding anniversary photo with family, 1960.
COURTESY OF HENDERSON FAMILY COLLECTION

E. B. and Nell were growing frustrated with the faster pace of life that Falls Church and metropolitan Washington had become. Because both were in their eighties and Nell was having problems with arthritis and mobility, neither was as fast or as stable on their feet as they once were. Wherever they decided to move, they would need a support system to aid them in their old age. They felt that it would be best to live close to family, meaning one of their two children.

TWO SONS

E. B. and Nell had two sons, Edwin (Ed) Meriwether Henderson (1912–1994) and James (Jimmy) Henry Meriwether Henderson (1917–2009). E. B. wrote, "I have not said much of the personal satisfaction that has come from the achievements of my own two sons, although I must admit it has been due more to their mother than to me."[3]

Ed had E. B.'s first name and Nell's maiden name, so he was not a junior. He was fun loving, a prankster and typical delinquent, always playing jokes on and bullying his younger brother, as most older brothers do. He was tall, handsome, and very fair-skinned, like his mother and father. Ed was Nell's favorite, even though most parents insist they love their children just the same. She surely loved them both, but she seemingly doted on Edwin more. Ed attended Dunbar High School, then Howard University for undergraduate college, before finishing at Howard Dental School.

During the Korean War, he spent time in a MASH unit, much like the one in the popular TV show starring Alan Alda. After the war, he was the dentist for the Washington, DC, prison at Lorton, Virginia, for many years. He finished his career for Group Health, an HMO that evolved into Kaiser Permanente. He lived in Northwest Washington, DC, near the Watergate complex. He married five times, but Ed had no biological children. In 1969, he married Anne Marie Gipson, whom he met while they were working at Group Health and later adopted her daughter, Christine. After E. B.'s death in 1977, they moved to Annapolis and eventually rebuilt a home on the site of "Loafing Holt," the charming summer cottage that belonged to E. B. and Nell on the banks of Black Walnut Lake in Highland Beach.

Jimmy was named for Nell's father, James Henry Meriwether. Jimmy was darker, a handsome child, but shorter and thinner than his brother. He didn't have his final growth spurt until after he finished high school and was attending college. Later, he grew to be taller than both his brother and his father but not by much, maybe an inch or two. He was always more serious-minded. Jimmy sought the attention and praise from his parents, particularly his mother.

Jimmy was also a graduate of Dunbar High School. He then attended Howard University, like his brother. He was interested in the biological sciences, particularly plants, or botany. His idol and mentor was the famous Howard University scientist Ernest Just, one of the founders of the Omega Psi Phi fraternity, of which E. B. was a member. Interestingly, Jimmy never joined the Omega Psi Phi fraternity, even though both his mentor and father, whom he adored, were members. But being the serious-minded person that he was, he kept his mind on his studies at Howard. Later he earned membership into the prestigious Phi Beta Kappa academic fraternity, which he was most proud of.

After finishing his bachelor's degree, Jimmy applied to the University of Virginia, knowing full well that the state of Virginia would not allow integration of their university. But there was a bill passed in the Virginia state legislature in 1936, the Dovell Act, that allowed for the state to pay full tuition for a student to attend any other university in the country, out of state, where the student was accepted.[4] Jimmy was able to "play the system," as many other African Americans did, and was granted a full scholarship to the University of Wisconsin at Madison, thanks to the state of Virginia. In 1943, Jimmy received his PhD in biology/plant physiology.

The United States was in the midst of World War II in 1943, so after receiving his PhD, Jimmy was put to work to support the war effort in laboratories involved in biological warfare at the University of Chicago. Not far from there, the theoretical work to produce the atomic bomb was being conducted in a laboratory under the university football field. As the war was coming to an end in the spring of 1945, two professors from Tuskegee Institute, one of which was the director of the George Washington Carver Research Foundation, visited Jimmy in Chicago and offered him a position at Tuskegee teaching and conducting research at the Carver Foundation. Jimmy spent the next fifty-four years teaching and doing research there. For many years, he was the director of the George Washington Carver Research Foundation, as well.

Some might have been hesitant to move to Tuskegee in 1965, with all that was going on just forty miles away in Montgomery, Alabama. But for E. B. and Nell, it wasn't that hard of a decision to make. They had been visiting Tuskegee ever since Nell's sister Edith married Booker T. Washington's younger son, Ernest (Dave) Washington. Jimmy was a professor at the university, and his wife, Betty, was also a professor of early childhood education and director of "Russell" nursery school at the Chambliss Children's House. Their four grandchildren were there to help out if needed. But part of the real joy for E. B. and Nell was to see their grandchildren grow.

Tuskegee was a progressive community with professional opportunities and lots of history. Its slower pace and country setting adjacent to a college campus was a nice combination for the elderly couple. As they settled into their new home and surroundings, life quickly fell into place, and before long, they felt right at home in this majority–African American southern community.

The Tuskegee Agricultural and Normal Institute (years later shortened to Tuskegee Institute and now Tuskegee University) was started when Lewis Adams asked his local state congressman to build a vocational school for African Americans in Tuskegee because he, being a local businessman, was unable to accommodate all the Blacks who wanted him to teach them his trade and employ them. House Bill 165 was passed in the Alabama state legislature, and a letter was written to General Samuel Armstrong at the Hampton Institute in Hampton, Virginia. Booker T. Washington was a teacher at the school, and Armstrong sent Washington to Tuskegee to start the school Adams had asked for on the grounds of Butler Chapel near his home. On July 4, 1881, instruction began in a building, no more than a shack with a leaky roof. That fall, Washington purchased an abandoned one-hundred-acre planation at the current location of the university.[5]

Washington was a pragmatic leader and orator, and within a decade, he had transformed his school into an example that attracted the attention of many "captains of industry," like Andrew Carnegie, George Eastman, J. P. Morgan, John D. Rockefeller, and Julius Rosenwald, to sit on the board of trustees and give money toward its improvement.[6] The students learned trades by which to make a living for themselves and provide goods, services, and employment for the communities in which they lived. Many people simply saw Washington's vision as one of vocational education, but in fact, it was an economic philosophy of Black empowerment through business development in the African American community.

By 1900, Tuskegee Institute had more than one hundred modern brick buildings on a mile-square campus. All were built by students at Tuskegee Institute. It was and still is the largest HBCU in area. Tuskegee had such a reputation that it was able to attract the best and brightest to come there to teach, like George Washington Carver (agricultural scientist) and Robert Taylor (architect). Presidents McKinley, Roosevelt, and Taft all visited Tuskegee to see what a Black man could accomplish with an idea put in motion and a little persuasion.[7]

Much has been made of a rift between Booker T. Washington and W. E. B. Du Bois, after Washington's Atlanta Exposition Speech, in which he was labeled as an "accommodationist," largely due to his comment, "In all things purely social we can be as separate as the fingers, yet one as the hand in all things essential to mutual progress."[8] However, W. E. B. Du Bois sent Washington a letter of congratulations after his speech in Atlanta. Washington was a realist. He knew Whites weren't ready to integrate or allow Blacks equal rights in the South in the late 1800s and early 1900s. But by learning trades and starting businesses in the Black community, Blacks could provide themselves with quality goods and services and thereby create a good life. Washington's philosophy had its basis in economic aspirations, not simply a vocational educational one, while Du Bois's philosophy was a sociopolitical one. There was no real conflict; they were different sides of the same coin.[9]

E. B. and especially Nell were familiar with and had visited Tuskegee going back to 1914, when Nell's sister Edith married Dave Washington.

In the absence of the bride's father, E. B. gave the bride away at the wedding. Sadly, a year later, Nell and E. B. attended the funeral of Edith's father-in-law, Booker T. Washington, in Tuskegee.

After E. B. retired in 1954, he and Nell drove to Tuskegee to spend Christmas and Easter with Jimmy, Betty, and their children. In the summers, Jimmy's family took that trip the other way, through the segregated South to Highland Beach. Betty Alice Francis, the granddaughter of Dr. John R. Francis Sr., had inherited her grandfather's house, one of the first cottages built in Highland Beach. This trip could be treacherous, though, because of the potential for racial violence that was prevalent before the mid-1960s.

In 1955, E. B. and Nell drove down for the birth of a grandchild, a boy this time. Now in his retirement, driving down for the birth of a grandchild was a pleasant getaway from the pace of Washington. When they arrived, the baby had just been delivered, and Jimmy and Betty were considering naming the child Dave Meriwether Henderson. After E. B. heard the news, he fell ill and soon retired to the bedroom for the evening. The drive from Washington was long, and everyone just thought he was tired.

He remained in bed the next day, which Betty and Jimmy thought unusual, so they asked if they should send for the doctor. The doctor came and told them that E. B. was tired and in some discomfort, but he couldn't find anything physically wrong with him, so he prescribed another day or two of bed rest. Betty and Jimmy started to have second thoughts about the choice of names they were considering for the newborn infant. Might the name be a problem? So they reconsidered and gave the baby boy E. B.'s name. They told E. B. the news, that the new baby would be named for him, Edwin Bancroft Henderson II. After hearing this, he smiled and immediately threw back the covers, came downstairs, and got something to eat. He was fine.

While visiting with the family and grandchildren, E. B. was able to meet with a number of people involved in human rights activities in Tuskegee. Tuskegee was majority African American, mostly due to two major entities that employed African Americans. One was Tuskegee

Institute, and the other was the Tuskegee Veterans Administration Hospital that had been built after World War I.

After World War I, African American soldiers were unable to receive proper medical care at many of the hospitals around the country, particularly in the southern states. Because of this, the president of Tuskegee Institute, Robert Russa Moton, and Booker T. Washington's personal physician, Dr. Howard Kenney, proposed building a VA hospital for the Black veterans who had served in World War I on land that would be donated by the university. In 1921, under the Warren G. Harding administration, the plan was approved for a segregated Black VA hospital to be built on 464 acres, 300 of which were donated by the university. The hospital opened in 1923 with twenty-seven buildings, including housing for staff and administrators, who were all Black.

This did not sit well with all the Whites in the town and the state, who wanted the staff and doctors to be White. But at the behest of the NAACP and the National Medical Association (an association for Black doctors), Mr. Moton and Dr. Kenney insisted that, because it was an African American VA hospital, it was also to be managed and operated by African Americans.[10]

This caused much consternation in Alabama. Death threats were made to Dr. Moton, Dr. Kenney, the university, and African American townspeople. The death threats to Dr. Kenney were so intense that he gathered his family and left Tuskegee. The KKK proposed to march through the town, right past the university. Dr. Moton asked all the faculty and staff to stay home, lock their doors, shutter their windows, and not to come out until the KKK finished their march through the town.[11]

However, Benjamin O. Davis Sr., a graduate of M Street High School in Washington, DC, and the first African American general in the army, lived just across from the Lincoln Gate, the entrance to the university. Davis vowed that he would not be intimidated by these cowardly, hooded Klansmen. He sat on his upper porch with his shotgun, as the crowd of KKK, in their white robes and hoods, marched past him through the campus.[12]

E. B. met with the Tuskegee Citizens' Association, which was in a battle with the White townspeople who had gerrymandered the university and 99 percent of the African Americans outside of the town boundaries. Another Washingtonian, Dr. C. G. Gomillion, a professor of sociology at the university, filed a lawsuit against the town. E. B. gave the group the benefit of his experience working for civil rights in Washington and Virginia and helped them to formulate strategies for their situation in their community. Their lawsuit eventually was heard in the US Supreme Court, *Gomillion v. Lightfoot*, which outlawed the town's actions.[13]

> When EB and Nell came back to Tuskegee for Christmas vacation to be with their grandchildren, they discovered a lot had gone on since EB's grandson had been born in September. Stemming from her frustration over many things, particularly the brutal lynching of Emmett Till in Mississippi, Mrs. Rosa Parks, a Black seamstress, refused to give up her seat on a Montgomery city bus in Alabama. This caused a whirlwind of activity in the community, which culminated in the NAACP and many other Black organizations in Montgomery gathering at the Dexter Avenue Baptist Church, thirty miles away, where a young twenty-six-year-old Baptist minister was selected to lead a boycott of the city's bus system. While EB was in Tuskegee, he took the opportunity to meet with the young minister, Dr. Martin Luther King Jr.. EB said, "I also had the pleasure of meeting Dr. King in Montgomery and talked to him at his home during the time of the bus boycott. It was very interesting, and I have kept up with what he has done ever since."[14]

After his visit, the trips to Tuskegee became more regular in his retirement. Jimmy was moving up in status at the university and was in line to become a department head. His research at the George Washington Carver Research Foundation was starting to bring him some notoriety, particularly in the field of tissue culturing. At California Institute of Technology (Cal Tech), Jimmy adapted his knowledge of cloning and tissue culture of plants to human cells.

Henrietta Lacks, a woman living in Baltimore, was diagnosed with cervical cancer. The doctors at Johns Hopkins Hospital took a biopsy from her cervix and found that her cells did not die. In other words, her cells were not limited by the Hayflick limit, where they no longer divided;

instead, they continued to divide and grow. These cells were cancer cells. When Johns Hopkins Hospital discovered the uniqueness of her cells, they licensed them and have been selling them for research and pharmaceutical purposes ever since. Her cells have made a lot of people very rich, while her family has not benefited until recently, once her story has become well known to the public through books and movies. Jimmy's knowledge was used to clone Lacks's "immortal cells" (known as HeLa cells) for a polio vaccine between 1953 and 1955, one of his accomplishments of which he was most proud during his career and which was big news in science circles.

In 1961, Jimmy went on a sabbatical from Tuskegee Institute. A former colleague of his, Dr. Jean Nitsch, whom he knew from his postdoctoral studies at Cal Tech in 1949, offered him an opportunity to spend the year at the laboratory Le Phytotron, in Gif-Sur Yvette, France, of which he was the director. Additionally, Jimmy applied for and received a grant from the National Science Foundation that would allow him to take the whole family with him to France.

This is where Jimmy would further conduct his cancer research, thirty kilometers outside Paris. The family lived in Bures-sur-Yvette, a few kilometers from the laboratory.

Traveling by airplane was not very practical for a family of six, so they traveled on the *Bremen*, a German steam liner, with sixteen pieces of luggage. When they arrived after six days at sea, there was a brand-new Peugeot station wagon waiting for them at the port. They all climbed in and traveled through the French countryside to Bures-sur-Yvette. They settled into a nice three-bedroom cottage, where they spent the year.

During E. B. and Nell's retirement years, they had the pleasure of doing a lot more traveling. They went on cruises together. They traveled to Haiti, where a colleague of E. B.'s had moved. They traveled to Mexico for vacation. And when they went to France to visit Jimmy and the family, they had a grand tour of Europe.

They spent two months touring Europe. They spent the first week in France with the family, and they went into Paris to sightsee. One time, Jimmy took them to an expensive restaurant, and when it was time to pay the bill, Jimmy said he had forgotten his wallet. Likely story, right?

After that week, they went to Naples, Rome, Genoa, the Blue Grotto, and Capri. Then they went along the Amalfi Drive and on to Pompeii. After leaving Italy, they visited four sites in Switzerland, including Lucerne. Afterward, they went to Germany, where E. B. had always wanted to visit. They had a whirlwind tour and headed home to get some rest. When they returned, they learned that E. B.'s mother Louisa had passed the night before her ninety-ninth birthday. Their arrival home was a sad occasion, especially for E. B.

In France, the children went to school in Gif-sur-Yvette, where Jimmy worked. All instruction was conducted in French, so the children had to learn the language. Uncharacteristically, the teachers were very understanding and accommodating to non-French speakers. Edwin struggled the most with French because they thought he was too young and immature to learn a foreign language at five years old, which was the conventional thinking in those days. The rest of the family prepared by taking lessons in French at their church in Tuskegee. At their school in Gif, Jay, the oldest boy, had trouble at first from some of the boys who called him Stupie, for *stupid boy,* trying to say *stupid* in English. After he blooded the nose of one French boy, he didn't have much trouble, and he made a few friends. The girls, Dena and Ellen, took lessons, made great strides in the language, and did well in school. Instruction for boys and girls were separate, so the girls went to L'Ecole des Filles, and the boys went to L'Ecole des Garcons.

The family took full advantage of the year abroad and traveled extensively throughout Europe. They went to Rome for Christmas and along the South of France. On another trip, they traveled through Switzerland and Austria, where they went skiing. They went behind the Iron Curtain to Czechoslovakia, then on to Germany, before making their way back to France. Their last trip was in the summer before coming home to the United States. On this trip, they toured Belgium, the Netherlands, Denmark, Sweden, and Norway.

At the end of their year abroad, they packed everything up, including their Peugeot station wagon, and climbed onboard the French steam liner *La France,* which set a record, arriving in New York in just four days. They arrived in late August, and because school would be starting soon, they could only spend a short time at Highland Beach with E. B. and Nell, then hightailing it back to Tuskegee to begin school for the fall semester: for Jimmy at the Carver Research Foundation, for Betty and the grandchildren at Chambliss Children's House, the laboratory school at the university, where she taught and they attended school.

Soon after their trip to France, Nell started to lose her mobility. She suffered terribly with arthritis, and not too long afterward, she broke her hip. In her infirmity, E. B. and Nell decided that they would move to be with Jimmy and the grandchildren. Their son Edwin, who lived close to Washington, didn't have any children and might not have been of assistance.

Jimmy had recently built a new house in Tuskegee. At first, the thought was that they would move into a house of their own in Tuskegee, but with Nell's mobility issues, they thought a part of the new house could be made into a place for the two of them. E. B., though not as nimble as he once was, was still in relatively good shape for eighty-two. Jimmy and his family moved into their new home in Tuskegee in 1963, and with some help from Nell and E. B., they were able to build out a comfortable apartment for his parents on the ground floor of his new home.

In 1965, E. B. and Nell moved to Tuskegee. Nell was excited about being closer to her sister Edith, with whom she could spend more time. This was a big selling point for her. Spending time with Jimmy, Betty, and the grandchildren surely was how they had imagined they would spend their last days. The two sisters visited each other and attended events together at the university, and the family had dinner together on Sundays after church. They were happy to be back together again.

Edith had established herself early on as an educator. She also graduated from Miner Teachers College, Normal School No. 2. When she married and moved to Tuskegee, she taught at the Chambliss Children's House, which taught kindergarten through eighth grade. The educational system in Alabama has never been one of the best, even to this day. The educational program at Tuskegee was superior, especially for African Americans. The university at Tuskegee was not only college level, but also included kindergarten through senior high school. Students boarded there and attended high school classes on the campus. Because there were no Colored schools in Tuskegee, the institute taught all grades to African Americans in the town.

E. B. continued to write letters to the editor of newspapers in Tuskegee, Montgomery, Birmingham, Atlanta, and the *Washington Post.* The faculty at the university was very welcoming of E. B. because of his pioneering work to establish athletics and physical education in the schools, as well as his status in the American Alliance for Health, Physical Education, Recreation, and Dance (AAHPERD). He was called on to lecture, and he enjoyed his new environment as a big fish in a very small pond. Those involved in social justice activities were well aware of him, and he was influential in starting a new branch of the NAACP in Macon County. E. B. continued to contribute to his publishing through his authority on Blacks in athletics, physical education, and civil rights.

In 1971, E. B. started to receive a number of accolades through his friendship with Dr. Bruce Bennett, a professor at Ohio State University. They became acquainted through AAHPERD, as Bennett was the historian for the organization. Later, Dr. Bennett interested one of his doctoral students, Leon Coursey, to choose E. B. as the topic of his dissertation. In March 1971, E. B. was invited to participate in the Big Ten Symposium on the campus of Ohio State University. Dr. Bennett and AAHPERD archivist Mabel Lee would become good friends. Between this time and E. B.'s death, they became good friends and were in constant correspondence with each other. Through this association, Bennett published E. B.'s presentation, "Rise of the Black Athlete," from the Big Ten Symposium. The following year, E. B. published a chapter, "Physical Education and Athletics among Negroes," in *The History of Physical Education and Sports*, edited by Bennett. E. B.'s final published work was a chapter, "The Black American in Sports," in Mabel Smythe's *The Black American Reference Book*.

E. B. was at a point in his life when a number of well-deserved honors and recognitions for his long career in physical education and athletics were bestowed on him. In 1973, the North American Society for Sports History was founded by none other than Bruce Bennett, and they had their first international meeting of the society, where E. B. was named as honorary president.

On March 14, 1974, E. B. was inducted into the inaugural class of the Black Sports Hall of Fame. The athletes honored were selected by sportswriters from recognized media around the country. E. B. was selected in the category of "Historian." Those honored were a long list of all the great athletes of the twentieth century, including Bill Russell, Muhammad Ali, Jackie Robinson, Jim Brown, and Jesse Owens.

Bennett and Lee started a campaign to have AAHPERD honor E. B. with their highest honor, the Luther Gulick Award. Every year from 1972, Bennett would nominate E. B. for the Gulick Award, and each year, they honored E. B. with a lesser honor or award—never their top honor. And it's a shame because many of the things Luther Gulick did during Jim Crow segregation, E. B. did for African Americans. In 2008, a nomination was put forth to honor E. B. for the Gulick Award, but in response, AAHPERD said that the award "cannot be granted posthumously." However, even without being honored with AAHPERD's most prestigious award, two auxiliary organizations within AAHPERD present a Dr. Edwin B. Henderson award of their own each year.[15]

Previous to their moving to Tuskegee, Jimmy purchased fifty-two acres and dammed the stream flowing through it to create a two-and-a-half-acre pond, stocked with bream and large-mouth bass. E. B.'s love of fishing would continue in his retirement to the country. Another area near the pond was cleared for E. B. to grow vegetables. He enjoyed tilling the soil and watching things grow in the spring and summer. He would fish, till a little bit, and enjoy the nature around the property at the lake. He had always enjoyed nature and fishing, so he felt right at home in his new surroundings.

When the weather got warmer, E. B. and Nell drove back to Washington to stay at their "Loafing Holt." They enjoyed going into Washington to visit with friends, but mostly they invited friends to come visit them at Highland Beach. Then, at the end of the season, after Labor Day, they would settle back in with Jimmy's family in Tuskegee.

During Christmas breaks, when Jimmy could take time off from the university and the kids were out of school, all the male members in the family would travel to Florida to go fishing. The goal was always to try to make it to Key West. Although a lofty goal, they never made it there before having to return to be back in time for school or for Jimmy to head back to his laboratory. But before turning back, they would catch a charter and do some deep-sea fishing. On these charters, E. B. always caught the most and the largest fish, just like old times in Highland Beach.

E. B. was very nurturing. He always encouraged everyone around him to strive for worthy goals. In his final years, E. B. doted on his grandchildren and taught them a lot about life. Whether it was the oldest granddaughter, Ellen, integrating the all-White high school with eleven other students in Tuskegee, or Dena taking over the administration building at Vassar College to bring in a Black studies program in 1969, or staying up past bedtime with the boys to watch the 1969 NBA Finals battle between Boston's Bill Russell and LA's Wilt Chamberlain, E. B. was there. E. B. attended his grandsons' sporting and scouting events. Living with his son Jimmy, Betty, and the grandchildren, E. B. was a very attentive grandparent. Two sayings sum up E. B.'s relationship with his children and grandchildren: "A good man leaves an inheritance to his children's children," and, "If you raise your children, you can spoil your grandchildren. But, if you spoil your children, then you'll have to raise your grandchildren."[16]

On a bright and breezy August day in 1975, E. B. and Nell's granddaughter Dena was married on the front lawn of the family's beach house in Highland Beach. Nell didn't want to miss her granddaughter's wedding day, but because of her lack of mobility, they felt it was best she sit in the car, where she would have a front-row seat to the ceremony.

While she was sitting there unattended, Nell suffered a massive stroke. With all the attention to the wedding ceremony and festivities, no one knew exactly when the stroke occurred. When they found her, she was unresponsive. And after rushing her to the hospital, the family's worst fears were confirmed. Shortly thereafter, arrangements were made, and Nell was admitted into a nursing home on Wisconsin Avenue in Washington. E. B., not wanting to be away from her at such a critical time, also checked into the nursing home, where they shared a room. For the next six months, he passed the time talking to her and reading to her in the room, only taking a break to get something to eat, which was not very often. On February 4, 1976, there in the nursing home, Nell took her last breath. Their love and their marriage lasted more than six decades. E. B. moved back to Tuskegee to be with Jimmy's family. It was apparent that his grief was too much to bear. He was inconsolable and cried often for his wife of sixty-six years.

E. B. continued to receive accolades. He received several testimonials in the communities where he spent his life. The North American Society for Sports History honored him as an honorary president. AAPHERD honored him again, and the *Washington Post* did a final article on him in the summer of 1976, "Never Too Old to Dream: NAACP Pioneer Recalls, at 92, the Milestones."

In late January 1977, E. B. was admitted into John Andrew Memorial Hospital on the campus of Tuskegee Institute. For three weeks, he would make sounds like he was trying to say something, but no one could understand the words coming out of his mouth. Finally, on February 3, one day less than a year after Nell's passing, E. B. took his last breath.

Often, when people have been together for many years and one dies, the other most likely will soon pass, too. It's like losing a part of yourself, like an arm or a leg. The family believed that, in the last three weeks, Nell was calling E. B. to be with her. And now they're together again in eternity.

One of the things that E. B. always said is that you are never too old to dream. We never really lose the ones we love. Their spirits stay with us until we pass on. This book is a testament to the life and work of Edwin Bancroft Henderson. It will hopefully inspire others to pursue their dreams to the fullest extent and never give up hope.

Epilogue

Resurrecting E. B. Henderson

For the past thirty years, I have lived in the home of E. B. and Nellie Henderson in Falls Church, Virginia. I have often felt their presence, walked in their footsteps, and nestled beneath the comfort and security it offered. I traveled to do research at the National Archives, the Library of Congress, the Moorland-Spingarn Research Center, the Fairfax County Courthouse, the Fairfax Regional Library, the Library of Virginia in Richmond, and the local Mary Riley Styles Library in Falls Church, making copies of deeds and wills of E. B. and his ancestors. I recorded the inventories of the enslaved members of E. B.'s family who toiled on the Fitzhugh Plantation. I copied census records, as well as articles written by and about E. B. I've listened to and saved his oral histories from interviews done during his lifetime. Ever since that eventful day when my sister and I found my grandfather's box in the attic, I have spent my time eating, drinking, and sleeping E. B. Henderson.

In December 2005, my wife and I submitted the first nomination for Dr. E. B. Henderson's induction to the Naismith Memorial Basketball Hall of Fame for his pioneering role in basketball for African Americans. We prepared a 138-page booklet hoping to convince the reviewers that the person who introduced the game of basketball to Black people on a wide-scale, organized basis; who formed the first athletic league; and who organized an early championship series between the teams of Washington and New York was worthy of enshrinement.

The introduction of inductees is always done at halftime during the NCAA basketball tournament's Final Four. As we watched the game, anticipating hearing my grandfather's name, we could clearly see that eight or nine of the ten players on the court were African Americans. At halftime, the announcement was made. Edwin Bancroft Henderson was not inducted that year. In our disappointment, we wondered, "Didn't they read the booklet we spent several months compiling to show that E. B. was worthy of enshrinement in the Hall of Fame?" Another nagging question was "Is the Basketball Hall of Fame more interested in the game's history or celebrity?" It was natural for a history teacher to think the former was more important than the latter. The final question we thought was, "What could we have done differently to make them see the importance of where the game began for those most present on the court?"

The Monday after the NCAA Final Four, my wife sent an email to the curator of the Basketball Hall of Fame asking him what happened. His answer was telling: "Nobody knew who he was. No one recognized his name." Most people's view of basketball is focused on the recent past; they know little of what basketball was before the advent of the National Basketball Association. When I would tell people I had nominated my grandfather to be inducted into the Basketball Hall of Fame, I was asked, "What team did he play for?" and "Is there any videotape of him playing?" Basketball was invented in 1891, fifty-six years before the NBA was formed. E. B. learned the game at Harvard University in 1904, forty-three years before the NBA would be formed, and videotape would not be used until about the same time.

But we were not deterred by the rejection. We knew it would not be easy. We knew that it would be somewhat, if not very, political. So the next year we decided to try a different tactic. For the 2007 nomination, we submitted a DVD in place of the booklet. We felt this would be a more concise and entertaining method of delivery. But still, during halftime at the NCAA Final Four, there was no mention of E. B. in the class of 2007. We felt they must need something *more* to convince them.

We submitted another nomination for 2008. We paid for footage from the *Today Show* with Bryant Gumbel, when he interviewed Arthur Ashe after he published his book *Hard Road to Glory* about the history of Black participation in athletics. This interview highlighted E. B.'s *The*

Negro in Sports. We included the part when Gumbel asked, "So why did you write a book on this topic? Surely it has been done before." And Ashe's response: "Yes, it had been done twice; first by Edwin Henderson, a gym teacher in the Washington, DC, Colored schools."[1] We also included an interview with Sheila Johnson, an owner of the WNBA's Washington Mystics, endorsing E. B. We then burned another twenty-eight DVDs and sent those to Springfield to the Hall of Fame.

Nothing came of it, but we were *still* not deterred. The following year, YouTube became a reality, so we sent the nomination again with the link to share with the twenty-eight reviewers. Still no favorable response.

Starting around 2008, we interested the curators of National Museum of African American History and Culture to partner with us to put on a two-day conference, "The Emergence and Legacy of the African American Basketball National Conference." Additional partners included the National YMCA and Howard University's Athletic Department. The event was scheduled to take place November 12–13, 2010. On November 12, there was a lecture at the American History Museum, moderated by sportswriter Bill Rhoden, and keynotes by Earl Lloyd and Dave Bing. On November 13, at the Burr Gymnasium, there was a full day of workshops and panel discussions regarding the history of Black basketball, which were open to the public. Synergy was building.

Fortuitously, earlier in the year, during African American History Month, Patrick Reynolds, who produces the *Flashback* comic strips, ran a month-long exposé on E. B. Henderson in the kid's section of the *Washington Post* once a week. The panels highlighted the story of E. B. introducing basketball to Washington, DC. Reynolds' comic strips were based on excerpts from Bob Kuska's book *Hot Potato*. These visuals in the *Washington Post* helped bring to light the E. B. Henderson story across the Washington metropolitan area, as well as nationally. So we asked the people at the Hall of Fame if we should prepare another nomination the following year, to which they responded, "No, please don't send another nomination. We have everything we need to make a decision on E. B. Henderson."

We waited but not silently. Newspapers were starting to take notice and were asking to interview us. We were highlighted in a couple

The author and his wife Nikki at the Naismith Memorial Basketball Hall of Fame induction ceremony, Springfield, Massachusetts, 2013.
PERSONAL PHOTO TAKEN BY MICHAEL HENDERSON

magazines. And we could feel the momentum building as more and more people were taking notice of the efforts to get E. B. inducted into the Basketball Hall of Fame.

Meanwhile in 2011, at the Hall of Fame, Chairman of the Board Mannie Jackson, owner of the Harlem Globetrotters, proposed a special elect category for African American pioneers for induction into the Basketball Hall of Fame to recognize those from an earlier era who had been passed over. We had met Mannie Jackson on a couple occasions. I met him once when the Globetrotters played nearby and another time the African American Ethnic Sports Hall of Fame that was honoring my grandfather. After reading his book *Boxcar to Boardroom*, published in 2012, I knew him as a man who overcame great obstacles and who had great integrity.

In 2013, E. B. Henderson was finally selected under the "Early African American Pioneers" Direct-Elect category of the Basketball Hall of Fame in Springfield, Massachusetts. The first I heard about the selection was from Turner Sports broadcaster David Aldridge in a Tweet. During Media Day at the 2013 Basketball Hall of Fame ceremony, he interviewed my wife and I. He admitted that, after reading our 138-page nomination, he felt that "this injustice cannot stand" and was tempted to give it a go that first year but did not. He did share with us that he was happy to see that we were tenacious and didn't give up.

In a 2014 documentary after the induction ceremony at the Naismith Basketball Hall of Fame, Aldridge was interviewed for the documentary. This is what he had to say said about the significance of E. B.'s induction:

> Basketball was invented in the early 1890s by James Naismith. The people he taught the game to, taught E. B. Henderson. So he is a direct link to James Naismith. . . . He [EB] was a one-man band. Not just in terms of playing, coaching, fundraising for basketball. This is the guy who gave Black basketball structure. Not just in the literal sense but also in a historical context. He really chronicled the origins of Black basketball. . . . If you think about [Black] basketball beginning in Washington, DC, on U Street and now you go a few blocks down the street to the Verizon (now Capital One) Center, where you see the best basketball players in the world play on a regular basis, almost all of them African American, geographically it's a short distance, but historically it's a huge leap. . . . It is very hard to bring people back to life. To kind of make this person whole in contemporary eyes. What Ed and Nikki did was to give Edwin B. Henderson some dimension, so that it wasn't just someone on the pages of a book.[2]

I hope that by writing this book I have proven David Aldridge right. I hope we have given him new life, making E. B. Henderson a recognizable name and giving the general public awareness of his contributions to basketball, interscholastic athletics, physical education, social justice, and sports history.

Although Dr. Edwin Bancroft Henderson was finally inducted into the Basketball Hall of Fame, it does not encapsulate the full story of his life. E. B. was much more than basketball. This story brings to life his family background, his early life, his courtship with his wife Nell, his role in establishing the Highland Beach community, and finally his retirement years in Tuskegee. On a professional level, this story tells of E. B.'s important role in history, as the first Black male to teach physical education in the nation. He created opportunities to implement physical training and athletics into school programs, believing it was a public health initiative vital to reducing the onset of diseases prevalent in the unsanitary, overcrowded cities during the Great Migration. He believed that athletics was a level playing field and advocated for interracial competitions before integration was commonplace, setting himself apart from other practitioners during his life. E. B. was a passionate pragmatist, a renaissance man, who deserves his rightful place in sports history.

Notes

Foreword

1. Jason P. Shurley, Jan Todd and Terry Todd, *Strength Coaching in America: A History of the Innovation That Transformed Sports*, University of Texas Press, 2019.

2. Theodore Roosevelt, "Professionalism" In Sports, *The North American Review*, Vol. 151, 1890.

3. Henry Cabot Lodge, "Speech at the Alumni Dinner," Harvard Commencement, June 1896, *Speeches and Addresses 1884–1909*, Houghton-Mifflin, 1909.

4. Arthur Ashe and Arnold Rampersad, *Days of Grace: A Memoir*, Ballantine Books, 1993.

5. A Man of Many Words," *Sports Illustrated*, Nov. 4, 1991.

Introduction

1. Ahmad Rashard, remarks at the Basketball Hall of Fame Induction Ceremony, September 8, 2013.

2. Edwin B. Henderson, "The Colored College Athlete," *Crisis Magazine* (July 1911).

3. Arthur R. Ashe Jr., *A Hard Road to Glory—Basketball: The African-American Athlete in Basketball* (Amistad, 1993), 51.

1

1. Claude Johnson, *The Black Fives: The Epic Story of Basketball's Forgotten Era* (Abrams Press, 2022), 24.

2. John Browne, *The Story of Ravensworth: A History of the Ravensworth Land-Grant in Fairfax County, Virginia* (CreateSpace, 2018), 6–17.

3.Ibid., 22.

4. Leon Coursey, "The Life of Edwin Bancroft Henderson and His Professional Contributions to Physical Education" (PhD diss., Ohio State University, 1971), 17.

5. Ibid.

6. Mordecai Fitzhugh, will.

7. Coursey, "Life of Edwin Bancroft Henderson," 17.

8. National Park Service, "Battle of Milliken's Bend, June 7, 1863," updated April 17, 2017, https://www.nps.gov/vick/learn/historyculture/battle-of-millikens-bend-june-7-1863.htm.

9. Edward E. Baptist, *The Half Has Never Been Told: Slavery and the Making of American Capitalism* (Basic Books, 2016), 32–42.

10. Melvin Lee Steadman Jr., Falls Church: By Fence and Fireside (Falls Church Public Library, 1964), 207–8, 215–16.

11. Coursey, "Life of Edwin Bancroft Henderson," 17–18.

2

1. Jacob E. Cooke, "The Compromise of 1790." *William and Mary Quarterly: A Magazine of Early American History and Culture* (1970): 524–45.

2. Matt Blum, "Benjamin Banneker: The First African-American Geek," *Wired*, February 27, 2010, https://www.wired.com/2010/02/benjamin-banneker-the-first-african-american-geek/.

3. Maxwell Whiteman, "Benjamin Banneker: Surveyor and Astronomer: 1731–1806: A Biographical Note," in *Banneker's Almanack, and Ephemeris for the Year of Our Lord 1793; Being the First after Bissextile or Leap Year: Banneker's Almanac, for the Year 1795: Being the Third after Leap Year*, ed. Maxwell Whiteman, Afro-American History Series, Rhistoric Publication No. 202 (Rhistoric, 1969).

4. Kathleen Lusk Brooke and Zoe G. Quinn, "The Founding of Washington D.C., United States," *Building the World* (blog), accessed June 26, 2023, https://blogs.umb.edu/buildingtheworld/founding-of-new-cities/the-founding-of-washington-d-c-united-states/.

5. Edward E., Baptist, *The Half Has Never Been Told: Slavery and the Making of American Capitalism* (Basic Books, 2016), 32–42.

6. Briana A. Thomas, *Black Broadway in Washington, D.C.* (History Press, 2021), 28.

7. Ibid., 30–32.

8. John H. Paynter, *Fugitives of the Pearl* (Associated Publishers, 1930).

9. Thomas, *Black Broadway*, 23–30.

10. Ibid., 32–34.

11. Terry Gross, "Lincoln's Evolving Thoughts on Slavery, and Freedom," *Fresh Air*, October 11, 2010, https://www.npr.org/2010/10/11/130489804/lincolns-evolving-thoughts-on-slavery-and-freedom.

12. National Archives, "Black Soldiers in the U.S. Military during the Civil War," accessed June 26, 2023, https://www.archives.gov/education/lessons/blacks-civil-war.

13. Thomas, *Black Broadway*, 40–43.

14. Mark Jones, "Contraband Camps of Northern Virginia," Boundary Stones, April 7, 2015, https://boundarystones.weta.org/2015/04/07/contraband-camps-northern-virginia.

15. Thomas, *Black Broadway*, 45–47.

16. Ibid., 48–50.

17. Alcione M. Amos, *Barry Farm-Hillsdale in Anacostia: A Historic African American Community* (History Press, 2021), 20.

18. Mrs. Blanche K. Bruce, letter to a newspaper in Philadelphia correcting the account of a game, including scores of the team for ten years. Henderson Collection.

19. National Museum of American Diplomacy, "The Diplomatic Career of Frederick Douglass," accessed June 26, 2023, https://diplomacy.state.gov/stories/the-diplomatic-career-of-frederick-douglass/.

20. Donna Hollie, "Grand Fountain of the United Order of True Reformers," *Encyclopedia Virginia*, updated December 14, 2020, https://encyclopediavirginia.org/entries/grand-fountain-of-the-united-order-of-true-reformers/#:~:text=The%20Grand%20Fountain%20of%20the,in%20Richmond%20in%20January%201881.

21. HouseHistoryMan, "The True Reformer Building at 1200 U 'You' Street NW," *The House History Man* (blog), May 9, 2020, http://househistoryman.blogspot.com/2020/05/the-true-reformer-building-at-1200-u.html.

22. Thomas, *Black Broadway*, 48.

23. Ibid.

24. Ibid.

25. Rachel Deborah Bernard, "These Separate Schools: Black Politics and Education in Washington, D.C., 1900–1930" (PhD diss., University of California, Berkeley, 2012), https://escholarship.org/uc/item/8h75g7n0.

3

1. Anna Buczkowska and Basen Saah, *Tinner Hill, Virginia: A Witness to Civil Rights*, Landscape Architecture Program, Washington Alexandria Architecture Center, Virginia Polytechnic Institute and State University, July 30, 2011, 8–9.

2. Deed of transfer, 1889, Fairfax County, Virginia Courthouse, Henderson Collection.

3. Claude Johnson, *The Black Fives: The Epic Story of Basketball's Forgotten Era* (Abrams Press, 2022), 30.

4. Ibid., 30.

5. Labor Commission on Racial and Economic Justice, "A Brief History of Labor, Race, and Solidarity," accessed June 26, 2023, https://racial-justice.aflcio.org/blog/est-aliquid-se-ipsum-flagitiosum-etiamsi-nulla.

6. Johnson, *Black Fives*, 32.

7. Edwin B. Henderson, "Looking Back on Fifty Years," *Baltimore Afro-American Newspaper*, September 7, 1954, 3.

8. Bob Kuska, *Hot Potato: How Washington and New York Gave Birth to Black Basketball and Changed America's Game Forever* (University of Virginia Press, 2004), 13.

9. Johnson, *Black Fives*, 33.

10. Ibid.

11. Dennis Dickerson, "Black Steelworkers in Western Pennsylvania," *Pennsylvania Heritage* (December 1977), http://paheritage.wpengine.com/article/black-steelworkers-western-pennsylvania/.

12. Paul Krause, The Battle for Homestead, 1880–1892: Politics, Culture, and Steel (University of Pittsburgh Press, 1951).

13. Charles McCollester, 2008, *The Point of Pittsburgh: Production and Struggle at the Forks of the Ohio*, 105.

14. AFL-CIO, "1892 Homestead Strike," accessed June 26, 2023, https://aflcio.org/about/history/labor-history-events/1892-homestead-strike.

15. McCollester, *The Point of Pittsburgh.*

16. AFL-CIO, "1892 Homestead Strike," accessed June 26, 2023, https://aflcio.org/about/history/labor-history-events/1892-homestead-strike.

4

1. John Caldbick, "Panic of 1893 and Its Aftermath," HistoryLink.org, October 1, 2019, https://www.historylink.org/file/20874.

2. Claude Johnson, *The Black Fives: The Epic Story of Basketball's Forgotten Era* (Abrams Press, 2022), 48.

3. Ibid, 48–49.

4. Geneva C. Turner, "For Whom Is Your School Named?" *Negro History Bulletin* (1958): 22–23.

5. Johnson, *Black Fives*, 49–50.

6. Ibid., 50.

7. Leon Coursey, "The Life of Edwin Bancroft Henderson and His Professional Contributions to Physical Education" (PhD diss., Ohio State University, 1971).

8. Johnson, *Black Fives*, 50.

9. Elizabeth Dowling Taylor, *The Original Black Elite: Daniel Murray and the Story of a Forgotten Era* (Amistad, 2017), 10.

10. Coursey, "Life of Edwin Bancroft Henderson," 21.

11. Ibid., 23.

5

1. Mary Gibson Hundley, *The Dunbar Story* (Vantage Press, 1965), 22.

2. Nina Tristani, "Separate and Unequal Education in 19th Century DC Schools," Hill-Rag, March 16, 2017, https://www.hillrag.com/2017/03/16/separate-unequal-education-19th-century-dc-schools/.

3. United States Senate, "Landmark Legislation: The Civil Rights Act of 1875," accessed June 26, 2023, https://www.senate.gov/artandhistory/history/common/generic/CivilRightsAct1875.htm#:~:text=Radical%20Republican%20senator%20Charles%20Sumner,schools%2C%20churches%2C%20and%20cemeteries.

4. Stephen G. Hall, "Revisiting the Tragic Era and the Nadir: Interrogating Individual and Collective African-American Lives in the Gilded Age and Progressive Era," *Journal of the Gilded Age and Progressive Era* 4, no. 4 (October 2005): 409–15.

5. Tristani, "Separate and Unequal Education."

6. BOTWC Staff, "Meet James Wormley, the Owner of Washington, D.C.'s First Integrated Hotel," Because of Them We Can, November 4, 2022, https://www.becauseofthemwecan.com/blogs/botwc-firsts/meet-james-wormley-the-owner-of-washington-d-c-s-first-integrated-hotel.

7. Ibid.

8. Ibid.

9. Hundley, *Dunbar Story.*

10. Ibid.

11. Carrie L. Thornhill, "Dunbar HS History," Dunbar Alumni Federation, accessed June 26, 2023, https://daf-dc.org/about/dunbar-history.

12. Camille Heung, "Robert H. Terrell (1857–1925)," BlackPast, June 24, 2008, https://www.blackpast.org/african-american-history/terrell-robert-h-1857-1925/.

13. Claudia Swain, "Dr. Anna J. Cooper: MVP of D.C. Education," July 6, 2016, https://boundarystones.weta.org/2016/07/06/dr-anna-j-cooper-mvp-dc-education.

14. Jacqueline Goggin, *Carter G. Woodson: A Life in Black History* (Lousiana State University Press, 1997).

15. Hundley, *Dunbar Story.*

16. Ibid.

17. Leon N. Coursey, "Anita J. Turner—Early Black Female Physical Educator," *Journal of Health, Physical Education, Recreation* 45, no. 3 (March 1974): 71–72, https://www.tandfonline.com/na101/home/literatum/publisher/tandf/journals/content/ujrd18/1974/ujrd18.v045.i03/00221473.1974.10612134/20130313/00221473.1974.10612134.fp.png_v03.

18. Leon Coursey, "The Life of Edwin Bancroft Henderson and His Professional Life in Physical Education" (PhD. diss., Ohio State University, 1971).

19. Ibid.

20. Ibid.

21. Photographs taken from a scrapbook belonging to EB, circa 1902, Henderson Collection.

22. Ibid.

6

1. Leon Coursey, "The Life of Edwin Bancroft Henderson and His Contributions to Physical Education" (PhD diss., Ohio State University, 1971), 34.

2. Ibid.

3. John H. Paynter, *Fugitives of the Pearl* (Associated Publishers,1930).

4. G. Smith Wormley, "Myrtilla Miner," Journal of Negro History 5, no. 4 (October 1920): 448–57, https://www.jstor.org/stable/2713679?searchText=au%3A%22G.+Smith+Wormley%22&searchUri=%2Faction%2FdoBasicSearch%3FQuery%3Dau%253A%2522G.%2520Smith%2520Wormley%2522&ab_segments=0%2Fbasic_phrase_search%2Fcontrol&refreqid=fastly-default%3A3d5bc3ff6f11aeb285478ba9f45a177f.

5. Ibid.

6. Ellen M. O'Connor, *Myrtilla Miner: A Memoir* (Houghton Mifflin, 1885).

7. Wormley, "Myrtilla Miner."

8. University of the District of Columbia, "Chronology of the University of Columbia and Its Predecessor Institutions, 1851–2009," accessed June 28, 2023, https://www.google.com/url?sa=t&rct=j&q=&esrc=s&source=web&cd=&ved=2ahUKEwiq9tqz97AhVZFlkFHWU2BOcQFnoECA4QAQ&url=https%3A%2F%2Fhbcudigitallibrary.auctr.edu%2Fdigital%2Fapi%2Fcollection%2FUDCW%2Fid%2F307%2Fdownload&usg=AOvVaw2Vubx0fPDomuU5dONrGHnl.

9. "Miner, Myrtilla (1815–1864)," *Women in World History: A Biographical Encylcopedia*, May 25, 2023, https://www.encyclopedia.com/women/encyclopedias-almanacs-transcripts-and-maps/miner-myrtilla-1815-1864.

10. "George Frederick Thompson Cooke, Superintendent of Colored Schools in DC, Dies at 77," *Crisis Magazine* (February 1913), https://www.flickr.com/photos/vieilles_annonces/4671321307.

11. Coursey, "Life of Edwin Bancroft Henderson," 34.

12. Edwin B. Henderson, diary entry, 1908, Henderson Collection.

13. Major Taylor, *The Fastest Bicycle Rider in the World* (Wormley, 1928).

14. Coursey, "Life of Edwin Bancroft Henderson," 37.

15. Ibid., 34.

16. Ibid, 37.

17. Ibid, 40.

7

1. Henderson, *Looking Back on Fifty Years, Baltimore Afro American Magazine* Magazine Section(July 31, 1954): 3.

2. Ibid.

3. Ibid.

4. RootsWeb, "James H. Meriwether," accessed June 28, 2023, https://freepages.rootsweb.com/~tmsirecords/genealogy/biographyjameshmeriwether.html.

5. Andrew Levy, *The First Emancipator: The Forgotten Story of Robert Carter: The Founding Father Who Freed His Slaves* (Random House, 2005).

6. *History of Lorain County Ohio, with Illustrations and Biographical Sketches of Some of Its Prominent Men and Pioneers* (Williams Brothers, 1879), 366.

7. Ibid.

8. Ibid.

9. Michael Todd, "A Short History of Home Mail Delivery," *Pacific Standard*, updated June 14, 2017, https://psmag.com/economics/a-short-history-of-mail-delivery-52444.

10. E. B. Henderson, letter to Nellie Henderson, Henderson Collection.

11. Nellie Henderson, letter to E. B. Henderson, Henderson Collection.

12. Anthony W. Neal, "Joseph Lee: Famed Hotelier, Restaurateur, Inventor," *Bay State Banner*, February 27, 2014, https://www.baystatebanner.com/2014/02/27/joseph-lee-famed-hotelier-restaurateur-inventor/.

13. Ocean City Beach Patrol, "125 Years of Ocean Lifesaving," accessed June 28, 2023, https://www.ocnj.us/departments/OCBP/OCBPHistory.

14. Nellie Henderson, letter to E. B. Henderson, Henderson Collection.

15. Leon Coursey, "The Life of Edwin Bancroft Henderson and His Professional Contributions to Physical Education," (PhD diss., Ohio State University, 1971), 24.

16. Ibid., 44–46.

17. Ibid., 46.

18. Ibid.

19. Ibid., 24.

8

1. Leon Coursey, "The Life of Edwin Bancroft Henderson and His Professional Contributions to Physical Education" (PhD diss., Ohio State University, 1971), 30–35.

2. Dudley Sargent (1883), quoted in Coursey, "Life of Edwin Bancroft Henderson," 13; George Harvey, "Belfast Man Pioneered Physical Education, Influenced Basketball's Creation and Field Hockey's U.S. Introduction," *Penobscot Bay Pilot*, October 4, 2020, https://www.penbaypilot.com/article/belfast-man-pioneered-physical-education-influenced-basketball-s-creation-and-field-h/134270.

3. PT Direct, "Vertical Jump Test (Sargent Jump)," accessed June 29, 2023, https://www.ptdirect.com/training-delivery/client-assessment/vertical-jump-test-sargent-jump-2013-a-predictive-test-of-lower-limb-power.

4. Harvey, "Belfast Man."

5. Coursey, "Life of Edwin Bancroft Henderson," 37.

6. Ibid., 40.

7. Ibid., 41–42.

8. Ibid., 41.

9. Ibid., 40.

10. Ibid.

11. Ibid.

12. Ibid.

13. Delia Cabe, "World Beaters," *Humanities* 31, no. 6 (November/December 2010), https://www.neh.gov/humanities/2010/novemberdecember/feature/world-beaters.

14. RetroSeasons, "National Basketball League I (NBL1): 1899–1904 (6 Seasons)," accessed June 29, 2023, https://www.retroseasons.com/leagues/nbl1/.

15. Wikiwand, "Basketball at the 1904 Summer Olympics," accessed June 29, 2023, https://www.wikiwand.com/en/Basketball_at_the_1904_Summer_Olympics.

16. Ibid.

9

1. Leon Coursey, "The Life of Edwin Bancroft Henderson and His Professional Contributions to Physical Education" (PhD diss., Ohio State University, 1971), 154.

2. Edwin B. Henderson, "Looking Back on Fifty Years," *Washington Afro-American Magazine* (July 24, 1954): 3.

3. Claude Johnson, *The Black Fives: The Epic Story of Basketball's Forgotten Era* (Abrams Press, 2022), 114.

4. Coursey, "Life of Edwin Bancroft Henderson," 43.

5. Ibid., 201.

6. Bob Kuska, *Hot Potato: How Washington and New York Gave Birth to Black Basketball and Changed America's Game Forever* (University of Virginia Press, 2004), 12.

7. Coursey, "Life of Edwin Bancroft Henderson," 201.

8. Edwin B. Henderson, *The Negro in Sports* (Associated Publishers, 1949), 284.

9. Coursey, "Life of Edwin Bancroft Henderson," 54.

10. D. W. Powell, *Black Georgetown Remembered* (Georgetown University Press, 2004).

11. Earl Telfair, *The Black Athletes of the District of Columbia during the Segregated Years: Remembering* (n.p., 1999), 8.

12. Edwin B. Henderson, "Public Recreation in the District," *Washington Tribune*, March 13, 1937.

13. Ibid.

14. Edwin B. Henderson, "Public Recreation in the District," *Washington Tribune*, April 3, 1937.

15. Edwin B. Henderson, "Public Recreation in the District," *Washington Tribune*, March 20, 1937.

16. Edwin B. Henderson, "Public Recreation in the District," *Washington Tribune*, April 3, 1937.

17. Edwin B. Henderson, "Public Recreation in the District," *Washington Tribune*, April 17, 1937.

10

1. Edwin B. Henderson, "Looking Back on 50 Years," *Afro American Magazine* (August 7, 1954), 5.

2. Edwin B. Henderson and William A. Joiner, eds., *Spalding Official Handbook of the Inter-Scholastic Athletic Association* (American Sports Publishing, 1910), 15.

3. Ibid., 17.

4. Ibid., 15.

5. Ibid., 17.

6. Ibid.

7. Ibid., 19.

8. "Track and Field Games," *Howard University Journal* 3, no. 25 (May 11, 1906): 5.

9. Henderson and Joiner, *Spalding Official Handbook* (1910), 19.

10. Black Fives Foundation, "In 1907, First Official African American Basketball Game, at 'Knickerbocker Court' in Brooklyn," November 13, 2014, https://www.blackfives.org/today-in-1907-first-official-african-american-basketball-game-at-knickerbocker-court-in-brooklyn/.

11. Edwin B. Henderson and William A. Joiner, eds., *Spalding Official Handbook of the Inter-Scholastic Athletic Association of Middle Atlantic States* (American Sports Publishing, 1911), 23.

12. Ibid.

13. Black Fives Foundation, "In 1907."

14. Henderson and Joiner, *Spalding Official Handbook* (1911), p. 3

15. Edwin B. Henderson, "An Experiment in Elementary School Athletics," *Journal of the American Association for Health, Physical Education, and Recreation* 22, no. 6 (June 1951):21–22.

16. Edwin B. Henderson, "Looking Back on Fifty Years," *Washington Afro-American Magazine* (July 24, 1954), 5.

11

1. Edwin B. Henderson and William A. Joiner, eds., *Spalding Official Handbook of the Inter-Scholastic Athletic Association of Middle Atlantic States* (American Sports Publishing, 1910), 83.

2. Edwin B. Henderson, "Looking Back on Fifty Years," *BaltimoreAfro American Magazine* (July 24, 1954), 5.

3. Ibid.

4. Edwin Bancroft Henderson, *The Negro in Sports* (Associated Publishers, 1949), 284.

5. Edwin Bancroft Henderson, *The Negro in Sports* (Associated Publishers, 1939), 246.

6. *Baltimore Afro American*, January 4, 1930, 11.

7. *Baltimore Afro American*, December 9, 1933, 21.

12

1. Delia Cabe, "World Beaters," *Humanities* 31, no. 6 (November/December 2010), https://www.neh.gov/humanities/2010/novemberdecember/feature/world-beaters.

2. Edwin B. Henderson and William A. Joiner, eds., *Spalding Handbook History of Inter-Scholastic Athletic Association of Middle Atlantic States* (American Sports Publishing, 1910), 19.

3. Leon Coursey, "The Life of Edwin Bancroft Henderson and His Professional Contributions to Physical Education" (PhD diss., Ohio State University, 1971), 29.

4. Edwin B. Henderson, "Looking Back on Fifty Years," *Washington Afro Magazine* (July 24, 1954), 5.

5. Bob Kuska, *Hot Potato: How Washington and New York Gave Birth to Black Basketball and Changed America's Game Forever* (University of Virginia Press, 2004), 1–2.

6. Historic Structures, "Twelfth Street YMCA Building (Anthony Bowen YMCA) Washington DC," October 25, 2010, https://www.historic-structures.com/washington_dc/dc/12th_ymca.php.

13

1. Al Tony Gilmore, *Bad Nigger! The National Impact of Jack Johnson* (Kennikat Press, 1975), 25–58.

2. Wikipedia, "Black Fives," updated April 10, 2023, https://en.wikipedia.org/wiki/Black_Fives.

3. Edwin Bancroft Henderson, *The Negro in Sports* (Associated Publishers, 1939), 128.

4. Black Fives Foundation, "Colored Basketball World's Champions, 1907–1925," accessed July 9, 2023, https://www.blackfives.org/champions/.

5. Claude Johnson, *The Black Fives: The Epic Story of Basketball's Forgotten Era* (Abrams Press, 2022), 159–60.

6. Ibid.

7. Ibid., 159.

8. *Washington Evening Star*, December 25, 1909, 9.

9. Daniel J. Middleton, "The Black Fives: The Pre-NBA Era of All-Black Basketball Teams," Unique Coloring, accessed July 1, 2023, https://www.uniquecoloring.com/articles/the-black-fives.

10. *New York Age*, February 17, 1910.

11. Johnson, *Black Fives*, 172–74.

12. Ibid.

13. Bob Kuska, *Hot Potato: How Washington and New York Gave Birth to Black Basketball and Changed America's Game Forever* (University of Virginia Press, 2004), 27–28.

14. Ibid., 29–30.

15. Ibid., 30.

16. Ibid.

14

1. Leon Coursey, "The Life of Edwin Bancroft Henderson and His Professional Contributions to Physical Education" (PhD diss., Ohio State University, 1971), 159.

2. J. E. Sullivan, letter to E. B. Henderson, October 16, 1909, Henderson Collection.

3. J. E. Sullivan, letter to E. B. Henderson, October 25, 1909, Henderson Collection.

4. Edwin B. Henderson and William A. Joiner, eds., *Spalding Official Handbook: The Inter-Scholastic Athletic Association of Middle Atlantic States* (American Sports Publishing, 1910).

5. Edwin B. Henderson and William A. Joiner, eds., *Spalding Official Handbook: The Inter-Scholastic Athletic Association of Middle Atlantic States* (American Sports Publishing, 1911).

6. Edwin B. Henderson and Garnet C. Wilkinson, eds., *Spalding Official Handbook: The Inter-Scholastic Athletic Association of Middle Atlantic States* (American Sports Publishing, 1912).

7. Edwin B. Henderson and Garnet C. Wilkinson, eds., *Spalding Official Handbook: The Inter-Scholastic Athletic Association of Middle Atlantic States* (American Sports Publishing, 1913).

8. Coursey, "Life of Edwin Bancroft Henderson," 160.

9.David Levering Lewis, *W. E. B. Du Bois: The Fight for Equality and the American Century, 1919–1963* (Henry Holt, 1994).

10. Edwin B. Henderson, "The Colored College Athlete," *Crisis Magazine* 2, no. 3 (July 16, 1911): 115.

11. Ibid.

15

1. Leon Coursey, "The Life of Edwin Bancroft Henderson and His Professional Contributions to Physical Education" (PhD diss., Ohio State University, 1971), 68.

2. Ibid.

3. Ibid.

4. Ibid.

5. Ibid., 180.

6. Ibid., 22.

7. National Park Service, "Charles Young and the 9th Ohio Battalion during the Spanish-American War," accessed July 6, 2023, https://www.nps.gov/articles/000/young9thohiobattalion.htm.

8. Vincent J. Cirillo, "Fever and Reform: The Typhoid Epidemic in the Spanish-American War," *Journal of the History of Medicine* 55 (October 2000): 363–97, https://vlp.cah.ucf.edu/instructionalmaterials/UCF-VLP-9th-12th-SPAM-DiseaseImpact-TyphoidArticle.pdf.

9. Coursey, "Life of Edwin Bancroft Henderson," 180.

16

1. Falls Church Town Council Minute Book, December 10, 1914.

2. Edwin B. Henderson and Edith Hussey, "History of the Fairfax County Branch of the NAACP," in *School Facilities for Negro Children in Fairfax County* (n.p., 1965), 1, http://100yearsblackfallschurch.org/items/show/288.

3. Colored Citizens Protective League (CCPL) minutes, January 8, 1915, Henderson Collection.

4. Anna Buczkowska and Basen Saah, HALS Report: *Tinner Hill, Virginia: A Witness to Civil Rights* (Landscape Architecture Program, Washington Alexandria Architecture Center, Virginia Polytechnic Institute and State University, July 30, 2011), 19.

5. Falls Church Town Council Minute Book, January 11, 1915.

6. W. E. B. DuBois, letter, February 1, 1915, Henderson Collection.

7. Town election flyer, 1915, Henderson Collection.

8. Buczkowska and Saah, HALS Report, 20.

9. Henderson and Hussey. *1965 History of the Fairfax County Branch of the NAACP*, p. 1.

10. Buchanan v. Warley, 245 U.S. 60 (1917), https://supreme.justia.com/cases/federal/us/245/60/.

11. Anne L. Mercer, "Tinner Hill and the Segregation Ordinance of 1915 (paper, George Washington University, 2000).

12. Leon Coursey, "The Life of Edwin Bancroft Henderson and His Professional Contributions to Physical Education" (PhD diss., Ohio State University, 1971), 72.

13. Ibid., 72–73.

14. "Falls Church Gleanings," *Washington Bee*, October 15, 1921, 5, http://100yearsblackfallschurch.org/items/show/550.

15. "New Item," *Washington Bee*, July 23, 1921, 1, http://100yearsblackfallschurch.org/items/show/537.

16. Mary Riley Styles Public Library, Local History Collection, Falls Church, VA, "Interview with E. B. Henderson (Part 1/2)," accessed July 6, 2023, http://100yearsblackfallschurch.org/items/show/256.

17. Morgan v. Virginia, 328 U.S. 373 (1946), https://supreme.justia.com/cases/federal/us/328/373/.

18. Farrell Evans, "How Jim Crow–Era Laws Suppressed the African American Vote for Generation," History, May 13, 2021, https://www.history.com/news/jim-crow-laws-black-vote#.

19. Ibid.

20. Henderson and Hussey, "History of Fairfax County Branch."

21. Mary Riley Styles Public Library, Local History Collection, Falls Church, VA, "Interview with E. B. Henderson (Part 2/2)," accessed July 6, 2023, http://100yearsblackfallschurch.org/items/show/255.

22. African and African American Studies, George Mason University, and the Tinner Hill Foundation, "A Brief Historical Sketch of the African American Presence in Falls Church, Virginia," accessed July 6, 2023, http://www.100yearsblackfallschurch.org/history.

23. Michelle Lee, "History of Luther Jackson High School (PhD diss., Virginia Polytechnical Institute, 1993); Nan Netherton, Donald Sweig, Janice Artemel, Patricia P. Hickin, and Patrick Reed, *Fairfax County, Virginia: A History* (Fairfax County Board of Supervisors, 1978).

24. Penny Gross, "A Penny for Your Thoughts," *Falls Church News-Press*, October 11, 2021, https://www.fcnp.com/2021/10/11/a-penny-for-your-thoughts-9/.

25. Ibid.

26. Wikipedia, "Mary Ellen Henderson," accessed July 6, 2023, https://en.wikipedia.org/wiki/Mary_Ellen_Henderson.

27. Henderson and Hussey. *1965 History of the Fairfax County Branch of the NAACP*, p. 5.

28. Juanita Smith, interview.

29. Henderson and Hussey, "History of the Fairfax County Branch," 6.

30. Wikipedia, "Lee Highway," accessed July 6, 2023, https://en.wikipedia.org/wiki/Lee_Highway.

31. Mary Riley Styles Public Library, Local History Collection, Falls Church, VA, "Interview (Part 1/2)."

32. Russell G. Brooker, "The Education of Black Children in the Jim Crow South," America's Black Holocaust Museum, accessed July 6, 2023, https://www.abhmuseum.org/education-for-blacks-in-the-jim-crow-south/.

33. Henderson and Hussey, "History of the Fairfax County Branch," 8.

34. Ibid.

35. African and African American Studies, George Mason University, and the Tinner Hill Foundation, "Brief Historical Sketch."

36. Ibid.

37. James H. Hershman, "Massive Resistance," in *Encyclopedia Virginia* (Virginia Humanities, December 7, 2020), https://encyclopediavirginia.org/entries/massive-resistance/.

38. Ibid.

39. Henderson and Hussey, "History of the Fairfax County Branch," 10–11.

40. Ibid., 11.

41. Geraldine L. Susi, *For My People: The Jennie Dean Story* (Manassas Museum System, 2003).

42. Ibid.

43. Lee, "History of Luther Jackson High School."

44. Ibid.

45. Ibid.
46. Ibid.
47. Ibid.
48. Ibid.
49. Susanna McBee, "26 Fairfax Negroes Ask US Court to End School Segregation at Once," *Washington Post*, August 21, 1959, A1.
50. Henderson and Hussey, "History of the Fairfax County Branch," 8–9.
51. Ibid., 10.
52. Cindy Long, "A Hidden History of Integration and the Shortage of Teachers of Color," *NEA Today*, March 11, 2020, https://www.nea.org/advocating-for-change/new-from-nea/hidden-history-integration-and-shortage-teachers-color.
53. W. E. Burghardt DuBois, "Does the Negro Need Separate Schools?" *Journal of Negro Education* 4, no. 3 (July 1935): 328–35.
54. Ibid.
55. Edwin B. Henderson, "The Colored College Athlete," *Crisis Magazine* 2, no. 3 (July 1911), 11.

17

1. Martin Luther King Jr., "I Have a Dream," August 28, 1963, https://www.npr.org/2010/01/18/122701268/i-have-a-dream-speech-in-its-entirety.
2. Library of Congress, "NAACP: A Century in the Fight for Freedom," accessed July 7, 2023, https://www.loc.gov/exhibits/naacp/founding-and-early-years.html.
3. [*Afro-American*, July 31, 1954, 9.
4. Brian Daugherity, *Keep on Keeping On: The NAACP and the Implementation of* Brown v. Board of Education *in Virginia* (University of Virginia Press, 2016), 40.
5. DC Historic Preservation Office, "M. J. Uline Ice Company and Arena (Washington Coliseum)," DC Historic Sites, accessed July 7, 2023, https://historicsites.dcpreservation.org/items/show/613.
6. Leon Coursey, "The Life of Edwin Bancroft Henderson and His Professional Contributions to Physical Education" (PhD diss., Ohio State University, 1971), 58.
7. DC Historic Sites, "M. J. Uline Ice Company."
8. *Washington Afro American*, August 10, 1954, Magazine Section, p. 3.
9. Coursey, "Life of Edwin Bancroft Henderson," 60.
10. Ibid., 61, 66.
11. Ibid., 64.
12. Briana A. Thomas, *Black Broadway in Washington, D.C.* (History Press, 2021), 69.
13. Coursey, "Life of Edwin Bancroft Henderson," 63.
14. Thomas, *Black Broadway in Washington, D.C.*, 69.
15. White House Historical Association, "Marian Anderson Performs at the White House," accessed July 7, 2023, https://www.whitehousehistory.org/marian-anderson-performs-at-the-white-house.
16. "Marian Anderson Citizens Committee," *Circulars, Pamphlets, Programs, Invitations, Flyers, Newsletters, Playbill and Broadsides* 16 (May 2018), https://dh.howard.edu/cgi/viewcontent.cgi?article=1015&context=og_circulars.

17. Coursey, "Life of Edwin Bancroft Henderson," 174.

18. Cary O'Dell, "NBC Radio Coverage of Marian Anderson's Recital at the Lincoln Memorial (April 9, 1939)," National Registry, 2008, https://www.loc.gov/static/programs/national-recording-preservation-board/documents/MarianAndersonLincolnMem.pdf.

19. Lafayette Matthews, "How Helen Hayes Helped Desegregate the National Theatre," Boundary Stones, June 22, 2016, https://boundarystones.weta.org/2016/06/22/how-helen-hayes-helped-desegregate-national-theatre.

20. The National Theatre, "Desegregation," *National Theatre, National Politics* (blog), accessed July 7, 2023, https://thenationaldcpolitics.org/desegregation/.

21. DC Historic Preservation Office, "Civil Rights Tour: Protest—National Theatre Goes Dark," DC Historic Sites, accessed July 7, 2023, https://historicsites.dcpreservation.org/items/show/956?tour=12&index=100.

22. The National Theatre, "Desegregation."

23. Coursey, "Life of Edwin Bancroft Henderson," 62–63.

24. Ibid., 64–65.

25. The National Theatre, "Desegregation."

26. Matthews, "How Helen Hayes Helped."

27. Coursey, "Life of Edwin Bancroft Henderson," 65.

28. Ibid., 125.

29. Ibid., 294.

30. Ibid., 300.

31. Ibid., 297.

32. Ibid.

33. Ibid., 303.

34. Cultural Tourism DC, "Cardozo (Business) High School Site, African American Heritage Trail," accessed July 7, 2023, https://www.culturaltourismdc.org/portal/cardozo-business-high-school-site-african-american-heritage-trail.

35. Thomas G. Smith, *Showdown: JFK and the Integration of the Washington Redskins* (Beacon Press, 2011), vii.

36. Ibid.

37. Ibid., 154.

38. Ibid.

39. Ibid., 113–14.

40. Ibid., 123–24.

41. King, "I Have a Dream."

42. F. L. Shuttlesworth and N. H. Smith, "Birmingham Manifesto," April 3, 1963, https://www.crmvet.org/docs/bhammanf.htm.

43. John F. Kennedy, "Report to the American People on Civil Rights," June 11, 1963, https://www.jfklibrary.org/learn/about-jfk/historic-speeches/televised-address-to-the-nation-on-civil-rights.

44. Zinn Education Project, "Jan. 25, 1941: A. Philip Randolph and March on Washington," accessed July 7, 2023, https://www.zinnedproject.org/news/tdih/a-philip-randolph-first-call-mow/.

18

1. Wendy Kail, "On the Track—Thomas Peter, Henry Clay, and the Duchess of Marlborough," Tudor Place, September 2013, https://tudorplace.org/wp-content/uploads/2020/07/On-the-Track-essay.pdf.

2. Ibid.

3. Ibid.

4. Eliza McGraw, "Remembering Benning's Racetrack," *Washington Post*, May 19, 2016, https://www.washingtonpost.com/blogs/all-opinions-are-local/wp/2016/05/19/remembering-bennings-race-track/.

5. Kentucky Derby, "Legacy of Black Jockeys," accessed July 8, 2023, https://www.kentuckyderby.com/history/legacy-of-black-jockeys.

6. Ibid.

7. David Berri, "The Disappearance of the African-American Jockey," *Forbes*, June 11, 2018, https://www.forbes.com/sites/davidberri/2018/06/11/the-disappearance-of-the-african-american-jockey/?sh=27261da53e13.

8. Edwin B. Henderson, "Early Negro Baseball: Washington Mutuals," *Baltimore Afro-American*, June 24, 1950.

9. Ibid.

10. Andrew C. Sharp, "D.C. and the Homestead Grays," Washington Baseball History, December 2, 2019, https://washingtonbaseballhistory.com/2019/12/02/d-c-and-the-homestead-grays/.

11. Ibid.

12. Marya Annette McQuirter, *African American Heritage Trail* (Cultural Tourism DC, 2003), https://www.culturaltourismdc.org/portal/c/document_library/get_file?uuid=e9ded752-0908-42f5-9d30-e4b01555db39&groupId=701982.

13. Deanwood History Project, *Deanwood: 1880–1950* (Deanwood History Project, 2005), https://planning.dc.gov/sites/default/files/dc/sites/op/publication/attachments/Deanwood_%2520Brochure.pdf.

14. Ibid.

15. Bob Kuska, *Hot Potato: How Washington and New York Gave Birth to Black Basketball and Changed America's Game Forever* (University of Virginia Press, 2004), 168–70.

16. Ibid., 183.

17. Claude Johnson, *The Black Fives: The Epic Story of Basketball's Forgotten Era* (Abrams Press, 2022), 243.

18. Ibid.

19. Kuska, *Hot Potato*, 182.

20. Armstrong Yearbook, 1923, Sumner School Archives.

21. Kuska, *Hot Potato*, 169.

22. Johnson, *Black Fives*, 380.

23. Kuska, *Hot Potato*, 164.

24. Ibid., 169.

25. Ibid., 164, 168.

26. Ibid., 171.

27. Ibid., 171.

28. Ibid., 171.
29. *Pittsburgh Courier*, December 31, 1927.
30. Kuska, *Hot Potato*, 171.
31. *Pittsburgh Courier*, December 31, 1927.
32. Kuska, *Hot Potato*, 173.
33. Ibid., 173.
34. Susan Rayl, interview.
35. Kuska, *Hot Potato*, 182.
36. Ibid., 183.
37. Ibid.
38. Black Fives Foundation, "R.I.P. Harold Jackson, 1915–2012: Was Black Fives Era Basketball Pioneer, among Many Major Contributions," May 24, 2012, https://www.blackfives.org/rip-harold-jackson-19152012-black-fives-era-basketball-pioneer/.
39. Phillip Jackson, "Forgotten Greatness: The Washington Bears Basketball Team," Boundary Stones, July 29, 2014, https://boundarystones.weta.org/2014/07/29/forgotten-greatness-washington-bears-basketball-team.
40. Kuska, *Hot Potato*, 183.
41. Ibid.
42. Rayl, interview.
43. Ibid.
44. Ibid.
45. Johnson, *Black Fives*, 407.
46. Jackson, "Forgotten Greatness."

19

1. Claude Johnson, *The Black Fives: The Epic Story of Basketball's Forgotten Era* (Abrams Press, 2022), 50.
2. Leon Coursey, "The Life of Edwin Bancroft Henderson and His Professional Contributions to Physical Education" (PhD diss., Ohio State University, 1971), 157–58.
3. Ibid., 158.
4. Ibid., 157.
5. Marion Holland, letter to E. B. Henderson, January 27, 1974, Henderson Collection.
6. Coursey, "Life of Edwin Bancroft Henderson."
7. Ibid.
8. Marion Holland, letter to E. B. Henderson, January 27, 1974, Henderson Collection.
9. Coursey, "Life of Edwin Bancroft Henderson."
10. Ibid.
11. Ibid.
12. Ibid.
13. Ibid.
14. *Today Show*, 1985.
15. Edwin B. Henderson, "Looking Back on Fifty Years," *Baltimore Afro-American*, August 28, 1954, 3.
16. Dr. Charles Drew, letter to E. B. Henderson, May 31, 1940, Henderson Collection.

17. Ibid.
18. Omega Psi Phi Brother Rohulamin Quander, Alpha Omega Chapter, Washington, DC.
19. Ibid.
20. Ibid.
21. Ibid., 91.
22. Coursey, "Life of Edwin Bancroft Henderson."
23. Henderson, "Looking Back."

20

1. Jack E. Nelson, Raymond L. Langston, and Margo Dean Pinson, *Highland Beach on the Chesapeake Bay: Maryland's First African American Incorporated Town* (Donning, 2008), 10.
2. Ibid., 9.
3. Ibid., 11–12.
4. Ibid., 13.
5. Ibid., 2.2
6. Betty Francis Henderson, interview.
7. Nelson, Langston, and Pinson, *Highland Beach*, 19–24.
8. E. B. Henderson, interview, Mary Riley Styles Library, Falls Church, Virginia.
9. Nelson, Langston, and Pinson, *Highland Beach*, 34–35.
10. Ibid., 35.
11. Ibid.
12. Leon Coursey, "The Life of Edwin Bancroft Henderson and His Professional Contributions to Physical Education" (PhD diss., Ohio State University, 1971), 178–79.
13. Nelson, Langston, and Pinson, *Highland Beach*, 42.
14. Ibid., 45.
15.Ibid., 42.
16. Coursey, "Life of Edwin Bancroft Henderson," 179.

21

1. Sargent White, tribute, Falls Church, 1974, Henderson Collection.
2. Testimonial, fiftieth wedding anniversary, 1960.
3. Edwin B. Henderson, "Looking Back on Fifty Years," *Afro-American*, August 31, 1954.
4. Chad Brock, "Desegregation in Virginia," Sutori, accessed July 9, 2023, https://www.sutori.com/en/story/desegregation-in-virginia--8iDDvVtHknA95pp4VJUc6Ce7.
5. Tuskegee University, "History of Tuskegee University," accessed July 9, 2023, https://www.tuskegee.edu/about-us/history-and-mission#:~:text=The%20founding%20date%20was%20July,but%20could%20read%20and%20write.
6. Linda Kenney Miller, *Beacon on the Hill: A Novel* (Harper House, 2008), 17–22.
7. "General Davis Promotion," C-Span, December 9, 1998, https://www.c-span.org/video/?116376-1/general-davis-promotion.

8. Booker T. Washington, "Atlanta Compromise Speech," History Matters, September 18, 1895, https://historymatters.gmu.edu/d/39/.

9. Gomillion v. Lightfoot, 364 U.S. 339 (1960), https://supreme.justia.com/cases/federal/us/364/339/.

10. Leon Coursey, "The Life of Edwin Bancroft Henderson and His Professional Contributions to Physical Education" (PhD diss., Ohio State University, 1971), 175.

11. Rebecca Skloot, *The Immortal Life of Henrietta Lacks* (Crown, 2009).

12. David K. Wiggins, *Glory Bound: Black Athletes in a White America* (, 1997), 236.

13. Ibid.

14. Ibid.

15. Ibid.

16. Proverbs 13:22; Manis Friedman and Rivka Goldstein, *Creating a Life That Matters: How to Live and Love with Meaning and Purpose* (It's Good to Know, 2021), https://www.goodreads.com/quotes/11459728-if-you-raise-your-children-well-you-can-spoil-you.

Epilogue

1. Arthur Ashe, interview with Bryant Gumbel, *Today Show*, 1988.

2. GVI, *E. B. Henderson*, video, August 1, 2014, https://www.youtube.com/watch?v=9TvUgSz6vEo&t=4s.

References

AFL-CIO. N.d. "1892 Homestead Strike." Accessed June 26, 2023. https://aflcio.org/about/history/labor-history-events/1892-homestead-strike.

African and African American Studies, George Mason University, and the Tinner Hill Heritage Foundation. N.d. "About." Accessed July 10, 2023. http://100yearsblackfallschurch.org/.

African and African American Studies, George Mason University, and the Tinner Hill Foundation. N.d. "A Brief Historical Sketch of the African American Presence in Falls Church, Virginia." Accessed July 6, 2023. http://www.100yearsblackfallschurch.org/history.

Amos, Alcione M. 2021. *Barry Farm-Hillsdale in Anacostia: A Historic African American Community*. History Press.

Armstrong Yearbook. 1923. Sumner School Archives.

Ashe, Arthur R., Jr. 1988. *A Hard Road to Glory—Basketball: The African-American Athlete in Basketball*. Amistad.

Baptist, Edward E. 2016. *The Half Has Never Been Told: Slavery and the Making of American Capitalism*. Basic Books.

Bernard, Rachel Deborah. 2012. "These Separate Schools: Black Politics and Education in Washington, D.C., 1900–1930." PhD diss., University of California, Berkeley. https://escholarship.org/uc/item/8h75g7n0.

Berri, David. 2018, June 11. "The Disappearance of the African-American Jockey." *Forbes*. https://www.forbes.com/sites/davidberri/2018/06/11/the-disappearance-of-the-african-american-jockey/?sh=27261da53e13.

Black Fives Foundation. N.d. "Colored Basketball World's Champions, 1907–1925." Accessed July 9, 2023. https://www.blackfives.org/champions/.

Black Fives Foundation. 2007, December 18. "The Hidden Story: Rens Break Pre-NBA Color Barrier, 1948." https://www.blackfives.org/rens-break-pre-nba-color-barrier-1948/.

Black Fives Foundation. 2012, May 24. "R.I.P. Harold Jackson, 1915–2012: Was Black Fives Era Basketball Pioneer, among Many Major Contributions." https://www.blackfives.org/rip-harold-jackson-19152012-black-fives-era-basketball-pioneer/.

Black Fives Foundation. 2014, November 13. "In 1907, First Official African American Basketball Game, at 'Knickerbocker Court' in Brooklyn." https://www

.blackfives.org/today-in-1907-first-official-african-american-basketball-game-at-knickerbocker-court-in-brooklyn/.

Blum, Matt. 2010, February 27. "Benjamin Banneker: The First African-American Geek." *Wired*. https://www.wired.com/2010/02/benjamin-banneker-the-first-african-american-geek/.

BOTWC Staff. 2022, November 4. "Meet James Wormley, the Owner of Washington, D.C.'s First Integrated Hotel." Because of Them We Can. https://www.becauseofthemwecan.com/blogs/botwc-firsts/meet-james-wormley-the-owner-of-washington-d-c-s-first-integrated-hotel.

Brock, Chad. N.d. "Desegregation in Virginia." Sutori. Accessed July 9, 2023. https://www.sutori.com/en/story/desegregation-in-virginia--8iDDvVtHknA95pp4VJUc6Ce7.

Brooke, Kathleen Lusk, and Zoe G. Quinn. N.d. "The Founding of Washington D.C., United States." *Building the World* (blog). Accessed June 26, 2023. https://blogs.umb.edu/buildingtheworld/founding-of-new-cities/the-founding-of-washington-d-c-united-states/.

Brooker, Russell G. N.d. "The Education of Black Children in the Jim Crow South." America's Black Holocaust Museum. Accessed July 6, 2023. https://www.abhmuseum.org/education-for-blacks-in-the-jim-crow-south/.

Browne, John. 2018. *The Story of Ravensworth: A History of the Ravensworth Land-Grant in Fairfax County, Virginia*, CreateSpace.

Buchanan v. Warley, 245 U.S. 60 (1917). https://supreme.justia.com/cases/federal/us/245/60/.

Buczkowska, Anna, and Basen Saah. 2011, July 30. *Tinner Hill, Virginia: A Witness to Civil Rights*. Landscape Architecture Program, Washington Alexandria Architecture Center, Virginia Polytechnic Institute and State University.

Cabe, Delia. 2010, November/December. "World Beaters." *Humanities* 31, no. 6. https://www.neh.gov/humanities/2010/novemberdecember/feature/world-beaters.

Caldbick, John. 2019, October 1. "Panic of 1893 and Its Aftermath." HistoryLink.org. https://www.historylink.org/file/20874.

Cirillo, Vincent J. 2020, October. "Fever and Reform: The Typhoid Epidemic in the Spanish-American War." *Journal of the History of Medicine* 55: 363–97. https://vlp.cah.ucf.edu/instructionalmaterials/UCF-VLP-9th-12th-SPAM-DiseaseImpact-TyphoidArticle.pdf.

Cooke, Jacob E. 1970. "The Compromise of 1790." *William and Mary Quarterly: A Magazine of Early American History and Culture*: 524–45.

Coursey, Leon. 1971. "The Life of Edwin Bancroft Henderson and His Professional Contributions to Physical Education." PhD diss., Ohio State University.

Coursey, Leon N. 1974, March. "Anita J. Turner—Early Black Female Physical Educator." *Journal of Health, Physical Education, Recreation* 45, no. 3: 71–72. https://www.tandfonline.com/na101/home/literatum/publisher/tandf/journals/content/ujrd18/1974/ujrd18.v045.i03/00221473.1974.10612134/20130313/00221473.1974.10612134.fp.png_v03.

Cultural Tourism DC. N.d. "Cardozo (Business) High School Site, African American Heritage Trail." Accessed July 7, 2023. https://www.culturaltourismdc.org/portal/cardozo-business-high-school-site-african-american-heritage-trail.

Daugherity, Brian. 2016. *Keep on Keeping On: The NAACP and the Implementation of* Brown v. Board of Education *in Virginia*. University of Virginia Press.

DC Historic Preservation Office. N.d. "Civil Rights Tour: Protest—National Theatre Goes Dark." DC Historic Sites. Accessed July 7, 2023. https://historicsites.dcpreservation.org/items/show/956?tour=12&index=100.

DC Historic Preservation Office. N.d. "M. J. Uline Ice Company and Arena (Washington Coliseum)." DC Historic Sites. Accessed July 7, 2023. https://historicsites.dcpreservation.org/items/show/613.

Deanwood History Project. 2005. *Deanwood: 1880–1950*. Deanwood History Project. https://planning.dc.gov/sites/default/files/dc/sites/op/publication/attachments/Deanwood_%2520Brochure.pdf.

Dickerson, Dennis. 1977, December. "Black Steelworkers in Western Pennsylvania." *Pennsylvania Heritage*. http://paheritage.wpengine.com/article/black-steelworkers-western-pennsylvania/.

Du Bois, W. E. Burghardt. 1935, July. "Does the Negro Need Separate Schools?" *Journal of Negro Education* 4, no. 3: 328–35.

Evans, Farrell. 2021, May 13. "How Jim Crow–Era Laws Suppressed the African American Vote for Generation." History. https://www.history.com/news/jim-crow-laws-black-vote#.

Fairfax County Public Schools. N.d. "School History: James Lee Elementary School." https://www.fcps.edu/about-fcps/history/records/desegregation/schools/james-lee.

"Falls Church Gleanings." 1921, October 15. *Washington Bee*, 5. http://100yearsblackfallschurch.org/items/show/550.

Falls Church Town Council. 1914, December 10. Minutes Book.

Falls Church Town Council. 1915, January 11. Minutes Book.

FDR Library and Museum. https://www.fdrlibrary.org/anderson org/.

Friedman, Manis, and Rivka Goldstein. 2021. *Creating a Life That Matters: How to Live and Love with Meaning and Purpose*. It's Good to Know. https://www.goodreads.com/quotes/11459728-if-you-raise-your-children-well-you-can-spoil-you.

"General Davis Promotion." 1998, December 9. C-Span. https://www.c-span.org/video/?116376-1/general-davis-promotion.

George, Nelson. 1992. *Elevating the Game: Black Men and Basketball*. HarperCollins..

"George Frederick Thompson Cooke, Superintendent of Colored Schools in DC, Dies at 77." 1913, February. *The Crisis*. https://www.flickr.com/photos/vieilles_annonces/4671321307.

Gilmore, Al Tony, 1975, *Bad Nigger! The National Impact of Jack Johnson*. Kennikat Press

Goggin, Jacqueline, 1997. *Carter G. Woodson: A Life in Black History*. Louisiana State University Press

Gomillion v. Lightfoot, 364 U.S. 339 (1960). https://supreme.justia.com/cases/federal/us/364/339/.

Gross, Penny. 2021, October 11. "A Penny for Your Thoughts." *Falls Church News-Press*. https://www.fcnp.com/2021/10/11/a-penny-for-your-thoughts-9/.

Gross, Terry. 2010, October 11. "Lincoln's Evolving Thoughts on Slavery, and Freedom." *Fresh Air*. https://www.npr.org/2010/10/11/130489804/lincolns-evolving-thoughts-on-slavery-and-freedom.

Gumbel, Bryant. 1988. Interview with Arthur Ashe. *Today Show*.

GVI. 2014, August 1. "E. B. Henderson." Video. https://www.youtube.com/watch?v=9TvUgSz6vEo&t=4s.

Hall, Stephen G. 2005, October. "Revisiting the Tragic Era and the Nadir: Interrogating Individual and Collective African-American Lives in the Gilded Age and Progressive Era." *Journal of the Gilded Age and Progressive Era* 4, no. 4: 409–15.

Harvey, George. 2020, October 4. "Belfast Man Pioneered Physical Education, Influenced Basketball's Creation and Field Hockey's U.S. Introduction." *Penobscot Bay Pilot*. https://www.penbaypilot.com/article/belfast-man-pioneered-physical-education-influenced-basketball-s-creation-and-field-h/134270.

Henderson Collection.

Henderson, Edwin B. 1911, July 16. "The Colored College Athlete." *The Crisis*:115.

Henderson, Edwin B. 1935, July. "The Courts and the Negro Separate School." *Journal of Negro Education* 4, no. 3: 328–35.

Henderson, Edwin B. 1937, March 13. "Public Recreation in the District." *Washington Tribune*.

Henderson, Edwin B. 1937, March 20. "Public Recreation in the District." *Washington Tribune*.

Henderson, Edwin B. 1937, April 3. "Public Recreation in the District." *Washington Tribune*.

Henderson, Edwin B. 1937, April 17. "Public Recreation in the District." *Washington Tribune*.

Henderson, Edwin Bancroft. 1939. *The Negro in Sports*. Associated Publishers.

Henderson, Edwin Bancroft. 1949. *The Negro in Sports*. Associated Publishers.

Henderson, Edwin B. 1950, June 24. "Early Negro Baseball: Washington Mutuals." *Baltimore Afro-American*.

Henderson, Edwin B. 1951, June. "An Experiment in Elementary School Athletics." *Journal of the American Association for Health, Physical Education, and Recreation* 2, no. 6: 21–22.

Henderson, Edwin B. 1954, July 24. "Looking Back on Fifty Years." *Washington Afro-American Magazine*: 3, 5.

Henderson, Edwin B. 1954, August 7. "Looking Back on Fifty Years." *Afro-American Magazine*: 5.

Henderson, Edwin B. 1954, August 28. "Looking Back on Fifty Years." *Baltimore Afro-American*, 3.

Henderson, Edwin B. 1954, August 31. "Looking Back on Fifty Years." *Baltimore Afro-American*.

Henderson, Edwin B. 1954, September 7. "Looking Back on Fifty Years." *Baltimore Afro-American*, 3.

Henderson, Edwin B. 1961, January. "Letter to the Editor: It Seems to Me." *Baltimore Afro-American.*

Henderson, Edwin B., and Edith Hussey. 1965. "History of the Fairfax County Branch of the NAACP." In *School Facilities for Negro Children in Fairfax County.* N.p.

Henderson, Edwin B., and the editors of *Sport* magazine. 1968. *The Black Athlete: Emergence and Arrival.* Publishers.

Henderson, Edwin, and Edith Hussey. 1940s. "School Facilities for Negro Children in Fairfax County." In *History of Fairfax County Branch.* http://100yearsblackfallschurch.org/items/show/288.

Henderson, Edwin B., and William A. Joiner. 1910. *Spalding Official Handbook: Inter-Scholastic Athletic Association of Middle Atlantic States.* American Sports Publishing.

Henderson, Edwin B., and William A. Joiner. 1911. *Spalding Official Handbook: Inter-Scholastic Athletic Association of Middle Atlantic States.* American Sports Publishing.

Henderson, Edwin B., and Garnet C. Wilkinson. 1912. *Spalding Official Handbook: Inter-Scholastic Athletic Association of Middle Atlantic States.* American Sports Publishing.

Henderson, Edwin B., and Garnet C. Wilkinson. 1913. *Spalding Official Handbook: Inter-Scholastic Athletic Association of Middle Atlantic States.* American Sports Publishing.

Henderson, James H. M., and Betty F. Henderson. 1985. *Molder of Men: Portrait of a "Grand Old Man," Edwin Bancroft Henderson.* Vantage Press.

Hershman, James H. 2020, December 7. "Massive Resistance." In *Encyclopedia Virginia.* Virginia Humanities. https://encyclopediavirginia.org/entries/massive-resistance/.

Heung, Camille. 2008, June 24. "Robert H. Terrell (1857–1925)." BlackPast. https://www.blackpast.org/african-american-history/terrell-robert-h-1857-1925/.

Historic Structures. 2010, October 25. "Twelfth Street YMCA Building (Anthony Bowen YMCA) Washington DC." https://www.historic-structures.com/washington_dc/dc/12th_ymca.php.

History of Lorain County Ohio, with Illustrations and Biographical Sketches of Some of Its Prominent Men and Pioneers. 1879. Williams Brothers.

Hollie, Donna. N.d. "Grand Fountain of the United Order of True Reformers." *Encyclopedia Virginia.* Updated December 14, 2020. https://encyclopediavirginia.org/entries/grand-fountain-of-the-united-order-of-true-reformers/#:~:text=The%20Grand%20Fountain%20of%20the,in%20Richmond%20in%20January%201881.

Hundley, Mary Gibson. 1965. *The Dunbar Story.* Vantage Press.

Jackson, Phillip. 2014, July 29. "Forgotten Greatness: The Washington Bears Basketball Team." Boundary Stones. https://boundarystones.weta.org/2014/07/29/forgotten-greatness-washington-bears-basketball-team.

Jeebus, A. P. K. Praise. 2020, May 9. "The True Reformer Building at 1200 U 'You' Street, NW." *House History Man* (blog). http://househistoryman.blogspot.com/2020/05/the-true-reformer-building-at-1200-u.html.

Johnson, Claude. 2022. *The Black Fives: The Epic Story of Basketball's Forgotten Era*. Abrams Press.

Jones, Mark. 2015, April 7. "Contraband Camps of Northern Virginia." Boundary Stones. https://boundarystones.weta.org/2015/04/07/contraband-camps-northern-virginia.

Jones, Mark. 2017, April 18. "Red Summer Race Riot in Washington, 1919." Boundary Stones. https://boundarystones.weta.org/2017/04/18/red-summer-race-riot-washington-1919.

Kail, Wendy. 2013, September. "On the Track—Thomas Peter, Henry Clay, and the Duchess of Marlborough." Tudor Place. https://tudorplace.org/wp-content/uploads/2020/07/On-the-Track-essay.pdf.

Kennedy, John F. 1963, June 11. "Report to the American People on Civil Rights." https://www.jfklibrary.org/learn/about-jfk/historic-speeches/televised-address-to-the-nation-on-civil-rights.

Kentucky Derby. N.d. "Legacy of Black Jockeys." Accessed July 8, 2023. https://www.kentuckyderby.com/history/legacy-of-black-jockeys.

King, Martin Luther, Jr. 1963, August 28. "I Have a Dream." https://www.npr.org/2010/01/18/122701268/i-have-a-dream-speech-in-its-entirety.

Krause, Paul. 1951. *The Battle for Homestead: Politics, Culture, and Steel*. University of Pittsburgh Press.

Kuska, Bob. 2004. *Hot Potato: How Washington and New York Gave Birth to Black Basketball and Changed America's Game Forever*. University of Virginia Press.

Labor Commission on Racial and Economic Justice. N.d. "A Brief History of Labor, Race, and Solidarity." Accessed June 26, 2023. https://racial-justice.aflcio.org/blog/est-aliquid-se-ipsum-flagitiosum-etiamsi-nulla.

Lee, Michelle. 1993. "History of Luther Jackson High School." PhD diss., Virginia Polytechnical Institute.

Levy, Andrew. 2005. *The First Emancipator: The Forgotten Story of Robert Carter, the Founding Father Who Freed His Slaves*. Random House.

Lewis, David Levering. 1994. *W. E. B. DuBois: The Fight for Equality and the American Century, 1919–1963*. Henry Holt.

Library of Congress. N.d. "NAACP: A Century in the Fight for Freedom." Accessed July 7, 2023. https://www.loc.gov/exhibits/naacp/founding-and-early-years.html.

Long, Cindy. 2020, March 11. "A Hidden History of Integration and the Shortage of Teachers of Color." *NEA Today*. https://www.nea.org/advocating-for-change/new-from-nea/hidden-history-integration-and-shortage-teachers-color.

"Marian Anderson Citizens Committee." 2018, May. *Circulars, Pamphlets, Programs, Invitations, Flyers, Newsletters, Playbill and Broadsides* 16. https://dh.howard.edu/cgi/viewcontent.cgi?article=1015&context=og_circulars.

Mary Riley Styles Public Library, Falls Church, Virginia.

Mary Riley Styles Public Library, Local History Collection, Falls Church, VA. N.d. "Interview with E. B. Henderson (Part 1/2)." Accessed July 6, 2023. http://100yearsblackfallschurch.org/items/show/256.

Mary Riley Styles Public Library, Local History Collection, Falls Church, VA. N.d. "Interview with E. B. Henderson (Part 2/2)." Accessed July 6, 2023. http://100yearsblackfallschurch.org/items/show/255.

Matthews, Lafayette. 2016, June 22. "How Helen Hayes Helped Desegregate the National Theatre." Boundary Stones. https://boundarystones.weta.org/2016/06/22/how-helen-hayes-helped-desegregate-national-theatre.

McBee, Susanna. 1959, August 21. "26 Fairfax Negroes Ask US Court to End School Segregation at Once." *Washington Post*, A1.

McCormick, Eliott. 2023, July 4. "July 4, 1910: Johnson vs Jeffries." Fight City. https://www.thefightcity.com/july-4-1910-johnson-vs-jeffries-jack-johnson-james-jeffries-corbett-sullivan-tommy-burns-fight-of-the-century/.

McGraw, Eliza. 2016, May 19. "Remembering Benning's Racetrack." *Washington Post*. https://www.washingtonpost.com/blogs/all-opinions-are-local/wp/2016/05/19/remembering-bennings-race-track/.

McQuirter, Marya Annette. 2003. *African American Heritage Trail*. Cultural Tourism DC. https://www.culturaltourismdc.org/portal/c/document_library/get_file?uuid=e9ded752-0908-42f5-9d30-e4b01555db39&groupId=701982.

Mercer, Anne L. 2000. "Tinner Hill, and the Segregation Ordinance of 1915." Paper, George Washington University.

Middleton, Daniel J. N.d. "The Black Fives: The Pre-NBA Era of All-Black Basketball Teams." Unique Coloring. Accessed July 1, 2023. https://www.uniquecoloring.com/articles/the-black-fives.

Miller, Linda Kenney. 2008. *Beacon on the Hill: A Novel*. Harper House.

"Miner, Myrtilla (1815–1864)." 2023, May 25. *Women in World History: A Biographical Encyclopedia*. https://www.encyclopedia.com/women/encyclopedias-almanacs-transcripts-and-maps/miner-myrtilla-1815-1864.

Morgan v. Virginia, 328 U.S. 373 (1946). https://supreme.justia.com/cases/federal/us/328/373/

National Archives. N.d. "Black Soldiers in the U.S. Military during the Civil War." Accessed June 26, 2023. https://www.archives.gov/education/lessons/blacks-civil-war.

National Museum of American Diplomacy. N.d. "The Diplomatic Career of Frederick Douglass." Accessed July 10, 2023. https://diplomacy.state.gov/stories/the-diplomatic-career-of-frederick-douglass/.

National Park Service. N.d. "Battle of Milliken's Bend, June 7, 1863." Updated April 17, 2017. https://www.nps.gov/vick/learn/historyculture/battle-of-millikens-bend-june-7-1863.htm.

National Park Service. N.d. "Charles Young and the 9th Ohio Battalion during the Spanish-American War." Accessed July 6, 2023. https://www.nps.gov/articles/000/young9thohiobattalion.htm.

The National Theatre. N.d. "Desegregation." *National Theatre, National Politics* (blog). Accessed July 7, 2023. https://thenationaldcpolitics.org/desegregation/.

Neal, Anthony W. 2014, February 27. "Joseph Lee: Famed Hotelier, Restaurateur, Inventor." *Bay State Banner*. https://www.baystatebanner.com/2014/02/27/joseph-lee-famed-hotelier-restaurateur-inventor/.

Nelson, Jack E., Raymond L. Langston, and Margo Dean Pinson. 2008. *Highland Beach on the Chesapeake Bay: Maryland's First African American Incorporated Town*. Donning.

Netherton, Nan, Donald Sweig, Janice Artemel, Patricia P. Hickin, and Patrick Reed. 1978. *Fairfax County, Virginia: A History*. Fairfax County Board of Supervisors.

"New Item." 1921, July 23. *Washington Bee*, 1. http://100yearsblackfallschurch.org/items/show/537.

New York Age. 1910, February 17.

Ocean City Beach Patrol. N.d. "125 Years of Ocean Lifesaving." Accessed June 28, 2023. https://www.ocnj.us/departments/OCBP/OCBPHistory.

O'Conner, Ellen M. 1885. *Myrtilla Miner: A Memoir*. Houghton, Mifflin, Riverside Press.

O'Dell, Cary. 2008. "NBC Radio Coverage of Marian Anderson's Recital at the Lincoln Memorial (April 9, 1939)." National Registry. https://www.loc.gov/static/programs/national-recording-preservation-board/documents/MarianAndersonLincolnMem.pdf.

Paynter, John H. 1930. *Fugitives of the Pearl*. Associated.

Pittsburgh Courier. 1927, December 31.

Powell, D. W. 2004. *Black Georgetown Remembered*. Georgetown University Press.

PT Direct. N.d. "Vertical Jump Test (Sargent Jump)." Accessed June 29, 2023. https://www.ptdirect.com/training-delivery/client-assessment/vertical-jump-test-sargent-jump-2013-a-predictive-test-of-lower-limb-power.

RetroSeasons. N.d. "National Basketball League I (NBL1): 1899–1904 (6 Seasons)." Accessed June 29, 2023. https://www.retroseasons.com/leagues/nbl1/.

RootsWeb. N.d. "James H. Meriwether." Accessed June 28, 2023. https://freepages.rootsweb.com/~tmsirecords/genealogy/biographyjameshmeriwether.html.

Sharp, Andrew C. 2019, December 2. "D.C. and the Homestead Grays." Washington Baseball History. https://washingtonbaseballhistory.com/2019/12/02/d-c-and-the-homestead-grays/.

Shuttlesworth, F. L., and N. H. Smith. 1963, April 3. "Birmingham Manifesto." https://www.crmvet.org/docs/bhammanf.htm.

Skloot, Rebecca. 2009. *The Immortal Life of Henrietta Lacks*. Crown.

Smith, Thomas G. 2011. *Showdown: JFK and the Integration of the Washington Redskins*. Beacon Press.

Steadman, Melvin Lee, Jr. 1964. *Falls Church: By Fence and Fireside*. Falls Church Public Library.

Susi, Geraldine L. 2002. *For My People: The Jennie Dean Story*. Manassas Museum System.

Swain, Claudia. 2016, July 6. "Dr. Anna J. Cooper: MVP of D.C. Education." Boundary Stones. https://boundarystones.weta.org/2016/07/06/dr-anna-j-cooper-mvp-dc-education.

Taylor, Elizabeth Dowling. 2017. *The Original Black Elite: Daniel Murray and the Story of a Forgotten Era*. Amistad.

Taylor, Major. 1928. *The Fastest Bicycle Rider in the World.* Wormley.

Telfair, Earl. 1999. *The Black Athletes of the District of Columbia during the Segregated Years: Remembering.* N.p.

Thomas, Briana A. 2021. *Black Broadway in Washington, D.C.* History Press.

Thornhill, Carrie L. N.d. "Dunbar HS History." Dunbar Alumni Federation. Accessed June 26, 2023. https://daf-dc.org/about/dunbar-history.

Todd, Michael. N.d. "A Short History of Home Mail Delivery." *Pacific Standard.* Updated June 14, 2017. https://psmag.com/economics/a-short-history-of-mail-delivery-52444.

"Track and Field Games." 1906, May 11. *Howard University Journal* 3, no. 25: 5.

Tristani, Nina. 2017, March 16. "Separate and Unequal Education in 19th Century DC Schools." HillRag. https://www.hillrag.com/2017/03/16/separate-unequal-education-19th-century-dc-schools/.

Turner, Geneva C. 1958. "For Whom Is Your School Named?" *Negro History Bulletin,* 22–23.

Tuskegee University. N.d. "History of Tuskegee University." Accessed July 9, 2023. https://www.tuskegee.edu/about-us/history-and-mission#:~:text=The%20founding%20date%20was%20July,but%20could%20read%20and%20write.

Ultimate History Project. http://ultimatehistoryproject.com/uline-arena.html.

United States Senate. N.d. "Landmark Legislation: The Civil Rights Act of 1875." Accessed June 26, 2023. https://www.senate.gov/artandhistory/history/common/generic/CivilRightsAct1875.htm#:~:text=Radical%20Republican%20senator%20Charles%20Sumner,schools%2C%20churches%2C%20and%20cemeteries.

University of the District of Columbia. N.d. "Chronology of the University of the District of Columbia and Its Predecessor Institutions, 1851–2009." Accessed June 28, 2023. https://www.google.com/url?sa=t&rct=j&q=&esrc=s&source=web&cd=&ved=2ahUKEwiq9tqz97AhVZFlkFHWU2BOcQFnoECA4QAQ&url=https%3A%2F%2Fhbcudigitallibrary.auctr.edu%2Fdigital%2Fapi%2Fcollection%2FUDCW%2Fid%2F307%2Fdownload&usg=AOvVaw2Vubx0fPDomuU5dONrGHnl.

Walker, Rhiannon. 2018, July 16. "The History of Black Baseball in D.C. Includes Frederick Douglass' Sons, Josh Gibson and the Fight for Equality." Andscape. https://andscape.com/features/the-history-of-black-baseball-in-d-c-includes-frederick-douglass-sons-josh-gibson-and-the-fight-for-equality/.

Ward, Geoffrey C. 2004. *Unforgiveable Blackness: The Rise and Fall of Jack Johnson.* A. A. Knopf.

Washington, Booker T. 1895, September 18. "Atlanta Compromise Speech." History Matters. https://historymatters.gmu.edu/d/39/.

Washington Evening Star. 1909, December 25, 9.

White House Historical Association. N.d. "Marian Anderson Performs at the White House." Accessed July 7, 2023. https://www.whitehousehistory.org/marian-anderson-performs-at-the-white-house.

Whiteman, Maxwell. 1969. "Benjamin Banneker: Surveyor and Astronomer: 1731–1806: A Biographical Note." In *Banneker's Almanack and Ephemeris for the Year of*

Our Lord 1793: Being the First after Bissextile or Leap Year and Banneker's Almanac, for the Year 1795: Being the Third after Leap Year, edited by Maxwell Whiteman. Repr. Afro-American History Series: Rhistoric Publication No. 202. Rhistoric.

Wiggins, David K. 1997. *Glory Bound: Black Athletes in a White America*. Syracuse University Press.

Wiggins, David K., and Patrick B. Miller, eds. 2003. *The Unlevel Playing Field: A Documentary History of the African American Experience in Sport*. University of Illinois Press.

Wikipedia. N.d. "Black Fives." Updated April 10, 2023. https://en.wikipedia.org/wiki/Black_Fives.

Wikipedia. N.d. "Lee Highway." Updated July 3, 2023. https://en.wikipedia.org/wiki/Lee_Highway.

Wikipedia. N.d. "Mary Ellen Henderson." Updated July 3, 2023. https://en.wikipedia.org/wiki/Mary_Ellen_Henderson.

Wikiwand. N.d. "Basketball at the 1904 Summer Olympics." Accessed June 29, 2023. https://www.wikiwand.com/en/Basketball_at_the_1904_Summer_Olympics.

Wormley, G. Smith. 1920, October. "Myrtilla Miner." *Journal of Negro History* 5, no. 4: 448–57. https://www.jstor.org/stable/2713679?searchText=au%3A%22G.+Smith+Wormley%22&searchUri=%2Faction%2FdoBasicSearch%3FQuery%3Dau%253A%2522G.%2520Smith%2520Wormley%2522&ab_segments=0%2Fbasic_phrase_search%2Fcontrol&refreqid=fastly-default%3A3d5bc3ff6f11aeb285478ba9f45a177f.

Zinn Education Project. N.d. "Jan. 25, 1941: A. Philip Randolph and March on Washington." Accessed July 7, 2023. https://www.zinnedproject.org/news/tdih/a-philip-randolph-first-call-mow/.

Index

About the Author

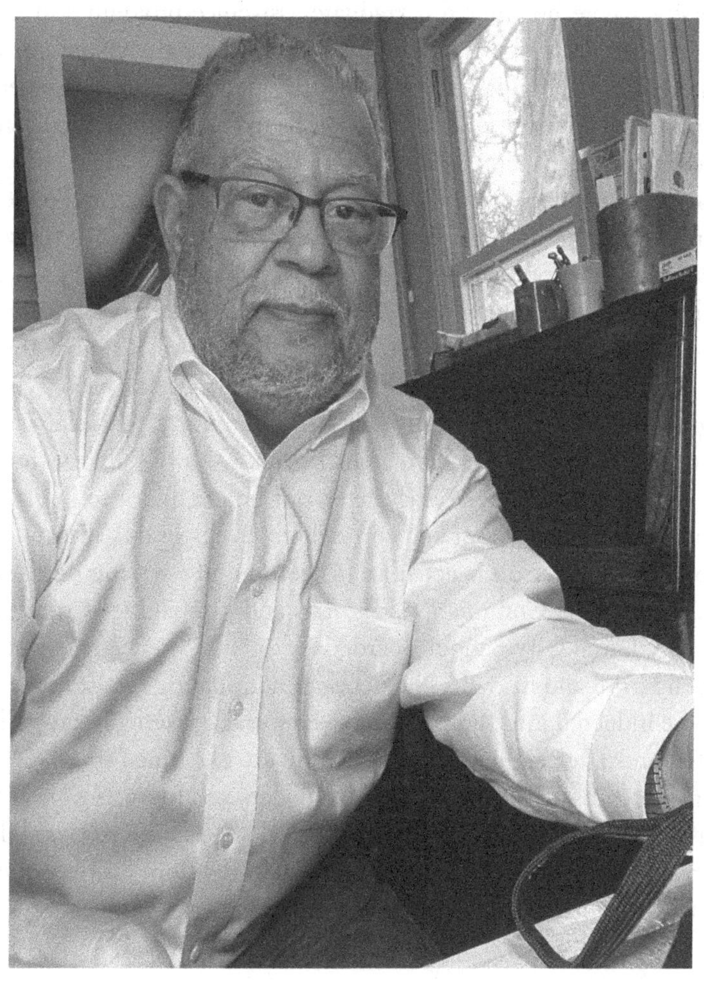

Edwin B. Henderson II is the grandson and namesake of Dr. E. B. Henderson. He was born in Tuskegee Institute, Alabama, where he attended the Laboratory School, Chambliss Children's House. Growing up on campus, he was exposed to a rich cultural experience, walking in the footsteps of Booker T. Washington, George Washington Carver, and the Tuskegee Airmen. Henderson enrolled in Tuskegee Institute and earned a bachelor's degree in history. He then studied photography and television engineering in California. It was in Compton, California, that he began his teaching career before matriculating back to Tuskegee University, where he entered a graduate assistance program and earned a master's degree in counseling education. Receiving a fellowship from the International Foundation for Education and Self-Help's Teachers for Africa program, he traveled to Nairobi, Kenya, and spent a year at the United States International University.

In 1993, Henderson moved to Falls Church, Virginia, and took possession of his grandfather Dr. E. B. Henderson's home. It is there that his training in history came full circle. He was instrumental in starting the Tinner Hill Heritage Foundation to research, preserve, and present African American and civil rights history in Northern Virginia. Through the Tinner Hill Heritage Foundation, Henderson has been active in changing the historical narrative in his community to make it more diverse and inclusive. He retired from Fairfax County Public Schools in 2012, ending a twenty-five-year career, but he continues to be involved in education as a consultant and curriculum developer on African American history. Henderson is active in his community, serving on the Falls Church Historical Commission, the Arts and Humanities Council, and the Falls Church City School Board.

Henderson and his wife, Nikki, began nominating Dr. E. B. Henderson to be inducted into the Naismith Memorial Basketball Hall of Fame in 2005, and after eight years, EB was finally enshrined in 2013. Henderson also runs two other entities, Henderson House, a nonprofit to preserve the intellectual property of Dr. E. B. Henderson, and Black Legacy Associates to consult with teachers to develop diverse, equitable, and inclusive curriculum.